Natural Philosophy

About the Author of This Book

"In a world increasingly rife with heresy and pseudo-religion, Guénon had to remind twentieth century man of the need for orthodoxy, which presupposes firstly a Divine Revelation and secondly a Tradition that has handed down with fidelity what Heaven has revealed. He thus restores to orthodoxy its true meaning, rectitude of opinion which compels the intelligent man not only to reject heresy but also to recognize the validity of faiths other than his own if they also are based on the same two principles, Revelation and Tradition."

—**Martin Lings**, author of *Ancient Beliefs and Modern Superstitions*

"If during the last century or so there has been even some slight revival of awareness in the Western world of what is meant by metaphysics and metaphysical tradition, the credit for it must go above all to Guénon. At a time when the confusion into which modern Western thought had fallen was such that it threatened to obliterate the few remaining traces of genuine spiritual knowledge from the minds and hearts of his contemporaries, Guénon, virtually single-handed, took it upon himself to reaffirm the values and principles which, he recognized, constitute the only sound basis for the living of a human life with dignity and purpose or for the formation of a civilization worthy of the name."

—**Philip Sherrard**, author of *Christianity: Lineaments of a Sacred Tradition*

"Apart from his amazing flair for expounding pure metaphysical doctrine and his critical acuteness when dealing with the errors of the modern world, Guénon displayed a remarkable insight into things of a cosmological order. . . . He all along stressed the need, side by side with a theoretical grasp of any given doctrine, for its concrete—one can also say its ontological—realization failing which one cannot properly speak of knowledge."

—**Marco Pallis**, author of *A Buddhist Spectrum*

"Guénon's mission was two-fold: to reveal the metaphysical roots of the 'crisis of the modern world' and to explain the ideas behind the authentic and esoteric teachings that still [remain] alive."

—**Harry Oldmeadow**, author of *Traditionalism: Religion in the Light of the Perennial Philosophy*

"To a materialistic society enthralled with the phenomenal universe exclusively, Guénon, taking the Vedanta as point of departure, revealed a metaphysical and cosmological teaching both macrocosmic and microcosmic about the hierarchized degrees of being or states of existence, starting with the Absolute . . . and terminating with our sphere of gross manifestation."
— **Whitall N. Perry**, editor of *A Treasury of Traditional Wisdom*

"Guénon established the language of sacred metaphysics with a rigor, a breadth, and an intrinsic certainty such that he compels recognition as a standard of comparison for the twentieth century."
— **Jean Borella**, author of *Guénonian Esoterism and Christian Mystery*

"René Guénon was the chief influence in the formation of my own intellectual outlook (quite apart from the question of Orthodox Christianity). . . . It was René Guénon who taught me to seek and love the truth above all else, and to be unsatisfied with anything else."
— **Fr. Seraphim Rose**, author of *The Soul After Death*

"His mixture of arcane learning, metaphysics, and scathing cultural commentary is a continent in itself, untouched by the polluted tides of modernity. . . . Guénon's work will not save the world—it is too late for that—but it leaves no reader unchanged."
— **Jocelyn Godwin**, author of *Mystery Religions in the Ancient World*

"René Guénon defies classification. . . . Were he anything less than a consummate master of lucid argument and forceful expression, his work would certainly be unknown to all but a small, private circle of admirers."
— **Gai Eaton**, author of *The Richest Vein*

"René Guénon is one of the few writers of our time whose work is really of importance. . . . He stands for the primacy of pure metaphysics over all other forms of knowledge, and presents himself as the exponent of a major tradition of thought, predominantly Eastern, but shared in the Middle Ages by the . . . West."
— **Walter Shewring**, translator of Homer's *Odyssey*

World Wisdom
The Library of Perennial Philosophy

The Library of Perennial Philosophy is dedicated to the exposition of the timeless Truth underlying the diverse religions. This Truth, often referred to as the *Sophia Perennis*—or Perennial Wisdom—finds its expression in the revealed Scriptures as well as the writings of the great sages and the artistic creations of the traditional worlds.

The Essential René Guénon: Metaphysics, Tradition, and the Crisis of Modernity appears as one of our selections in the Perennial Philosophy series.

The Perennial Philosophy Series

In the beginning of the twentieth century, a school of thought arose which has focused on the enunciation and explanation of the Perennial Philosophy. Deeply rooted in the sense of the sacred, the writings of its leading exponents establish an indispensable foundation for understanding the timeless Truth and spiritual practices which live in the heart of all religions. Some of these titles are companion volumes to the Treasures of the World's Religions series, which allows a comparison of the writings of the great sages of the past with the perennialist authors of our time.

René Guénon in Egypt

THE ESSENTIAL
RENÉ GUÉNON

Metaphysics, Tradition,
and the Crisis of Modernity

Edited by
John Herlihy

Introduction by
Martin Lings

World Wisdom

The Essential René Guénon: Metaphysics, Tradition,
and the Crisis of Modernity
© 2009 World Wisdom, Inc. and Sophia Perennis

Library of Congress Cataloging-in-Publication Data

Guénon, René.
[Selections. English. 2009]
The essential René Guénon : metaphysics, tradition, and the crisis of modernity /
edited by John Herlihy ; introduction by Martin Lings.
 p. cm. -- (The perennial philosophy series)
Includes bibliographical references and index.
ISBN 978-1-933316-57-4 (pbk. : alk. paper) 1. Tradition (Philosophy) 2.
Religion. I. Herlihy, John. II. Title.
 B2430.G82E54 2009
 194--dc22

2009027980

Cover: Tile decoration from the Alhambra Palace, Granada, Spain

Printed on acid-free paper in The United States of America.

For information address World Wisdom, Inc.
P.O. Box 2682, Bloomington, Indiana 47402-2682
www.worldwisdom.com

If you do not know, ask the people who know.
(Koran 16:43)

Spirit is still, but it sings sweetly
and universes are born.
They live in the infinite ocean of the Spirit
like ice floating on water.
(Swami Ramdas)

CONTENTS

PREFACE

The respective worldviews of tradition and science frame the nature of reality in starkly contrasting ways, and in this divided house of our time, it is clear which of the two views has gained the greater share of our attention and respect. The rational, material, and secular worldview of modern science threatens to overwhelm the traditional human quest for the metaphysical and spiritual realities that underlie the grand design of the natural world. The ascending ladder of the multiple states of being no longer inspires the mind to reach beyond itself; the hierarchical orders of knowledge have vanished in the mist; the great cycles of the cosmos have been rolled up like an ancient scroll; and eternity and infinity have been reduced to the here-and-now of sensorial perception. An intellectual and moral haze hangs around our souls and obscures the promise of supreme Mystery that awakens human consciousness to a vision beyond the stars.

Already early in the twentieth century, René Guénon identified the deep chasm that separates ancient from modern, sacred from profane, and true knowledge from empirical science, a series of deep wounds such as can fully be healed only by the ending of this cosmic cycle and the beginning of another. Is it surprising that a person emerged to explain the nature of the great divide we experience as spiritual beings living in an anti-spiritual world of our own making? The answer must be a resounding "no" given the beneficence of Heaven. Do we, however, still have the capacity to appreciate the message of this voice that speaks to us from across the decades like a grand patriarch and true visionary? The answer must be an equally resounding "yes" given the native intelligence of the human heart.

The burden of our age lies in responding to Guénon's penetrating critique of the modern world and his assessment of its near total state of disarray. Guénon resurrected a truly universal vision that draws upon an ultimate mystery that was revealed at the beginning of time and which continues to haunt the dark night of the modern soul with its promise of unity and perfection. Are we in today's sophisticated world willing to heed the warning of this man whose message has struck a celestial cord, or do our hearts only feel the faint rhythms of a distant bell that will never be struck in reality?

*   *   *

In the 1970s, I came across a dusty little hardback with a cracked spine that had been published during the Second World War, entitled *The Crisis of the Modern World.*[1] The title struck me, like the sting of a whip, with its seemingly accusatory reference to the modern world, a world in which I had been raised to believe in the myth of a progressive, technological society that was on the brink of a brave new world. After briefly skimming its Foreword, I reached into my pocket for the dollar bill that would buy me this treasure.

In this short but intense book, Guénon invokes such notions as a "primordial spirituality" now "obscured", truths once "within the reach of all" that are now "hidden and inaccessible", and the "absence of principle" that now dominates today's anti-traditional worldview. It was as though someone had lowered a bucket into the well of my being allowing me to draw upon our deepest resources—the water of "pure spirituality" that lies within human nature. In buying the book I had unknowingly sown the seeds of a new understanding that in time would lead me out of the *cul de sac* of the modern worldview and point me down the path of a spiritual future.

Thirty years later, having read through the entire range of the Guénonian corpus, I feel that I have emptied myself of the false hopes and opaque dreams that the modern world offers the unsuspecting soul. I have immersed myself instead in a comprehensive body of traditional knowledge that is not as distant as thunder and as fragile as ashes—as are the promises of the modern world—but that exists as a living reality, open to those who partake in one of the orthodox pathways that lead back to God.

*   *   *

Guénon is considered one of the founders, together with Frithjof Schuon and Ananda Coomaraswarmy, of the "traditionalist" or

---

[1] London: Luzac & Co., 1942 (the original French edition was published in 1927). Its first chapter, entitled "The Dark Age", opens the present anthology of Guénon's writings. See Appendix 2 for a full listing of Guenon's works in the original French editions, along with a complete listing of English translations by Sophia Perennis publishers (the Collected Works of Rene Guenon series).

"perennialist" school of thinking that has flowered in the present era. Schuon wrote that "in a series of remarkable works" Guénon "took upon himself the task of interpreting the still living intellectuality of the East and more especially India",[2] while Rusmir Mahmutćehajić characterized him as the "bearer of a lost and forgotten knowledge, of the universal experience of movement along the *axis mundi*, of the ascent towards the Absolute".[3] Martin Lings, a close friend of Guénon during his final years in Cairo, revealed that he "was conscious of being a pioneer":[4] one who reminded the modern world of the need for orthodoxy through revelation, followed by a tradition that can preserve the revelation in some practical manner from generation to generation.

Much of Guénon's writing could be described as a meditation on the first principle that there must exist a non-individual, non-formal body of knowledge—a Primordial Tradition—which acts like the hub of a cosmic wheel whose spokes radiate outwards into the world of formal manifestation. Through this emphasis on metaphysical knowledge as the source material for the great world religions, Guénon prepared the way for an understanding of what Frithjof Schuon described as "the transcendent unity" of the world's religious traditions, wherein each religion casts the same universal truth within the mold of an individual form that suits a particular mentality and a given era. As to the question of the source or derivation of the metaphysical doctrines of this one Primordial Tradition, Guénon states emphatically that "The origin of tradition, if indeed the word 'origin' has any place at all in such a case, is as 'non-human' as is metaphysics itself".[5] In his mind, "metaphysical truth is eternal"; it is all the rest that is subject to change and contingency.

In the Guénonian worldview, the thinking man or woman is by nature a metaphysician and only later a scientist, teacher, or craftsman. As metaphysicians, we are equipped with inner faculties and senses not

---

[2] *The Transcendent Unity of Religions* (London: Faber & Faber, 1953), p. 13.

[3] *Dialogue*, Sarajevo, 5 June 1997.

[4] "René Guénon", *Sophia*, Vol. 1, No. 1, Oakton, 1995, pp. 36-37.

[5] "Eastern Metaphysics", in *Studies in Hinduism* (Hillsdale, NY: Sophia Perennis, 2001), p. 100.

only to navigate our way through "this world", but also to see things in themselves, just as our forefather Adam, by knowing the "names of things", knew their inner meaning. In principle and as a part of human nature, we can perceive this essential knowledge through the intellect with its capacity to capture directly and without question the nature of reality, a revelatory perception that paves the way for human consciousness to reach higher realms of spiritual awareness. Today, sadly, this capacity often goes unused, for we see the forms of things and want to know what they can do for us, but we are not interested in what lies beyond the outer shell. We see an object but no horizon, and we hear a myth that entertains us, but no meaning beyond the telling of the tale. We are aware of this man and that woman, but not of the soul and the spirit that vivifies the human form.

People today are searching for something, though they may not know what exactly. What they instinctively feel lacking within themselves is precisely what Guénon has endeavored to proclaim and preserve in the hearts of modern-day generations who need not be irrevocably excluded from the knowledge that, since time immemorial, has effectively resolved the mystery of life and provided a sense of wonder. Imagine a sacred wand that has the power to transform existential truths into celestial realities; picture a universal symbol that when gazed upon could raise human consciousness to a higher order of perception, or a word that when remembered could transform nature's images into archetypal verities of a transcendent order, truths that trace their source and ultimate origin to a Primordial Tradition that leads us back to the edge of time. What Guénon has accomplished is nothing less than the restatement of the traditional doctrines, rites of worship, and universal symbols and planted them as the seeds they were meant to be within the ground of the human soul.

*　　*　　*

Four adjectives come to mind that help characterize Guénon's unique style: exactness, intelligibility, harmony, and purity. His writing displays a mathematical precision on all planes, a clarity of language that bespeaks a spiritual intelligence, a harmony of composition that is remarkably consistent throughout his *oeuvre*, and a crystalline purity of style. Glimpses of Guénon the man may occasionally shine through his sober, intellectual style, but essentially he remains in the shadows, allowing instead his spirit to shine through the art of his language and the depth of his perceptions.[6]

In order to give some definition and shape to the vast array of subjects Guénon wrote about, ranging from pure metaphysics to the symbolism of the Holy Grail, we have chosen to group selected excerpts of his writings under four headings: the Modern World, the Metaphysical World, the Hindu World, and the Traditional World. Each part has its own clear identity and relevance for today's readership, and taken together they provide a point of departure for readers who have enduring questions about the source and true nature of metaphysical knowledge, the role of the world religions in preserving the traditional doctrines, and the means and methods of spiritual realization. These sections may be described briefly as follows:

Part I: The Modern World—Guénon identifies a crisis of the modern world that, in keeping with the Hindu cosmological principle of cycles, could lead to the end of this particular world, and by doing so he touches a nerve that is near to breaking. For Guénon, the emergence of a spiritually darkened modern world is the natural result of a gradual process in which primordial spirituality and the truth to which it aspires "have become more and more hidden and inaccessible".[7] This downward spiral from higher to lower has created a host of antagonisms: Unity has become a multiplicity without center or purpose, while the sublimity of a wondrous spirituality has become a pedantic display of materialism dressed in the pretensions of rationality. The intellectual witnessing of divine ideas has become the cognitive search for the cold logic of facts. The multiple states of being and the hierarchical order of knowledge have been leveled. Spirit has become matter; quality has been reduced to quantity; pure intellectuality has degenerated into rationalism, or worse, sentimentality. The traditional sciences that found their legitimacy in the genuine sources of knowledge have disappeared just as surely as the prehistoric civilization of Atlantis vanished through cataclysm.

---

[6] For biographical details on René Guénon, see the Introduction by Martin Lings as well as Appendix 1.

[7] *The Crisis of the Modern World* (Hillsdale, NY: Sophia Perennis, 2001) p. 7.

Part II: The Metaphysical World—Already in his first work, *Introduction to the Study of the Hindu Doctrines*, published in 1921 when he was only 36 years old, Guénon clearly identified the metaphysical foundation upon which his thought rests. With a certitude that he says is an "intrinsic characteristic" of intuitive knowledge, he affirms that metaphysics is "essentially the knowledge of the Universal"[8] which he further clarifies as a "knowledge of principles belonging to the universal order". The rest of Guénon's *oeuvre* can be seen as an identification of the universal principals that exist within the world of manifestation and form. In this perspective, which can be found particularly in the Hindu tradition, but also in Taoism and Buddhism, as well as in the more inward and esoteric dimension of Christianity and Islam, myths, rites, symbols, and the rhythms of nature are considered as "signs" of a higher order of knowledge or as echoes of celestial ideas that in themselves are beyond form and words. As Guénon at one point clearly states, "Metaphysics, because it opens out a limitless vista of possibilities, must take care never to lose sight of the inexpressible, which indeed constitutes its very essence."[9]

Part III: The Hindu World—Guénon understood Hinduism to represent "a traditional order purely and exclusively [that] has no need to depend upon any more or less exterior form of organization, or upon the support of any authority other than that of the doctrine itself".[10] Hinduism has the additional advantage of having arisen in a remote epoch in which the knowledge of metaphysical reality could be presented directly to the people of that time, living as they did in closer proximity to the Primordial Era that forms the velvet backcloth of Guénon's thinking. That Hinduism has come down into the modern era essentially unchanged, that it is a living tradition which still has the capacity to produce men and women of great sanctity, Guénon attributes, in part, to its having been founded and fully grounded upon the Vedic scriptures, and, in part, to the survival of the caste system in which the Brahmins are the chosen safeguarders of the Hindu way

---

[8] *Introduction to the Study of the Hindu Doctrines* (Hillsdale, NY: Sophia Perennis, 2002), p. 71.

[9] Ibid., p. 75.

[10] Ibid., p. 123.

of life. We are, however, reminded by Marco Pallis, one of Guénon's translators, that there is no question of Guénon choosing to write on a "special subject", and that his writing "might just as well serve as a key to the understanding of any of the traditional doctrines, or all of them. As for the Hindu doctrines themselves, . . . they have simply been selected to exemplify the principles and workings of a traditional civilization".[11]

Part IV: The Traditional World—We conclude this summative anthology with some of Guénon's writings on the root symbols that both enrich and transcend the individual religions. Considerations of space allow us to include only a representative sampling of his numerous articles on various aspects of symbolism; interested readers are encouraged to refer to the work *Symbols of Sacred Science*, a posthumous collection in which is spread out a rich tapestry of symbolic exegesis that actually forms the foundation for a universal and esoteric symbology.

In his writings on symbolism, Guénon places great emphasis on the fact that "in the strict sense [symbolism] is essentially synthetic and thereby as it were intuitive, which makes it more apt than language to serve as a support for intellectual intuition which is above reason, and which must not be confused with that lower intuition to which numerous contemporary philosophers so often refer".[12] He points out that man himself "is a symbol by the very fact that he is 'created in the image of God' (Gen. 1:26-27)" and reminds us that the sensible realities of nature are not to be used for purely human benefit, rather they should be seen as signposts of a higher domain and pictograms of a higher reality. "In nature the sensible can symbolize the supra-sensible; the natural order in its entirety can in its turn be a symbol of the divine order."[13] In seeing the sun lifting itself over the horizon, one can see not only a flaming orb but the Supreme Light of the Heavens and in the image of the cross one can witness at a glance the axis between the horizontal plane of this world and the vertical

---

[11] Translator's Preface to *Introduction to the Study of Hindu Doctrines.*

[12] *Symbols of Sacred Science* (Hillsdale, NY: Sophia Perennis, 2004), pp. 7-8.

[13] Ibid., p. 10.

perspective that cuts through the cosmos with the sword of Heaven, thereby creating the duality of creation.

We must understand the things of this world as symbols of a higher order of reality, but the bud of understanding finds its fulfillment only in the flower of realization. We can surpass the domain of manifestation, "only through liberating ourselves entirely from the limiting conditions of individual existence by metaphysical realization".[14] Given this human requirement, Part IV also includes several of Guénon's articles on initiation in which he provides "spiritual direction", including a description of the function of a spiritual master and the obstacles an aspirant is likely to encounter on the way.

* * *

In his essay "Experience", Ralph Waldo Emerson writes that: "Man is a golden impossibility. The line he must walk is a hair's breadth. The wise through excess of wisdom is made a fool."[15] It is a stunning thought that fits well with the themes of Guénon's work. The miracle of the human being would be an "impossibility" without the creative hand of a Supreme Intelligence; the line dividing the traditional from the modern world is indeed finer than a hair's breadth and sharper than a razor's edge; and all the deductions of modern science would add up to nothing more than the "wisdom of a fool" without the guiding principles of metaphysics. René Guénon has shown us that the human being is an "impossibility" made possible by virtue of the golden thread of perennial truth that is woven into the very fabric of existence. Perhaps this mystery is the true point of departure in our journey of return to that mythical land beyond the celestial horizon, where "Spirit is still, but it sings sweetly and universes are born".[16]

John Herlihy

---

[14] *The Multiple States of Being* (Hilladale, NY: Sophia Perennis, 2002), p. 23.

[15] *Essays* (Boston: Houghton, Mifflin and Company, 1891), p. 59.

[16] *The Essential Swami Ramdas*, ed. Susunaga Weeraperuma (Bloomington, IN: World Wisdom, 2005), p. 18.

INTRODUCTION[1]

As regards the early part of the life of René Guénon our knowledge is very limited because of his extreme reticence. His objectivity, which is one aspect of his greatness, made him realize the evils of subjectivism and individualism in the modern world, and impelled him perhaps too far in the opposite direction; he shrank at any rate from speaking about himself. Since his death book after book has been written about him and the authors have no doubt felt often extremely frustrated at being unable to find out various things and as a result, book after book contains factual errors.

What we do know is that he was born at Blois in France in 1886, that he was the son of an architect; he had a traditional Catholic upbringing and at school he excelled in philosophy and mathematics. But at the age of 21 he was already in Paris, in the world of occultism, which was in full ferment at that time, about 1906-1908. And the dangers of that world were perhaps counteracted for him by the fact that it was more open to wider perspectives. It seems to be about this time, in Paris, that he came in contact with some Hindus of the Advaita Vedanta school, one of whom initiated him into their own Shivaite line of spirituality. We have no details of time or place and he seems never to have spoken about these Hindus nor does he seem to have had further contact with them after one or two years. But what he learned from them is in his books and his meeting with them was clearly providential. His contact with them must have been extremely intense while it lasted. His books are just what was and is needed as antidote to the crisis of the modern world.

By the time he was nearly 30, his phenomenal intelligence had enabled him to see exactly what was wrong with the modern West, and that same intelligence had dug him out of it altogether. I myself remember that world in which and for which Guénon wrote his earliest books, in the first decade after the First World War, a monstrous world made impenetrable by euphoria: the First World War had been

---

[1] This is a transcript of a lecture entitled "René Guénon", given in the autumn of 1994 at the Prince of Wales Institute in London and reprinted in the first issue of *Sophia*, Vol. 1, No. 1, 1995. ED

the war to end war. Now there would never be another war; and science had proved that man was descended from the ape, that is, he had progressed from apehood, and now this progress would continue with nothing to impede it; everything would get better and better and better. I was at school at that time and I remember being taught these things with just one hour a week being taught the opposite in religious lessons. But religion in the modern world had long before then been pushed into a corner. From its corner it protested against this euphoria, but to no avail.

Today the situation is considerably worse and considerably better. It is worse because human beings have degenerated still further. One sees far more bad faces than one did in the 1920s, if I may say so, at least, that is my impression. It is better because there is no euphoria at all. The edifice of the modern world is falling into ruin. Great cracks are appearing everywhere through which it can be penetrated as it could not be before. But it is again worse because the Church, anxious not to be behind the times, has become the accomplice of modernity.

But to return to the world of the twenties, I remember a politician proclaiming, as who would dare to do today, "We are now in the glorious morning of the world". And at this same time, Guénon wrote of this wonderful world, "It is as if an organism with its head cut off were to go on living a life which was both intense and disordered" (from *East and West* first published in 1924).

Guénon seems to have had no further contact with the Hindus and no doubt they had returned to India. Meantime, he had been initiated into a Sufi order which was to be his spiritual home for the rest of his life. Among the ills which he saw all around him he was very much preoccupied with the general anti-religious prejudice which was particularly rife among the French so-called intelligentsia. He was sure that some of these people were nonetheless virtually intelligent and would be capable of responding to the truth if it were clearly set before them. This anti-religious prejudice arose because the representatives of religion had gradually become less and less intelligent and more and more centered on sentimental considerations. In the Catholic Church especially, where the division of the community into clergy and laity was always stressed, a lay figure had to rely on the Church, it was not his business to think about spiritual things. Intelligent laymen would ask questions of priests who would not be able to answer these questions and who would take refuge in the idea that intelligence and pride were very closely connected. And so it is not difficult to see how this very anti-religious prejudice came into being especially in France.

Now Guénon put himself the question: Since these people have rejected Christianity would they be able to accept the truth when expressed in the Islamic terms of Sufism, which are closely related to Christian terms in many respects? He decided that they would not, that they would say that this is another religion; we have had enough of religion. However Hinduism, the oldest living religion, is on the surface very different from both Christianity and Islam, and so he decided to confront the Western world with the truth on the basis of Hinduism. It was to this end that he wrote his general *Introduction to the Study of Hindu Doctrines*. The French was published in 1921 to be followed in 1925 by what is perhaps the greatest of all of Guénon's books, *Man and His Becoming according to the Vedanta*.

He could not have chosen a better setting for his message of truth to the West because Hinduism has a directness which results from its having been revealed to man in a remote age when there was not yet a need to make a distinction between esoterism and exoterism, and that directness means that the truth did not have to be veiled. Already in Classical Antiquity the Mysteries, that is esoterism, were for the few. In Hinduism however they were the norm and the highest truths could be spoken of directly. There was no question of "Cast not your pearls before swine" and "Give not holy things to dogs". The sister religions of Hinduism, for example, the religions of Greece and Rome, have long since perished. But thanks to the caste system with the Brahmins as safeguarders of religion we have today a Hinduism which is still living and which down to this century has produced flowers of sanctity.

One of the points to be mentioned first is the question of the distinction which has to be made at the divine level and which is made in all esoterisms but cannot be made exoterically, that is, in religions as given to the masses today—the distinction between the Absolute and the beginnings therein of relativity. The Absolute which is One, Infinite, Eternal, Immutable, Undetermined, Unconditioned, is represented in Hinduism by the sacred monosyllable *Aum*, and it is termed *Ātmā*, which means Self, and *Brahma* which is a neuter word that serves to emphasize that it is beyond all duality such as male and female. And it is also termed *Tat* (That), just as in Sufism, the

Absolute is sometimes termed *Huwa* (He). Then we have what corresponds in other religions to the personal God, *Īshvara*, which is the beginning already of relativity, because it is concerned with manifestation, the term that Hindus use for creation, and creation is clearly the beginning of a duality—Creator and created. *Īshvara* is at the divine level, yet it is the beginning of relativity.

In all esoterism one finds the same doctrine. Meister Eckhart came into difficulties with the Church because he insisted on making a distinction between God and Godhead—*Gott und Gottheit.* He used the second term for the Absolute, that is for the absolute Absolute, and he used God for the relative Absolute. It could have been the other way around, it was just that he needed to make some difference. In Sufism one speaks of the Divine Essence and the Essential Names of God such as the One, the Truth, the All-Holy, the Living, and the Infinitely Good, *al-Rahmān,* which contains the roots of all goodness and which is also a name of the Divine Essence. Below that there are the Names of Qualities, like Creator, the Merciful, in the sense of one who has Mercy on others, and that is clearly the beginning of a duality. In every esoterism this distinction is made even at the level of the Divinity. It cannot exist below esoterism because it would result in the idea of two Gods; a division in the Divinity would be exceedingly dangerous in the hands of the mass of believers. The Divine Unity has to be maintained at all costs.

Now Guénon, in this book, traces with all clarity the hierarchy of the universe from the Absolute, from the personal God, down to the created logos, that is *buddhi,* which is the word which means intellect and which has three aspects—Brahmā (this time the word is masculine), Vishnu, and Shiva. Strictly speaking in the hierarchy of the universes these *deva*s (this is the same word linguistically as the Latin *deus*), have the rank of what we would call archangels. Hinduism is so subtle however that though they are created they can be invoked as Names of the Absolute because they descend from the Absolute and they return to the Absolute. They can be invoked in the sense of the Absolute *Brahma,* in the sense of *Ātmā,* in the sense of *Aum.*

The Hindu doctrine, like Genesis, speaks of the two waters. The Koran speaks of the two seas, the upper waters and the lower waters. The upper waters represent the higher aspect of the created world, that is, of the manifested world, corresponding to the different heavens in which are the different paradises. It is all part of the next world from the point of view of this world. The lower waters represent the world of body and soul, and all is a manifestation of the Absolute.

In *Man and His Becoming According to the Vedanta*, Guénon, having traced the manifestation of man and having shown what is the nature of man in all its details, then proceeds to show how, according to Hindu doctrine, man can return to his absolute source. It ends with the supreme spiritual possibility of oneness with the Absolute, a oneness which is already there. A Brahmin boy at the age of eight is initiated by his father and the words are spoken into his ear, "Thou art That", meaning thou art the Absolute, *tat tvam asi*. This shows how far we are from religion as understood in the modern world. But that truth which is called in Sufism the secret, *al-sirr*, is necessary in all esoterism in the present day, otherwise it would not deserve the name esoterism.

Another aspect of Hinduism which made it the perfect vehicle for Guénon's message is the breadth of its structure. In the later religions it is as if Providence had shepherded mankind into a narrower and narrower valley: the opening is still the same to heaven but the horizontal outlook is narrower and narrower because man is no longer capable of taking in more than a certain amount. The Hindu doctrine of the *samsāra*, that is, of the endless chain of innumerable worlds which have been manifested, and of which the universe consists, would lead to all sorts of distractions. Nonetheless, when one is speaking of an Absolute, Eternal Divinity, the idea that that Infinitude produced only one single world in manifesting itself does not satisfy the intelligence. The doctrine of the *samsāra* does, on the other hand, satisfy, but the worlds are innumerable that have been manifested.

Another point in this respect is that Hinduism has an amazing versatility. It depends first of all on Divine Revelation. The Vedas and the Upanishads are revealed; the *Bhagavad Gītā* is generally considered as revealed but not the *Mahābhārata* as a whole, this "inspired" epic to which the *Gītā* belongs. In Hinduism this distinction between revelation, *sruti*, and inspiration, *smriti*, is very clearly made, as it also is in Judaism and in Islam: the Pentateuch, that is, the first five books of the Old Testament, were revealed to Moses, the Psalms to David, the Koran to Muhammad. That is something which Christians as a rule do not understand. They have difficulty in realizing, in the Old Testament for example, the difference between the Pentateuch and the Books of Kings and Chronicles which are simply sacred history, inspired no doubt, but in no sense revealed. For Christians the revelation is Jesus Christ, the Word made flesh; the concept of "the Word made book", which is a parallel revelation, does not enter into their perspective.

Hinduism also has the *avatāra*s, and that a Christian can well understand, that is, the manifestations, the descents, of the Divinity. Of course a Christian would not recognize the descents of the Hindu *avatāra*s because for the average Christian there has only ever been one descent and that is Christ Himself, but Hinduism recognizes the descent as an inexhaustible possibility and it names ten *avatāra*s who have helped maintain the vitality of the religion down to the present day. The ninth *avatāra*, which is called the foreign *avatāra*, is the Buddha himself because, although he appeared in India, he was not for Hindus but clearly for the Eastern world. The breadth of Hinduism is seen also in its prefiguration of exoterism which is the recognition of the Three Ways. These are still Ways back to God—the three *mārga*s—the way of knowledge, the way of love, and the way of action—three ways which correspond to the inclinations and affinities of different human beings.

Another point which makes the terms of Hinduism so right for giving Europeans the message is that they have as Aryans an affinity with Hinduism because they are rooted in the religions of Classical Antiquity which are sister religions to Hinduism; their structure was clearly the same as the structure of Hinduism. Of course they degenerated into complete decadence and have now disappeared. Nonetheless our heritage lies in them and Guénon gives us, one might say, the possibility of a mysterious renascence in a purely positive sense by his message of the truth in Hindu terms. This affinity must not be exaggerated however, and Guénon never advised anybody who was not a Hindu, as far as I know, to become a Hindu.

His message was always one of strict orthodoxy in one esoterism, but at the same time of equal recognition of all other orthodoxies, but his purpose was in no sense academic. His motto was *vincit omnia veritas*, "Truth conquers all", but implicitly his motto was "Seek and ye shall find, knock and it shall be opened unto you". Implicit in his writings is the certainty that they will come providentially to those who are qualified to receive his message and they will impel them to seek and therefore to find a way.

Guénon was conscious of having a function and he knew what belonged to this function and what did not belong to it. He knew that it was not his function to have disciples; he never had any. It was his function to teach in preparation for a way that people would find for themselves, and this preparation meant filling in gaps which are left by modern education. The first of these gaps is the failure to understand the meaning of the transcendent and the meaning of the word intellect in consequence, a word which always continues to be used, but the intellect in the traditional sense of the word, corresponding to the Sanskrit *buddhi*, had simply been forgotten in the Western world. Guénon insisted in his writings on giving this word its true meaning which is perception of transcendent realities, the faculty which can perceive the things of the next world, and its prolongations in the soul are what might be called intellectual intuitions which are the preliminary glimmerings before intellection in the full sense takes place.

One has the impression that Guénon must have himself had an intellectual illumination at quite an early age. He must have perceived directly spiritual truths with the intellect in the true sense. He fills in gaps by explaining the meaning of rites, the meaning of symbols, the hierarchy of the worlds. In modern education the next world is left out altogether whereas in the Middle Ages students were taught about the hierarchy of the faculties and correspondingly the hierarchy of the universe.

Now I must for the moment speak on a rather personal level, but perhaps it may not be without interest. When I read the books of Guénon in the early thirties it was as if I had been struck by lightning and realized that this was the truth. I had never seen the truth before set down as in this message of Guénon's that there were many religions and that they must all be treated with reverence; they were different because they were for different people. It made sense and it also was at the same time to the glory of God because a person with even a reasonable intelligence when taught what we were taught at school would inevitably ask, well what about the rest of the world? Why were things managed in this way? Why was the truth given first of all only to the Jews, one people only? And then Christianity was ordered to spread over the world, but why so late? What about previous ages? These questions were never answered, but when I read Guénon I knew that what he said was the truth and I knew that I must do something about it.

I wrote to Guénon. I translated one of his first books, *East and West*, into English and I was in correspondence with him in connection with that. In 1930 Guénon left Paris, after the death of his first wife, and went to Cairo where he lived for twenty years until his death in 1951. One of my first ideas upon reading Guénon's books was to send copies to my greatest friend who had been a student with me at Oxford, because I knew he would have just the same reaction as I had. He came back to the West and took the same way that I had already found, a way of the kind that Guénon speaks of in his books. Then being in need of work he was given a lectureship at Cairo University, and I sent him Guénon's *poste restante* number. Guénon was extremely secretive and would not give his actual address to anybody; he wanted to disappear. He had enemies in France and he suspected that they wished to attack him by magic. I do not know this for certain but I know that Guénon was very much afraid of being attacked by certain people and he wished to remain unknown, to sink himself into the Egyptian world where he was, the world of Islam. And so my friend had to wait a long time before Guénon agreed to see him. But when the meeting finally took place Guénon became immediately attached to him, and told him that he could always come to his house whenever he liked.

In the summer of 1939 I went to visit my friend in Cairo and when I was there the war broke out. I had a lectureship in Lithuania at that time and, being unable to return there, I was forced to stay in Egypt. My friend, who had become like a member of Guénon's household, collecting his mail from *poste restante* and doing many other things for him, took me to see Guénon. A year later I was out riding in the desert with my friend when his horse ran away with him and he was killed as the result of an accident. I shall never forget having to go to tell Guénon of his death. When I did he just wept for an hour. I had no option but to take my friend's place. I had already been given the freedom of the household and very quickly I became like one of the family. It was a tremendous privilege of course. Guénon's wife could not read and she spoke only Arabic. I quickly learned Arabic so I was able to talk to her. It was a very happy marriage. They had been married for seven years without children and Guénon, who was getting fairly old—he was much older than she was—had had no children with his first wife, so it was unexpected when they began to have children. They had four children altogether. I went to see Guénon nearly every day. I was the first person to read *The Reign of Quantity*, the only book he wrote while I knew him since the other books had all been written earlier. He gave it to me chapter by chapter. And I was able also to give him my own first book when I wrote it, *The Book of Certainty*, which I gave him also chapter by chapter. It was a very great privilege to have known such a person.

During this time a rather important question was resolved. The Hindus with whom Guénon had made contact in Paris had given him a wrong idea, not a strictly Hindu idea, about Buddhism. Hinduism recognizes the Buddha as the ninth *avatāra* of Vishnu but some Hindus maintain that he was not an *avatāra*, that he was just a revolted Kshatriya, that is a member of the royal caste, against the Brahmins and it was this latter view which Guénon had accepted. Consequently he wrote about Buddhism as though it was not one of the great religions of the world. Now Ananda Coomaraswamy, Frithjof Schuon, and Marco Pallis altogether decided that they would remonstrate with Guénon about this point. Guénon was very open to being persuaded and in 1946 I took Marco Pallis to see him with the result that he agreed that he had been mistaken and that the mistakes must be rectified in his books. Marco Pallis started sending him lists of many pages that needed correction.

Guénon almost never went out except when he came to visit us. I would send a car to fetch him and he would come with his family to our house about twice a year. We lived at that time just near the pyramids outside of Cairo. I went out with him only once and we went to visit the mosque of Sayyidnā Husayn near al-Azhar. He had a remarkable presence; it was striking to see the respect with which he was treated. As he entered the mosque you could hear people on all sides saying, "*Allāhumma salli ʿalā Sayyidnā Muhammad*", that is, "May God rain blessings on the Prophet Muhammad", which is a way of expressing great reverence for someone. He had a luminous presence and his very beautiful eyes, one of his most striking features, retained their luster into early old age.

With his book on the Vedanta ranks his book on symbols, entitled *Fundamental Symbols: The Universal Language of Sacred Science,*[2] which was published after his death from all the articles which were written about symbols in his journal, *Études Traditionnelles*. It was marvelous to read these articles when they came out month after

---

[2] Also entitled *Symbols of Sacred Science*. ED

month, but this book takes us back almost to prehistoric times as does *Man and His Becoming According to the Vedanta* but in a wider sense. Everything is a symbol of course, it could not exist if it were not a symbol, but the fundamental symbols are those which express eloquently aspects of the Supreme Truth and the Supreme Way. For example, one of these aspects of both the Way and the Truth is what is called the "axis of the world", the axis which runs through all the higher states from the center of this state. That is the meaning of what is called the Tree of Life. The Tree of Life is symbolized by many particular trees: the oak, the ash, the fig and others throughout the world. The axis is the Way itself, the way of return to the Absolute. It is also symbolized by man-made things: the ladder, the mast, weapons like the lance, and the central pillar of edifices. As architects know, many buildings are built round a central axis which is not in fact there, which is not materialized. Very often in traditional houses the hearth is the center of the house and the chimney through which the smoke rises is another figure of the axis. And things which are normally horizontal are symbols of the axis: a bridge is also a symbol of the world axis. Witness the title Pontifex, the maker of the bridge, which is given to the highest spiritual authority of the Church—the bridge, which is the bridge between Heaven and earth.

Another fundamental symbol is the river. There are three aspects to the river: the crossing of the river symbolizes the passage from this world to a higher world, always, but then there is the river itself. There is the difficulty of moving upstream which symbolizes the difficulties of the spiritual path, of returning to one's source against the current. There is also the symbolism of moving in the other direction to the ocean, of returning finally to the ocean; that is another symbol of the Way. In this book amongst many other symbols, Guénon also treats of the symbolism of the mountain, the cave, the temporal cycle. In the temporal cycle the solstices of summer and winter are the gates of the gods according to Hinduism. The gate of the gods is the winter solstice, in the sign of Capricorn; the gate of the ancestors is the summer solstice, in the sign of Cancer.

As I have said, Guénon did not like to talk about himself and I respected his reticence; I did not ask him questions and I think he was pleased with that. To sum up what his function was, one might say that it was his function, in a world increasingly rife with heresy and pseudo religion, to remind twentieth century man of the need for orthodoxy which itself presupposes firstly a divine intervention, and secondly a tradition which hands down with fidelity from generation to generation what Heaven has revealed. In this connection we are deeply indebted to him for having restored to the world the word orthodoxy in the full rigor of its original meaning, that is, rectitude of opinion, a rectitude which compels the intelligent man not merely to reject heresy, but also to recognize the validity of all those faiths which conform to those criteria on which his own faith depends for its orthodoxy.

On the basis of this universality, which is often known as *religio perennis*, it was also Guénon's function to remind us that the great religions of the world are not only the means of man's salvation, but that they offer him beyond that, even in this life, two esoteric possibilities which correspond to what were known in Graeco-Roman Antiquity as *mysteria pava* and *mysteria magna*, the "Lesser Mysteries" and the "Greater Mysteries". The first of these is the way of return to the primordial perfection which was lost in the fall. The second, which presupposes the first, is the way to gnosis, the fulfillment of the precept, "know thyself". This one ultimate end is termed in Christianity *deificatio*, in Hinduism, *yoga*, union, and *moksha*, deliverance, in Buddhism, *nirvāna*, that is, extinction of all that is illusory. And in Islamic mysticism, that is Sufism, *tahaqquq*, which means realization and which was glossed by a Sufi shaykh as self-realization in God. The Mysteries and especially the Greater Mysteries are explicitly or implicitly the main theme of Guénon's writing, even in *The Crisis of the Modern World* and *The Reign of Quantity*. The troubles in question are shown to have sprung ultimately from loss of the mysterial dimension, that is, the dimension of the mysteries of esoterism. He traces all the troubles in the modern world to the forgetting of the higher aspects of religion. He was conscious of being a pioneer, and I will end simply by quoting something he wrote of himself, "All that we shall do or say will amount to giving those who come afterwards facilities which we ourselves were not given. Here as everywhere else it is the beginning of the work that is hardest."

Martin Lings

PART 1

THE MODERN WORLD

Guénon states the problem of the modern world in unequivocal terms, claiming that the modern mentality lives only for what "previous civilizations had no use". The crisis that Western civilization suffers from lies in its inability "to recognize the higher principles of a metaphysical order". As a result it bases the pursuit of reality on a "negation of principles" leading to an age of darkness preceding the end of the present world. This in essence is the "true nature of the modern world".

1

The Dark Age

The Hindu doctrine teaches that a human cycle, to which it gives the name *Manvantara*, is divided into four periods marking so many stages during which the primordial spirituality becomes gradually more and more obscured; these are the same periods that the ancient traditions of the West called the Golden, Silver, Bronze, and Iron Ages. We are now in the fourth age, the *Kali-Yuga* or "dark age", and have been so already, it is said, for more than six thousand years, that is to say since a time far earlier than any known to "classical" history. Since that time, the truths which were formerly within reach of all have become more and more hidden and inaccessible; those who possess them grow fewer and fewer, and although the treasure of "nonhuman" (that is, supra-human) wisdom that was prior to all the ages can never be lost, it nevertheless becomes enveloped in more and more impenetrable veils, which hide it from men's sight and make it extremely difficult to discover. This is why we find everywhere, under various symbols, the same theme of something that has been lost—at least to all appearances and as far as the outer world is concerned—and that those who aspire to true knowledge must rediscover; but it is also said that what is thus hidden will become visible again at the end of the cycle, which, because of the continuity binding all things together, will coincide with the beginning of a new cycle.

It will doubtless be asked why cyclic development must proceed in this manner, in a downward direction, from higher to lower, a course that will at once be perceived to be a complete antithesis to the idea of progress as the moderns understand it. The reason is that the development of any manifestation necessarily implies a gradually increasing distance from the principle from which it proceeds; starting from the highest point, it tends necessarily downward, and, as with heavy bodies, the speed of its motion increases continuously until finally it reaches a point at which it is stopped. This fall could be described as a progressive materialization, for the expression of the principle is pure spirituality; we say the expression and not the principle itself, for the latter, being beyond all oppositions, cannot be described by any term appearing to suggest an opposite. Moreover, words such as "spirit" and "matter", which we borrow here from Western terminology for the sake of convenience, have for us little more than a symbolical value; in any case, they can be made to fit the question in hand only on condition that we exclude the special interpretations given them by modern philosophy, whose "spiritualism" and "materialism" are, in our eyes, only two complementary forms that imply each other and are both negligible for anyone who wishes to go beyond these contingent points of view. However, since it is not of pure metaphysics that we propose to treat here, if all due precautions are taken to avoid ambiguity, and if the essential principles are never lost from sight, we may accept the use of terms that, although inadequate, nevertheless serve to make things more easily understandable, so long, of course, as this can be done without distorting what is to be understood.

What has been said of the development of manifestation gives a picture that is accurate when viewed as a whole, but is nonetheless too simplified and rigid in that it may give the idea of development along a straight line—in one direction only and without oscillations of any sort—whereas the truth is actually far more complex. In point of fact, . . .[1] two contrary tendencies are to be traced in everything, the one descending and the other ascending, or, in other words, one centrifugal and the other centripetal; and, from the predominance of one or the other tendency result two complementary phases of manifestation, the one a departure from the principle and the other a return to it, two phases often symbolically compared to the beating of the heart or the process of breathing. Although these two phases are usually described as successive, the two tendencies to which they correspond must in reality be conceived as always acting simultaneously—although in different proportions—and it sometimes happens, at moments when the downward tendency seems on the point of prevailing definitively in the course of the world's development, that some special action intervenes to strengthen the contrary tendency, and to restore a certain equilibrium, at least relative, such as the conditions of the moment

---

[1] Due to the collective nature of this book, with selections ranging from Guénon's complete works, references that he makes within the text to earlier comments and/or chapters have been deleted to preserve the continuity of the text within this volume. ED

allow; and this causes a partial readjustment through which the fall may seem to be checked or temporarily neutralized.[2]

It is obvious that these traditional data, of which we can give only a bare outline here, open the way to conceptions that are deeper, wider, and altogether different from the various attempts at a "philosophy of history" that are so popular with modern writers. However, we have for the moment no intention of going back to the origin of the present cycle, or even to the beginning of the *Kali-Yuga*; we shall only be concerned, directly at least, with a far more limited field, namely with the last phases of the *Kali-Yuga*. Actually, within each of the great periods of which we have spoken it is possible to go further, and distinguish secondary phases constituting so many subdivisions of it, and since each part is analogous after its own fashion to the whole, these subdivisions reproduce, so to speak, on a much smaller scale, the general course of the greater cycle in which they are contained; but here also a complete investigation of the ways in which this law applies to particular cases would carry us beyond the limits of the present study.

We shall conclude these preliminary remarks by mentioning only one or two particularly critical periods among those through which mankind has more recently passed, that is, among those falling within the period usually called "historical", as it is in fact the only one really accessible to ordinary or "profane" history; and this will lead us directly to the real object of our study, since the last of these critical periods is none other than the one that constitutes what is termed the modern age.

It is a strange fact, and one which appears never to have received proper attention, that the strictly "historical" period—in the sense that we have just indicated—goes back exactly to the sixth century before the Christian era, as though there were at that point a barrier in time impossible to penetrate by the methods of investigation at the disposal of ordinary research. Indeed, from this time onward there is everywhere a fairly precise and well-established chronology, whereas

---

[2] This is connected with the function of "divine preservation", which is represented in the Hindu tradition by Vishnu, and more particularly by the doctrine of *Avatāras* or "descents" of the divine Principle into the manifested world, a doctrine that we cannot undertake to develop here.

for everything that occurred prior to it only very vague approximations are usually obtained, and the dates suggested for the same events
often vary by several centuries. This is very noticeable even in the case
of countries of whose history we possess more than a few scattered
vestiges, such as Egypt, for example; but what is perhaps even more
astonishing is that in an exceptional and privileged case like that of
China, which possesses annals relating to far more distant periods and
dated by means of astronomical observations that leave no room for
doubt, modern writers nonetheless class these periods as "legendary",
as if they saw in them a domain in which they have no right to any certainty, and in which they do not allow themselves to obtain any. So-
called "classical" antiquity is therefore a very relative antiquity, and far
closer to modern times than to real antiquity, since it does not even go
back to the middle of the *Kali-Yuga*, whose length is itself, according
to the Hindu doctrine, only a tenth part of the whole *Manvantara*;
and this is sufficient indication of how far the moderns are justified in
priding themselves on the extent of their historical knowledge. They
will doubtless seek to justify themselves by replying that all this refers
only to "legendary" periods and is therefore unworthy of consideration; but this reply in itself is an admission of ignorance and of a lack
of comprehension that can be explained only by their contempt for
tradition; the specifically modern outlook is in fact, as we shall explain
further on, identical with the anti-traditional outlook.

In the sixth century before the Christian era considerable changes
took place for one reason or another among almost all peoples, changes
which however varied in character from country to country. In some
cases it was a readaptation of the tradition to conditions other than
those previously prevailing, a readaptation that was accomplished in
a rigorously orthodox sense. This is what occurred for example in
China, where the doctrine, primitively established as a single whole,
was then divided into two clearly distinct parts: Taoism, reserved
for an elite and comprising pure metaphysics and the traditional sciences of a properly speculative nature, and Confucianism, which was
common to all without distinction, and whose domain was that of
practical and mainly social applications. Among the Persians there
seems also to have been a readaptation of Mazdaism, for this was the

time of the last Zoroaster.[3] In India on the other hand this period saw the rise of Buddhism,[4] that is to say of a revolt against the traditional spirit, amounting to a denial of all authority and resulting in a veritable anarchy, in the etymological sense, of "absence of principle", both in the intellectual and social realms. It is a curious fact that there are no monuments in India dating from before this period, the orientalists having tried to make this fact tell in favor of their tendency to find the origins of everything in Buddhism, the importance of which they strangely exaggerate.[5] The explanation of the fact is nevertheless quite simple; it is that all earlier constructions were of wood and have therefore left no trace.[6] Such a change in the mode of construction must have corresponded however to a profound modification of the general conditions governing the existence of the people concerned.

Moving westward we see that for the Jews this was the time of the Babylonian captivity and perhaps one of the most astonishing of all these happenings is the fact that a short period of seventy years should have sufficed for the Jews to forget even their alphabet, so that after-

---

[3] It should be noted that the name Zoroaster does not really designate any particular person, but a function that is both prophetic and legislative; there were several Zoroasters, who lived at very different periods; it is probable that it was a function of a collective nature, as was that of Vyāsa in India; likewise in ancient Egypt, what was attributed to Thoth or Hermes represented the work of the whole sacerdotal caste.

[4] The question of Buddhism is by no means so simple as this brief account of it might suggest; and it is interesting to note that if, as far as their own tradition is concerned, the Hindus have always condemned the Buddhists, this is not the case with the Buddha himself, for whom many of them have a great reverence, some going so far as to see in him the ninth *Avatāra*. As for Buddhism such as it is known today, one should be careful, in dealing with it, to distinguish between its *Mahāyāna* and its *Hīnayāna* forms, that is, between the "Greater" and the "Lesser" Vehicles; in general one may say that Buddhism outside India differs markedly from the original Indian form, which began to lose ground rapidly after the death of Ashoka and eventually disappeared.

[5] In later writings, Guenon changed somewhat his views on Buddhism (see pt. 4, chap. 30, note 4 for a further explanation on this point). Note 4 above was later added by Guénon to attenuate his criticism of Buddhism in this section. ED

[6] This is a state of affairs not peculiar to India, but met with in the West as well; it is for the same reason that no traces remain of the cities of the Gauls, the existence of which is however undeniable, being testified to by contemporary witnesses; and here also modern historians have profited by the lack of monuments to depict the Gauls as savages living in forests.

ward the sacred books had to be reconstructed in quite different characters from those in use up to that time. It would be possible to cite many other events belonging more or less to the same date: we will only mention that for Rome it was the beginning of the "historical" period, which followed on the "legendary" period of the kings, and it is also known, though somewhat vaguely, that there were important movements among the Celtic peoples at this time; but without elaborating these points we must pass on to consider what happened in Greece. There too, the sixth century was the starting-point of the so-called "classical" civilization, which alone is entitled—according to the moderns—to be considered "historical", everything previous to it being so little known as to be treated as "legendary", even though recent archeological discoveries no longer leave room for doubt that there was a very real civilization; and we have reasons for supposing that this first Hellenic civilization was far more interesting intellectually than what followed, and that the relationship between the two is to some extent analogous to that between medieval and modern Europe. It should be noted however that the breach was not so complete as in the latter case, for at least a partial readaptation was carried out in the traditional order, principally in the domain of the "mysteries"; one may refer here to the case of Pythagorism, which was primarily a restoration, under a new form, of the earlier Orphic tradition, and whose connection with the Delphic cult of the Hyperborean Apollo bears witness to an unbroken and regular line of descent from one of the most ancient traditions of mankind. But on the other hand there very soon appeared something of which there had been no previous example, and which, in the future, was to have an injurious effect on the whole Western world: we refer to that special form of thought that acquired and retained the name of "philosophy"; and this point is important enough to warrant our dwelling on it at somewhat greater length.

It is true that the word "philosophy" can, in itself, be understood in quite a legitimate sense, and one which without doubt originally belonged to it, especially if it be true that Pythagoras himself was the first to use it: etymologically it denotes nothing other than "love of wisdom"; in the first place, therefore, it implies the initial disposition required for the attainment of wisdom, and, by a quite natural extension of this meaning, the quest that is born from this same disposition and that must lead to knowledge. It denotes therefore a preliminary and preparatory stage, a step as it were in the direction of wisdom or a degree corresponding to a lower level of wisdom;[7] the perversion that ensued consisted in taking this transitional stage for an end in itself and in seeking to substitute "philosophy" for wisdom, a process which implied forgetting or ignoring the true nature of the latter. It was in this way that there arose what may be described as "profane" philosophy, in other words, a pretended wisdom that was purely human and therefore entirely of the rational order, and that took the place of the true, traditional, supra-rational, and "nonhuman" wisdom. However, there still remained something of this true wisdom throughout the whole of antiquity, as is proven primarily by the persistence of the "mysteries", whose essentially initiatic character is beyond dispute; and it is also true that the teachings of the philosophers themselves usually had both an "exoteric" and an "esoteric" side, the latter leaving open the possibility of connection with a higher point of view, which in fact made itself clearly—though perhaps in some respects incompletely—apparent some centuries later among the Alexandrians. For "profane" philosophy to be definitively constituted as such, it was necessary for exoterism alone to remain and for all esoterism simply to be denied, and it is precisely this that the movement inaugurated by the Greeks was to lead to in the modern world. The tendencies that found expression among the Greeks had to be pushed to the extreme, the undue importance given to rational thought had to grow even greater, before men could arrive at "rationalism", a specifically modern attitude that consists in not merely ignoring, but expressly denying, everything of a supra-rational order. . . .

In what has been said above, there is one thing that has particular bearing on the point of view with which we are concerned: it is that some of the origins of the modern world may be sought in "classical" antiquity; the modern world is therefore not altogether wrong in claiming to base itself on the Greco-Latin civilization and to be a continuation of it. At the same time, it must be remarked that the continuation is rather remote from, and unfaithful to, the original, for

---

[7] The relation is almost the same as that which exists in the Taoist doctrine between the "gifted man" and the "transcendent man" or "true man".

classical antiquity still possessed many things pertaining to the intellectual and spiritual order, to which no equivalent is to be found in
the modern world; in any case, the two civilizations mark two quite
different degrees in the progressive obscuration of true knowledge.
One could indeed conceive of the decadence of the civilization of
antiquity leading gradually, and without any breach of continuity, to a
state more or less similar to that which we see today; but in fact this
did not occur, and in the meanwhile there intervened another critical
period for the West, a period that was at the same time one of those
readjustments to which we have already referred.

This was the epoch that witnessed the rise and spread of Christianity, which coincided on the one hand with the dispersion of the
Jews and on the other with the last phase of Greco-Latin civilization.
We can pass over these events more rapidly, despite their importance,
because they are more generally known than those we have previously
spoken of, and also because their coincidence has received more attention, even by historians with the most superficial views. Attention has
also frequently been drawn to certain features common to the decadence of the "classical" world and to the present time; and, without
wishing to push the parallel too far, it must be recognized that there
are in reality striking resemblances. Purely "profane" philosophy had
gained ground: the appearance of skepticism on the one hand, and of
Stoic and Epicurean moralism on the other, are sufficient to show to
what point intellectuality had declined. At the same time, the ancient
sacred doctrines, scarcely understood any longer by anyone, had
degenerated through this lack of understanding into "paganism" in the
true sense of the word, that is to say they had become no more than
"superstitions", things which, having lost their profound meaning,
survived for their own sake as merely outward manifestations. There
were attempts to react against this decadence: Hellenism itself strove
to acquire new vigor by the help of elements borrowed from those
Eastern doctrines with which it was able to come in touch; but such
means were no longer adequate; the Greco-Latin civilization had to
end, and the readjustment had to come from outside and be realized
in a totally different form. It was Christianity that accomplished this
transformation; and it may be noted in this connection that the comparison that can be established in certain respects between that time
and our own is, perhaps, one of the factors responsible for the disordered "messianism" to be met with today. After the troubled period

of the barbarian invasions, necessary to complete the destruction of the old order of things, a normal order was re-established for a period of some centuries; this period was that of the Middle Ages, of which the moderns—unable to understand its intellectuality—have so false an idea that it certainly appears to them far more alien and distant than classical antiquity.

For us, the real Middle Ages extend from the reign of Charlemagne to the opening of the fourteenth century, at which date a new decadence set in that has continued, through various phases and with gathering impetus, up to the present time. This date is the real starting-point of the modern crisis: it is the beginning of the disruption of Christendom, with which the Western civilization of the Middle Ages was essentially identified: at the same time, it marks the origin of the formation of "nations" and the end of the feudal system, which was very closely linked with the existence of Christendom. The origin of the modern period must therefore be placed almost two centuries further back than is usual with historians; the Renaissance and Reformation were primarily results, made possible only by the preceding decadence; but, far from being a readjustment, they marked an even deeper falling off, consummating, as they did, the definitive rupture with the traditional spirit, the former in the domain of the arts and sciences, and the latter in that of religion itself, although this was the domain in which it might have seemed the most difficult to conceive of such a rupture.

As we have said on previous occasions, what is called the Renaissance was in reality not a rebirth but the death of many things; on the pretext of being a return to the Greco-Latin civilization, it merely took over the most outward part of it, since this was the only part that could be expressed clearly in written texts; and in any case, this incomplete restoration was bound to have a very artificial character, as it meant a re-establishment of forms whose real life had gone out of them centuries before. As for the traditional sciences of the Middle Ages, after a few final manifestations around this time, they disappeared as completely as those of distant civilizations long since destroyed by some cataclysm; and this time nothing was to arise in their place. Henceforth there was only "profane" philosophy and "profane" science, in other words, the negation of true intellectuality, the limitation of knowledge to its lowest order, namely, the empirical and analytical study of facts divorced from principles, a dispersion in an indefinite multitude of insignificant details, and the accumulation of unfounded and mutually destructive hypotheses and of fragmentary views leading to nothing other than those practical applications that constitute the sole real superiority of modern civilization—a scarcely enviable superiority, moreover, which, by stifling every other preoccupation, has given the present civilization the purely material character that makes of it a veritable monstrosity.

An altogether extraordinary fact is the rapidity with which Medieval civilization was completely forgotten; already in the seventeenth century, men had lost all idea of what it had been, and its surviving monuments no longer had any meaning for them, either intellectually or even esthetically; all this is proof enough of how far the general mentality had changed. We shall not here investigate the factors—and they are certainly complex—that contributed to bringing about a change so radical that it seems difficult to admit that it can have occurred spontaneously, without the intervention of some directing will whose exact nature must remain rather enigmatic. In this connection, one may note some very strange circumstances, such as the popularization at a certain moment, under the form of new discoveries, of things that had in reality been known for a very long time, but not generally disclosed, since the disadvantages of so doing ran the risk of outweighing the advantages.[8] It is also improbable that the legend alleging that the Middle Ages were a time of gloom, ignorance, and barbarism could have arisen and become accepted, or that the veritable falsification of history in which the moderns have indulged, could have been accomplished in the absence of some preconceived idea; but we shall pursue this question no further, for, in whatever manner these processes may have taken place, our main concern for the moment is to make clear their results.

A word that rose to honor at the time of the Renaissance, and that summarized in advance the whole program of modern civilization is "humanism". Men were indeed concerned to reduce everything to

---

[8] We will quote only two examples, which were to have consequences of the most serious kind: the pretended invention of printing, which had been known by the Chinese before the Christian era, and the "official" discovery of America, with which continent far more extensive relations than is supposed had existed throughout the Middle Ages.

purely human proportions, to eliminate every principle of a higher order, and, one might say, symbolically to turn away from the heavens under pretext of conquering the earth; the Greeks, whose example they claimed to follow, had never gone as far in this direction, even at the time of their greatest intellectual decadence, and with them utilitarian considerations had at least never claimed the first place, as they were very soon to do with the moderns. Humanism was the first form of what has subsequently become contemporary secularism; and, owing to its desire to reduce everything to the measure of man as an end in himself, modern civilization has sunk stage by stage until it has reached the level of the lowest elements in man and aims at little more than satisfying the needs inherent in the material side of his nature, an aim that is in any case quite illusory since it constantly creates more artificial needs than it can satisfy.

Will the modern world follow this fatal course right to the end, or will a new readjustment intervene once more, as it did in the case of the Greco-Latin decadence, before it reaches the bottom of the abyss into which it is being drawn? It would seem that a halt midway is no longer possible since, according to all the indications furnished by the traditional doctrines, we have in fact entered upon the last phase of the *Kali-Yuga*, the darkest period of this "dark age", the state of dissolution from which it is impossible to emerge otherwise than by a cataclysm, since it is not a mere readjustment that is necessary at such a stage, but a complete renovation. Disorder and confusion prevail in every domain and have been carried to a point far surpassing all that has been known previously, so that, issuing from the West, they now threaten to invade the whole world; we know full well that their triumph can never be other than apparent and transitory, but such are the proportions which it has reached, that it would appear to be the sign of the gravest of all the crises through which mankind has passed in the course of its present cycle. Have we not arrived at that terrible age, announced in the Sacred Books of India, "when the castes shall be mingled, when even the family shall no longer exist"? It is only necessary to look around in order to be convinced that this state is truly that of the world of today, and to see on all sides that profound degeneracy which the Gospel terms "the abomination of desolation". The gravity of the situation cannot be minimized; it should be envisaged such as it is, without optimism but also without pessimism, for as we have already said, the end of the old world will be also the beginning of a new one.

This gives rise to the question: what is the reason for a period such as the one in which we now live? Indeed, however abnormal present conditions may be when considered in themselves, they must nevertheless enter into the general order of things, that order which, according to a Far-Eastern formula, is made up of the sum of all disorders; the present age, however painful and troubled it may be, must also, like all the others, have its allotted place in the complete course of human development, and indeed the very fact of its being predicted by the traditional doctrines is indication enough that this is so. What we have already said regarding the general trend of a cycle of manifestation toward progressive materialization gives a direct explanation of such a state, and shows that what is abnormal and disordered from a particular point of view is nevertheless but the consequence of a law implied in a higher and more extensive point of view. We will add, without dwelling upon the question, that like every change of state the passage from one cycle to another can take place only in darkness; this is another law of great importance and with numerous applications; but for that very reason a detailed exposition of it would carry us too far from our subject.[9]

Nor is this all: the modern period must necessarily correspond with the development of certain possibilities that have lain within the potentiality of the present cycle ever since its origin, and however low the rank of these possibilities in the hierarchy of the whole, they like the others were bound to manifest themselves at their appointed time. In this connection, it might be said that what, according to tradition, characterizes the ultimate phase of a cycle is the realization of all that has been neglected or rejected during the preceding phases; and indeed, this is exactly the case with modern civilization, which lives as it were only by that for which previous civilizations had no use. To confirm this fact, it is enough to observe how the genuine and

---

[9] This law was represented in the Eleusinian mysteries by the symbolism of the grain of wheat; the alchemists represented it by "putrefaction" and the color black, which marks the beginning of the "Great Work"; what the Christian mystics call the "dark night of the soul" is the application of this law to the spiritual development of the being in its ascent to superior states; and it would be easy to indicate many other concordant applications.

traditional representatives of such of the more ancient civilizations as have endured in the East up to the present appraise Western sciences and their industrial applications. These lower forms of knowledge, so worthless to anyone possessing knowledge of a different and higher order, had nevertheless to be realized, but this could not occur except at a stage where true intellectuality had disappeared. Such research, exclusively practical in the narrowest sense of the word, was inevitable, but it could only be carried out in an age at the opposite pole to primordial spirituality, and by men so embedded in material things as to be incapable of conceiving anything beyond them. The more they have sought to exploit matter, the more they have become its slaves, thus dooming themselves to ever increasing agitation without rule or objective, to a dispersion in pure multiplicity leading to final dissolution.

Such, in broad outline and taking note only of essentials, is the true explanation of the modern world; but let it be stated quite clearly that this explanation can in no way be taken as a justification. An inevitable ill is nonetheless an ill, and even if good is to come out of evil, this does not change the evil character of the evil itself: we use the words "good" and "evil" here only to make ourselves clear and without any specifically "moral" intention. Partial disorders cannot but exist, since they are necessary elements in the total order, but a period of disorder is in itself nevertheless comparable to a monstrosity, which, though the consequence of certain natural laws, is still a deviation and an error, or to a cataclysm, which, though resulting from the normal course of events, is nevertheless a subversion and an anomaly when viewed in itself. Modern civilization, like all things, has of necessity its reason for existing, and if indeed it represents the state of affairs that terminates a cycle, one can say that it is what it should be and that it comes in its appointed time and place; but it should nonetheless be judged according to the words of the Gospel, so often misunderstood: "Offense must needs come, but woe unto him through whom offense cometh."

2

Sacred and Profane Science

. . . In civilizations of a traditional nature, intellectual intuition lies at the root of everything; in other words, it is the pure metaphysical doctrine that constitutes the essential, everything else being linked to it, either in the form of consequences or applications to the various orders of contingent reality. Not only is this true of social institutions, but also of the sciences, that is, branches of knowledge bearing on the domain of the relative, which in such civilizations are only regarded as dependencies, prolongations, or reflections of absolute or principial knowledge. Thus a true hierarchy is always and everywhere preserved: the relative is not treated as non-existent, which would be absurd; it is duly taken into consideration, but is put in its rightful place, which cannot but be a secondary and subordinate one; and even within this relative domain there are different degrees of reality, according to whether the subject lies nearer to or further from the sphere of principles.

Thus, as regards science, there are two radically different and mutually incompatible conceptions, which may be referred to respectively as traditional and modern. We have often had occasion to allude to the "traditional sciences" that existed in antiquity and the Middle Ages and which still exist in the East, though the very idea of them is foreign to the Westerners of today. It should be added that every civilization has had "traditional sciences" of its own and of a particular type. Here we are no longer in the sphere of universal principles, to which pure metaphysics alone belongs, but in the realm of adaptations. In this realm, by the very fact of its being a contingent one, account has to be taken of the whole complex of conditions, mental and otherwise, of a given people and, we may even say, of a given period in the existence of this people, since, as we have seen above, there are times at which "readaptations" become necessary. These readaptations are no more than changes of form, which do not touch the essence of the tradition: with a metaphysical doctrine, only the expression can be modified, in a manner more or less comparable to a translation from one language into another; whatever be the forms it assumes for the sake of expressing itself—insofar as expression is possible—metaphysics remains one, just as truth itself is one. The case is different however when one passes to the realm of applications: with sciences, as with social institutions, we are in the world of form and multiplicity; therefore different forms can be said to constitute different sciences, even when the object of study remains at least partially the same. Logicians are apt to regard a science as being defined entirely by its object, but this is over-simplified and misleading; the angle from which the object is envisaged must also affect the definition of the science. The number of possible sciences is indefinite; it may well happen that several sciences study the same things, but under such different aspects and therefore by such different methods and with such different intentions that they are in reality different sciences. This is especially liable to be the case with the traditional sciences of different civilizations, which though mutually comparable nevertheless cannot always be assimilated to one another, and often cannot rightly be given the same name. The difference is even more marked if instead of comparing the different traditional sciences—which at least all have the same fundamental character—one tries to compare the sciences in general with the sciences of the modern world; it may sometimes seem at first sight that the object under study is the same in both cases, and yet the knowledge of it that the two kinds of science provide is so different that on closer examination one hesitates to say that they are the same in any respect.

A few examples may make our meaning clearer. To begin with, we will take a very general one, namely "physics", as understood by the ancients and by the moderns respectively; here the profound difference between the two conceptions can be seen without leaving the Western world. The term "physics", in its original and etymological sense, means precisely the "science of nature" without qualification; it is therefore the science that deals with the most general laws of "becoming", for "nature" and "becoming" are in reality synonymous, and it was thus that the Greeks, and notably Aristotle, understood this science. If there are more specialized sciences dealing with the same order of reality, they can amount to no more than "specifications" of physics, dealing with one or another more narrowly defined sphere. Already, therefore, one can see the significant deviation of meaning to which the modern world has subjected the word "physics", using it to designate exclusively one particular science among others, all of which are equally natural sciences, and this is an example of that process of subdivision we have already mentioned as being one of the characteristics of modern science. This "specialization", arising from an analytical attitude of mind, has been pushed to such a point that those who have undergone its influence are incapable of conceiving of a science that deals with nature in its entirety. Some of the drawbacks of this specialization have not passed altogether unnoticed, especially the narrowness of outlook that is its inevitable outcome; but even those who perceive this most clearly seem nonetheless resigned to accept it as a necessary evil entailed by the accumulation of detailed knowledge such as no man could hope to take in at once; on the one hand, they have been unable to perceive that this detailed knowledge is insignificant in itself and not worth the sacrifice of synthetic knowledge which it entails, for synthetic knowledge, though it too is restricted to what is relative, is nevertheless of a much higher order; and on the other hand, they have failed to see that the impossibility of unifying the multiplicity of this detailed knowledge is due only to their refusal to attach it to a higher principle; in other words, it is due to a persistence in proceeding from below and from outside, whereas it is the opposite method that would be necessary if one wished to have a science of any real speculative value.

If one were to compare ancient physics, not with what the moderns call by this name, but with the totality of all the natural sciences as at present constituted—for this is its real equivalent—the first difference to be noticed would be the division it has undergone into multiple "specialities" that are, so to speak, foreign to one another. This however is only the most outward side of the question, and it is not to be supposed that by joining together all these particular sciences one would arrive at an equivalent of ancient physics. The truth is that the point of view is quite different, and therein lies the essential difference between the two conceptions referred to above: the traditional conception, as we have said, attaches all the sciences to the principles of which they are the particular applications, and it is this attachment that the modern conception refuses to admit. For Aristotle, physics was only "second" in its relation to metaphysics—in other words, it was dependent on metaphysics and was really only an application to the province of nature of principles that stand above nature and are reflected in its laws; and one can say the same for the Medieval cosmology. The modern conception on the contrary claims to make the various sciences independent, denying everything that transcends them, or at least declaring it to be "unknowable" and refusing to take it into account, which in practice comes to the same thing. This negation existed *de facto* long before it was erected into a systematic theory under such names as "positivism" or "agnosticism", and it may truly be said to be the real starting-point of all modern science. It was however only in the nineteenth century that men began to glory in their ignorance—for to proclaim oneself an agnostic means nothing else—and claimed to deny to others any knowledge to which they had no access themselves; and this marked yet one more stage in the intellectual decline of the West.

By seeking to sever the connection of the sciences with any higher principle, under the pretext of assuring their independence, the modern conception robs them of all deeper meaning and even of all real interest from the point of view of knowledge; it can only lead them down a blind alley, by enclosing them, as it does, in a hopelessly limited realm.[1] Moreover, the development achieved in this realm is not a deepening of knowledge, as is commonly supposed, but on the contrary remains completely superficial, consisting only of the dispersion in detail already referred to and an analysis as barren as it is laborious; this development can be pursued indefinitely without coming one step closer to true knowledge. It must also be remarked that it is not for its own sake that, in general, Westerners pursue science; as they interpret it, their foremost aim is not knowledge, even of an inferior order, but practical applications, as can be deduced from the ease with which the majority of our contemporaries confuse science and industry, and from the number of those for whom the engineer represents the typical man of science; but this is connected with another question that we shall have to deal with more fully further on.

In assuming its modern form, science has lost not only in depth but also, one might say, in stability, for its attachment to principles enabled it to share in their immutability to the extent that its sub-

---

[1] It should be noted that an analogous rupture has occurred in the social order, where the moderns claim to have separated the temporal from the spiritual. We do not mean to deny that the two are distinct, since they are in fact concerned with different provinces, just as are metaphysics and the sciences; but due to an error inherent in the analytical mentality, it has been forgotten that distinction does not mean separation. Because of this separation, the temporal power has lost its legitimacy—which is precisely what can be said, in the intellectual order, of the sciences.

ject-matter allowed, whereas being now completely confined to the world of change, it can find nothing in it that is stable, and no fixed point on which to base itself; no longer starting from any absolute certainty, it is reduced to probabilities and approximations, or to purely hypothetical constructions that are the product of mere individual fantasy. Moreover, even if modern science should happen by chance to reach, by a roundabout route, certain conclusions that seem to be in agreement with some of the teachings of the ancient traditional sciences, it would be quite wrong to see in this a confirmation—of which these teachings stand in no need; it would be a waste of time to try to reconcile such utterly different points of view or to establish a concordance with hypothetical theories that may be completely discredited before many years are out.[2] As far as modern science is concerned, the conclusions in question can only belong to the realm of hypothesis, whereas the teachings of the traditional sciences had a very different character, coming as the indubitable consequences of truths known intuitively, and therefore infallibly, in the metaphysical order.[3] Modern experimentalism also involves the curious illusion that a theory can be proven by facts, whereas in reality the same facts can always be equally well explained by several different theories; some of the pioneers of the experimental method, such as Claude Bernard, have themselves recognized that they could interpret facts only with the help of preconceived ideas, without which they would remain "brute facts" devoid of all meaning and scientific value.

Since we have been led to speak of experimentalism, the opportunity may be taken to answer a question that may be raised in this connection: why have the experimental sciences received a development in modern civilization such as they never had in any other? The reason is that these sciences are those of the sensible world, those of

---

[2] Within the religious realm, the same can be said about that type of "apologetics" that claims to agree with the results of modern science—an utterly illusory undertaking and one that constantly requires revision; one that also runs the risk of linking religion with changing and ephemeral conceptions, from which it must remain completely independent.

[3] It would be easy to give examples of this: we will mention only one of the most striking: the difference in the conceptions of ether of Hindu cosmology and modern physics.

matter, and also those lending themselves most directly to practical applications; their development, proceeding hand in hand with what might well be called the "superstition of facts", is therefore in complete accord with specifically modern tendencies, whereas earlier ages could not find sufficient interest in them to pursue them to the extent of neglecting, for their sake, knowledge of a higher order. It must be clearly understood that we are not saying that any kind of knowledge can be deemed illegitimate, even though it be inferior; what is illegitimate is only the abuse that arises when things of this kind absorb the whole of human activity, as we see them doing at present. One could even conceive, in a normal civilization, of sciences based on an experimental method being attached to principles in the same way as other sciences, and thus acquiring a real speculative value; if in fact this does not seem to have happened, it is because attention was turned for preference in a different direction, and also because, even when it was a question of studying the sensible world as far as it could appear interesting to do so, the traditional data made it possible to undertake this study more advantageously by other methods and from another point of view.

We said above that one of the characteristics of the present age is the exploitation of everything that had hitherto been neglected as being of insufficient importance for men to devote their time and energy to, but which nevertheless had to be developed before the end of the cycle, since the things concerned had their place among the possibilities destined to be manifested within it; such in particular is the case of the experimental sciences that have come into existence in recent centuries. There are even some modern sciences that represent, quite literally, residues of ancient sciences that are no longer understood: in a period of decadence, the lowest part of these sciences became isolated from all the rest, and this part, grossly materialized, served as the starting-point for a completely different development, in a direction conforming to modern tendencies; this resulted in the formation of sciences that have ceased to have anything in common with those that preceded them. Thus, for example, it is wrong to maintain, as is generally done, that astrology and alchemy have respectively become modern astronomy and modern chemistry, even though this may contain an element of truth from a historical point of view; it contains, in fact, the very element of truth to which we have just alluded, for, if the latter sciences do in a certain sense come from the former, it is not by "evolution" or "progress"—as is claimed—but on the contrary by degeneration. This seems to call for further explanation.

In the first place, it should be noted that the attribution of different meanings to the terms "astrology" and "astronomy" is relatively recent; the two words were used synonymously by the Greeks to denote the whole ground now covered by both. It would seem at first sight then that we have here another instance of one of those divisions caused by "specialization" between what originally were simply parts of a single science. But there is a certain difference in this case, for whereas one of the parts, namely that representing the more material side of the science in question, has taken on an independent development, the other has on the contrary entirely disappeared. A measure of the truth of this lies in the fact that it is no longer known today what ancient astrology may have been, and that even those who have tried to reconstruct it have managed to create nothing more than parodies of it. Some have tried to assimilate it to a modern experimental science by using statistics and the calculation of probabilities, a method arising from a point of view which could not in any way be that of the ancient or medieval world. Others again confined their efforts to the restoration of an "art of divination", which existed formerly, but which was merely a perversion of astrology in its decline and could at best be regarded as only a very inferior application unworthy of serious consideration, as may still be seen in the civilizations of the East.

The case of chemistry is perhaps even more clear and characteristic; and modern ignorance concerning alchemy is certainly no less than in the case of astrology. True alchemy was essentially a science of the cosmological order, and it was also applicable at the same time to the human order, by virtue of the analogy between the "macrocosm" and the "microcosm"; apart from this, it was constructed expressly so as to permit a transposition into the purely spiritual domain, and this gave a symbolical value and a higher significance to its teaching, making it one of the most typical and complete of the "traditional sciences". It is not from this alchemy, with which as a matter of fact it has nothing in common, that modern chemistry has sprung; the latter is only a corruption and, in the strictest sense of the word, a deviation from that science, arising, perhaps as early as the Middle Ages, from the incomprehension of persons who were incapable of penetrating the true meaning of the symbols and took everything literally. Believing that no more than material operations were in question, they launched out upon a more or less confused experimentation; it is these men, ironically referred to by the alchemists as "puffers" and "charcoal burners", who are the real forerunners of the present-day chemists; and thus it is that modern science is constructed from the ruins of ancient sciences with the materials that had been rejected and left to the ignorant and the "profane". It should be added that the so-called restorers of alchemy, of whom there are a certain number among our contemporaries, are merely continuing this same deviation, and that their research is as far from traditional alchemy as that of the astrologers to whom we have just referred is from ancient astrology; and that is why we have a right to say that the traditional sciences of the West are really lost for the moderns.

We will confine ourselves to these few examples, although it would be easy to give others taken from slightly different realms, and showing everywhere the same degeneration. One could show for instance that psychology as it is understood today—that is, the study of mental phenomena as such—is a natural product of Anglo-Saxon empiricism and of the eighteenth-century mentality, and that the point of view to which it corresponds was so negligible for the ancient world that, even if it was sometimes taken incidentally into consideration, no one would have dreamed of making a special science of it, since anything of value that it might contain was transformed and assimilated in higher points of view. In quite a different field, one could show also that modern mathematics represents no more than the outer crust or "exoteric" side of Pythagorean mathematics; the ancient idea of numbers has indeed become quite unintelligible to the moderns, because, here too, the higher portion of the science, which gave it its traditional character and therewith a truly intellectual value, has completely disappeared—a case that is very similar to that of astrology. But to pass all the sciences in review, one after another, would be somewhat tedious; we consider that we have said enough to make clear the nature of the change to which modern sciences owe their origin, a change that is the direct opposite of "progress", amounting indeed to a veritable regression of intelligence. We will now return to considerations of a general order concerning the purposes served respectively by the traditional sciences and the modern sciences, so as to show the profound difference that exists between the real purpose of the one and of the other.

According to the traditional conception, any science is of interest less in itself than as a prolongation or secondary branch of the doctrine, whose essential part consists in pure metaphysics.[4] Actually, though every science is legitimate as long as it keeps to the place that belongs to it by virtue of its own nature, it is nevertheless easy to understand that knowledge of a lower order, for anyone who possesses knowledge of a higher order, is bound to lose much of its interest. It remains of interest only, so to speak, as a function of principial knowledge, that is, insofar as it is capable, on the one hand, of reflecting this knowledge in a contingent domain, and on the other, of leading to this knowledge itself, which, in the case that we have in mind, must never be lost sight of or sacrificed to more or less accidental considerations. These are the two complementary functions proper to the traditional sciences: on the one hand, as applications of the doctrine, they make it possible to link the different orders of reality and to integrate them into the unity of a single synthesis, and on the other, they constitute, at least for some, and in accordance with their individual aptitudes, a preparation for a higher knowledge and a way of approach to it—forming by virtue of their hierarchical positioning, according to the levels of existence to which they refer, so many rungs as it were by which it is possible to climb to the level of pure intellectuality.[5] It is only too clear that modern sciences cannot in any way serve either of these purposes; this is why they can be no more than "profane science", whereas the "traditional sciences", through their connection with metaphysical principles, are effectively incorporated in "sacred science".

The co-existence of the two roles we have just mentioned does not imply a contradiction or a vicious circle, as those who take a superficial view of the question might suppose, but it is a point calling for further discussion. It could be explained by saying that there are two points

---

[4] This is expressed, for example, in such a designation as *upaveda*, used in India for certain traditional sciences and showing their subordination to the *Veda*, that is, sacred knowledge.

[5] In our study *The Esoterism of Dante* we spoke of the symbolism of the ladder, the rungs of which correspond, in several traditions, to certain sciences and, at the same time, to states of being; this necessarily implies that these sciences were not regarded in a merely "profane" manner, as in the modern world, but allowed of a transposition bestowing on them a real initiatic significance.

of view, one descending and the other ascending, one corresponding to the unfolding of knowledge starting from principles and proceeding to applications further and further removed from them, and the other implying a gradual acquisition of this knowledge, proceeding from the lower to the higher, or, if preferred, from the outward to the inward. The question does not have to be asked, therefore, whether the sciences should proceed from below upward or from above downward, or whether, to make their existence possible, they should be based on knowledge of principles or on knowledge of the sensible world; this question can arise from the point of view of "profane" philosophy and seems, indeed, to have arisen more or less explicitly in this domain in ancient Greece, but it cannot exist for "sacred science", which can be based only on universal principles; the reason why this is pointless in the latter case is that the prime factor here is intellectual intuition, which is the most direct of all forms of knowledge, as well as the highest, and which is absolutely independent of the exercise of any faculty of the sensible or even the rational order. Sciences can only be validly constituted as "sacred sciences" by those who, before all else, are in full possession of principial knowledge and are thereby qualified to carry out, in conformity with the strictest traditional orthodoxy, all the adaptations required by circumstances of time and place. However, when these sciences have been so established, their teaching may follow an inverse order: they then serve as it were as "illustrations" of pure doctrine, which they render more easily accessible to certain minds, and the fact that they are concerned with the world of multiplicity gives them an almost indefinite variety of points of view, adapted to the no less great variety of the individual aptitudes of those whose minds are still limited to that same world of multiplicity. The ways leading to knowledge may be extremely different at the lowest degree, but they draw closer and closer together as higher levels are reached. This is not to say that any of these preparatory degrees are absolutely necessary, since they are mere contingent methods having nothing in common with the end to be attained; it is even possible for some persons, in whom the tendency to contemplation is predominant, to attain directly to true intellectual intuition without the aid of such means;[6] but this is a more or less exceptional case,

---

[6] This is why, according to Hindu doctrine, Brahmins should keep their minds con-

and in general it is accepted as being necessary to proceed upward gradually. The whole question may also be illustrated by means of the traditional image of the "cosmic wheel": the circumference in reality exists only in virtue of the center, but the beings that stand upon the circumference must necessarily start from there or, more precisely, from the point thereon at which they actually find themselves, and follow the radius that leads to the center. Moreover, because of the correspondence that exists between all the orders of reality, the truths of a lower order can be taken as symbols of those of higher orders, and can therefore serve as "supports" by which one may arrive at an understanding of these; and this fact makes it possible for any science to become a sacred science, giving it a higher or "anagogical" meaning deeper than that which it possesses in itself.[7]

Every science, we say, can assume this character, whatever may be its subject-matter, on the sole condition of being constructed and regarded from the traditional standpoint; it is only necessary to keep in mind the degrees of importance of the various sciences according to the hierarchical rank of the diverse realities studied by them; but whatever degree they may occupy, their character and functions are essentially similar in the traditional conception. What is true of the sciences is equally true of the arts, since every art can have a truly symbolic value that enables it to serve as a support for meditation, and because its rules, like the laws studied by the sciences, are reflections and applications of fundamental principles: there are then in every normal civilization "traditional arts", but these are no less unknown to the modern West than are the "traditional sciences".[8] The truth is that there is really no "profane realm" that could in any way be opposed to a "sacred realm"; there is only a "profane point of view",

---

stantly turned toward supreme knowledge, whereas Kshatriyas should rather apply themselves to a study of the successive stages by which this is gradually to be reached.

[7] This is the purpose, for example, of the astronomical symbolism so commonly used in the various traditional doctrines; and what we say here can help to indicate the true nature of ancient astrology.

[8] The art of the medieval builders can be cited as a particularly remarkable example of these traditional arts, whose practice moreover implied a real knowledge of the corresponding sciences.

which is really none other than the point of view of ignorance.[9] This is why "profane science", the science of the moderns, can as we have remarked elsewhere be justly styled "ignorant knowledge", knowledge of an inferior order confining itself entirely to the lowest level of reality, knowledge ignorant of all that lies beyond it, of any aim more lofty than itself, and of any principle that could give it a legitimate place, however humble, among the various orders of knowledge as a whole. Irremediably enclosed in the relative and narrow realm in which it has striven to proclaim itself independent, thereby voluntarily breaking all connection with transcendent truth and supreme wisdom, it is only a vain and illusory knowledge, which indeed comes from nothing and leads to nothing.

This survey will suffice to show how great is the deficiency of the modern world in the realm of science, and how that very science of which it is so proud represents no more than a deviation and, as it were, a downfall from true science, which for us is absolutely identical with what we have called "sacred" or "traditional" science. Modern science, arising from an arbitrary limitation of knowledge to a particular order—the lowest of all orders, that of material or sensible reality—has lost, through this limitation and the consequences it immediately entails, all intellectual value; as long, that is, as one gives to the word "intellectuality" the fullness of its real meaning, and refuses to share the "rationalist" error of assimilating pure intelligence to reason, or, what amounts to the same thing, of completely denying intellectual intuition. The root of this error, as of a great many other modern errors—and the cause of the entire deviation of science that we have just described—is what may be called "individualism", an attitude indistinguishable from the anti-traditional attitude itself and whose many manifestations in all domains constitute one of the most important factors in the confusion of our time. . . .

[9] To see the truth of this, it is sufficient to note facts such as the following: cosmogony, one of the most sacred of the sciences—and one that has its place in all the inspired books, including the Hebrew Bible—has become for the modern world a subject for completely "profane" hypotheses; the domain of the science is indeed the same in both cases, but the point of view is utterly different.

3

A Material Civilization

. . . Easterners are justified in reproaching modern Western civilization for being exclusively material: it has developed along purely material lines only, and from whatever point of view it is considered, one is faced with the more or less direct results of this materialization. However, there is still something to be added to what we have already said about this: in the first place, we must explain the different meanings that can be given to a word such as "materialism", for if we use it to characterize the contemporary world, people who claim to be very modern, without considering themselves in any way materialistic, will be sure to protest and will feel convinced that this is mere calumny; we must therefore begin with an explanation that will remove in advance any ambiguity that might arise on this point.

It is significant in itself that the very word "materialism" does not go any further back than the eighteenth century; it was invented by the philosopher Berkeley, who used it to designate any theory that accepted the real existence of matter; it is scarcely necessary to say that it is not this meaning of the word that concerns us here, since we are not raising the question of the existence of matter. A little later the same word took on a narrower meaning, the one in fact that it still retains: it came to denote a conception according to which nothing else exists but matter and its derivatives. It should be remarked that such a conception is something altogether new and essentially a product of the modern outlook, and therefore corresponds to at least some of the tendencies that are inherent in this outlook.[1] But we intend at present to speak of materialism mainly in another, much wider, and yet very definite sense: in this sense, materialism stands for a complete state of mind, of which the conception that we have just described is only one manifestation among many others, and which, in

---

[1] Prior to the eighteenth century there were "mechanistic" theories, from Greek atomism down to Cartesian physics, but mechanism should not be confused with materialism, despite certain affinities that may have subsequently brought about a kind of fellowship between them.

itself, is independent of any philosophical theory. This state of mind is one that consists in more or less consciously putting material things, and the preoccupations arising out of them, in the first place, whether these preoccupations claim to be speculative or purely practical; and it cannot be seriously disputed that this is the mentality of the immense majority of our contemporaries. The whole of the "profane" science that has developed in the course of recent centuries is a study of only the sensible world, is enclosed entirely within this world, and works by methods that can be applied only to this domain; these methods alone are proclaimed to be "scientific", which amounts to rejecting any science that does not deal with material things. Among those who think in this way, and even among those who have specialized in the sciences in question, there are nevertheless many who would refuse to call themselves materialists, or accept the philosophical theory that bears this name. There are even some who gladly profess a religious faith, and whose sincerity is not in doubt; but their scientific attitude does not differ appreciably from that of the avowed materialists. The question has often been raised whether, from the religious point of view, modern science should be denounced as atheistic or materialistic, but the question has usually been badly put: it is quite certain that this science does not explicitly profess atheism or materialism, it merely, because of its prejudices, ignores certain things, without formally denying them, as this or that philosopher may have done; in connection with modern science, therefore, one can only speak of *de facto* materialism, or what might be called practical materialism; but the evil is perhaps even more serious, as it is deeper and more widespread. A philosophical attitude may be something very superficial, even with the "professional" philosophers; and besides, there are people whose mind would recoil from actual negation, but who have no objection to complete indifference; this is what is most to be feared, for to deny something one must think about it to some extent, however little that may be, whereas an attitude of indifference makes it possible not to think about it at all. When an exclusively material science claims to be the only science possible, and when men are accustomed to accept, as an unquestionable truth, that there can be no valid knowledge outside this science, and when all the education they receive tends to instill into them the superstition of this science—or "scientism" as it should really be called—how could these men not in fact be materialists, or in other words, how could they fail to have all their preoccupations turned in the direction of matter?

It seems that nothing exists for modern men beyond what can be seen and touched; or at least, even if they admit theoretically that something more may exist, they immediately declare it not merely unknown but unknowable, which absolves them from having to think about it. There are, it is true, people who try to create for themselves some idea of an "other world" but, relying as they do on nothing but their imagination, they represent it in the likeness of the terrestrial world, and endow it with all the conditions of existence that belong to this world, including space and time and even a sort of "corporeality"; we have shown elsewhere, in speaking of spiritist[2] conceptions, some particularly striking examples of this kind of grossly materialized representation. But if these conceptions represent an extreme case, in which this trait is exaggerated to the point of caricature, it would be wrong to suppose that this sort of thing is confined to spiritism and to the sects that are more or less akin to it. Indeed, in a more general manner, the intrusion of the imagination into realms in which it can be of no service, and which should normally be closed to it, shows very clearly the inability of modern Westerners to rise above the sensible domain. There are many who can see no difference between "conceiving" and "imagining", and some philosophers—such as Kant—have gone so far as to declare "inconceivable" or "unthinkable" everything that is not susceptible of representation. Likewise, what is called "spiritualism" or "idealism" is usually only a sort of transposed materialism; and this is true not only of what we have termed "neo-spiritualism", but also of philosophical spiritualism itself, even though this holds itself to be the opposite of materialism. Indeed spiritualism and materialism, in the philosophical sense of these words, cannot be understood apart from each other, being merely the two halves of the Cartesian dualism, whose radical separation has been transformed into a sort of antagonism; since that time, the whole of philosophy has oscillated between these two terms, without being able to get beyond them. Despite its name, spiritualism has nothing in common with spirituality; its war with materialism cannot be of the slightest interest to those who adopt a higher point of view, and who see that these two

---

[2] For a detailed exposition of "spiritism", see the author's *The Spiritist Fallacy*. ED

alleged opposites are basically close to being simple equivalents, and that on many points their pretended opposition ultimately amounts to no more than a mere verbal dispute.

Modern persons in general cannot conceive of any other science than that of things that can be measured, counted, and weighed, in other words material things, since it is to these alone that the quantitative point of view can be applied; the claim to reduce quality to quantity is very typical of modern science. This tendency has reached the point of supposing that there can be no science, in the real meaning of the word, except where it is possible to introduce measurement, and that there can be no scientific laws except those that express quantitative relations. It is a tendency that arose with the mechanism of Descartes; since then it has become more and more pronounced, notwithstanding the rejection of Cartesian physics, for it is not bound up with any particular physical theory, but with a general conception of scientific knowledge. Today, attempts are made to apply measurement even in the psychological field, the very nature of which excludes such a method. The point has been reached of no longer understanding that the possibility of measurement derives from a quality inherent in matter, that is to say from its indefinite divisibility; or else it is thought that this quality is to be found in all that exists, which comes to the same as materializing everything. As we have said before, matter is the principle of division and of all that is multiplicity; the predominance given to the quantitative point of view—a predominance to be found . . . even in the social domain—is thus really materialism in the sense that we defined above; this materialism is not necessarily connected with philosophical materialism, which, in fact, it preceded in the development of the tendencies inherent in the modern outlook. We will not dwell on the mistake of seeking to reduce quality to quantity, or on the inadequacy of all attempts at explanation that are more or less of the "mechanistic" type. That is not our present purpose, and we will remark only, in this connection, that even in the sensible order, a science of this kind has but little connection with reality, the greater part of which is bound to elude it.

Speaking of "reality" leads us to mention another fact, which might easily be overlooked, but which is very significant as a sign of the state of mind we are speaking of: it is that people commonly use the word "reality" to denote exclusively reality of the sensible order. As language expresses the mentality of a people or a period, one must conclude that, for such people, everything that cannot be grasped by the senses is "unreal", that is to say illusory or even nonexistent. They may not be clearly aware of it, but this negative conviction is nonetheless deeply held and, if they deny it, one can be certain that though they may not be aware of it their denial is merely the expression of something even more outward, and indeed may be no more than verbal. If anyone should be tempted to think that we are exaggerating, he has only to consider, for example, what the so-called religious convictions of many people amount to, namely a few notions learnt by heart, in a purely mechanical and schoolboy way, which they have never assimilated, to which they have never devoted serious thought, but which they store in their memory and repeat on occasion as part of a certain convention or formal attitude which is all they understand by the name of religion. . . . This "minimization" of religion, of which the "verbalism" in question represents one of the final stages, . . . explains why so-called "believers" in no wise fall short of "unbelievers" as regards practical materialism. We shall return to this point later, but first we must complete our description of the materialistic character of modern science, for this is a subject that requires to be treated from various angles.

We must recall once more a point that has already been mentioned: modern sciences do not possess the character of disinterested knowledge, nor is their speculative value, even for those who believe in it, much more than a mask beneath which purely practical considerations are hidden; but this mask makes it possible to retain the illusion of a false intellectuality. Descartes himself, in working out his physics, was primarily interested in extracting from it a system of mechanics, medicine, and morality; but a still greater change was brought about by the diffusion of the influence of Anglo-Saxon empiricism. It is almost exclusively the practical results that science makes possible that gives it so much prestige in the eyes of the general public, because here again are things that can be seen and touched. We have said that pragmatism represents the outcome of all modern philosophy, and the last stage in its decline; but outside philosophy there is also, and has been for a long time, a widespread and unsystematized pragmatism that is to philosophical pragmatism what practical is to theoretical materialism, and which is really the same as what people call "common sense". What is more, this almost instinctive utilitarianism is inseparable from the materialist tendency, for "common sense" consists in not going beyond the things of this earth, as well as in ignoring all that does not make an immediate practical appeal. In particular, it is "common sense" that sees only the world of the senses as real, and that admits of no knowledge other than the one that comes from the senses; moreover, it ascribes value to this narrow form of knowledge only insofar as it offers a possibility of satisfying either material needs or a certain sentimentalism, for in reality sentiment—and this must be frankly stated at the risk of shocking contemporary moralism—lies quite close to matter. In all this there remains no place for intelligence, or at most only insofar as intelligence may consent to serve for the attainment of practical ends, and to become a mere instrument subordinated to the requirements of the lowest and most corporeal part of the human individual—"a tool for making tools", to quote a significant expression of Bergson: it is an utter indifference to truth that begets pragmatism in all its forms.

Under such conditions, industry is no longer merely an application of science, an application from which science should, in itself, remain completely independent; it has become the reason for, and justification of, science to such an extent that here too the normal relations between things have been reversed. What the modern world has striven after with all its strength, even when it has claimed in its own way to pursue science, is really nothing other than the development of industry and machinery; and in thus seeking to dominate matter and bend it to their service, men have only succeeded, as we said at the beginning of this book,[3] in becoming its slaves. Not only have they limited their intellectual ambition—if such a term can still be used in the present state of things—to inventing and constructing machines, but they have ended by becoming in fact machines themselves. Indeed, it is not only scholars but also technicians and even workers who have to undergo the specialization that certain sociologists praise so highly under the name of "division of labor"; and for the "workers", it makes intelligent work quite impossible. Very different from the craftsmen of former times, they have become mere slaves of machines with which they may be said to form part of a single body. In a purely mechanical way they have constantly to repeat certain specific movements, which are always the same and always performed in the same

---

[3] *Crisis of the Modern World.* ED

way, so as to avoid the slightest loss of time; such at least is required by the most modern methods which are supposed to represent the most advanced stage of "progress". Indeed, the object is merely to produce as much as possible; quality matters little, it is quantity alone that is of importance, which brings us back once more to the remark we have already made in other contexts, namely, that modern civilization may truly be called a quantitative civilization, and this is merely another way of saying it is a material civilization.

Anyone who wants still further evidence of this truth can find it in the tremendous importance that economic factors take on nowadays, both in the lives of peoples and of individuals: industry, commerce, finance—these seem to be the only things that count; and this is in agreement with the fact already mentioned that the only social distinction that has survived is the one based on material wealth. Politics seem to be altogether controlled by finance, and trade competition seems to be the dominant influence in determining the relations between peoples; it may be that this is only so in appearance, and that these factors are really not so much causes as means of action, but the choice of such means is a clear sign of the character of the period to which they are suited. Moreover, our contemporaries are convinced that it is almost exclusively economic conditions that dictate historical events, and they even imagine that it has always been so; a theory has even been invented according to which everything is to be explained by economic factors alone, and has been named, significantly, "historical materialism". Here also may be seen the effect of one of those suggestions to which we referred above, suggestions whose power is all the greater in that they correspond to the tendencies of the general mentality; and the result of this suggestion is that economic factors have really come to decide almost everything that occurs in the social sphere. It is true that the masses have always been led in one manner or another, and it could be said that their part in history consists primarily in allowing themselves to be led, since they represent a merely passive element, a "matter" in the Aristotelian sense of the word. But, in order to lead them today, it is sufficient to dispose of purely material means, this time in the ordinary sense of the word, and this shows clearly to what depths our age has sunk. At the same time, the masses are made to believe that they are not being led, but that they are acting spontaneously and governing themselves, and the fact that they believe this is a sign from which the extent of their stupidity may be inferred.

As we are speaking of economic factors, we will take the opportunity to mention a widespread illusion on this subject, namely that of supposing that relations established in the field of commerce can serve to draw peoples closer together and bring about an understanding between them, whereas in reality they have exactly the opposite effect. Matter, as we have often pointed out, is essentially multiplicity and division, and therefore the source of struggles and conflicts; also, whether with peoples or individuals, the economic field is and can only be that of rival interests. In particular, the West cannot count on industry, any more than on the modern science that is inseparable from it, to serve as a basis for an understanding with the East; if Easterners bring themselves to accept this industry as an unpleasant and transitory necessity, it will only be as a weapon to enable them to resist the invasion of the West and to safeguard their own existence. It should be clearly understood that this is bound to be so: Easterners who bring themselves to consider economic competition with the West, despite the repugnance they feel for this kind of activity, can do so only with one purpose, namely to rid themselves of a foreign domination that is based on mere brute force, and on the material power that industry itself supplies; violence breeds violence, but it should be recognized that it is certainly not the Easterners who have sought war in this field.

Moreover, apart from the question of the relations between East and West, it is easy to see that one of the most conspicuous results of industrial development is that engines of war are being constantly perfected and their power of destruction increased at an ominous rate. This alone should be enough to shatter the "pacifist" dreams of some of the admirers of modernist "progress"; but the dreamers and idealists are incorrigible, and their gullibility seems to know no bounds. The "humanitarianism" that is so much in fashion is certainly not worth taking seriously; but it is strange that people should talk so much about ending all war at a time when the ravages it causes are greater than they have ever been, not only because the means of destruction have been multiplied, but also because, as wars are no longer fought between comparatively small armies composed solely of professional soldiers, all the individuals on both sides are flung against each other indiscriminately, including those who are the least qualified for this kind of function. Here again is a striking example of modern confusion, and it is truly portentous, for those who care to reflect upon it, that a "mass uprising" or a "general mobilization" should have come to be considered quite natural, and that with very few exceptions the minds of all should have accepted the idea of an "armed nation". In this also can be seen an outcome of the belief in the power of numbers alone: it is in keeping with the quantitative character of modern civilization to set in motion enormous masses of combatants; and at the same time, egalitarianism also finds its expression here, as well as in systems such as "compulsory education" and "universal suffrage". Let it be added that these generalized wars have only been made possible by another specifically modern phenomenon, that is, by the formation of "nations"—a consequence on the one hand of the destruction of the feudal system, and on the other of the disruption of the higher unity of medieval Christendom; and, without pausing over considerations that would carry us too far afield, let us point out that matters have been made still worse by the non-recognition of any spiritual authority which, under normal conditions, could be an effective arbiter, standing as it does by its very nature above all conflicts of the political order. Denial of the spiritual authority is the same thing as practical materialism; and even those who in theory claim to recognize such an authority refuse in practice to allow it any real influence or power of intervention in the social domain, in exactly the same way as they fence off religion from the concerns of their every-day existence: whether in public or in private life, it is the same mental outlook that prevails.

Even if we admit that material development does have certain advantages—though, indeed, from a very relative point of view—the sight of consequences such as those just mentioned leads one to question whether they are not far outweighed by the inconveniences. We say this without referring to the many things of incomparably greater value that have been sacrificed to this one form of development—we do not speak of the higher knowledge that has been forgotten, the intellectuality that has been overthrown, and the spirituality that has disappeared. Simply taking modern civilization on its merits, we affirm that, if the advantages and inconveniences of what has been brought about were set against each other, the result might well on balance prove to be negative. The inventions, whose number is at present growing at an ever-increasing pace, are all the more dangerous in that they bring into play forces whose real nature is quite unknown to the men who utilize them; and this ignorance is the best proof of the worthlessness of modern science as an explanatory means, that is to say considered as knowledge, even were one's attention confined entirely to the physical realm. At the same time, the fact that such ignorance in no way interferes with practical applications proves that this science is in reality directed only to practical ends, and that it is industry that is the only real object of all its research. The danger inherent in these inventions, even in those that are not expressly created for a purpose destructive to mankind—but which nonetheless cause just as many catastrophes, without mentioning the unsuspected disturbances that they create in the physical environment—will undoubtedly continue to grow, and that to an extent difficult to foretell, so that, as we have already shown, it is by no means improbable that it will be through these inventions that the modern world will bring about its own destruction, unless it can check its course in this direction while there is still time.

It is not enough however to withhold approval of modern inventions on the grounds of their dangerous side alone; there is more than this to the affair. One hears of the "benefits" claimed for what men have agreed to call "progress", and that one might even consent so to call, provided one take care to make it clear that there is no question of any but a purely material progress; but are not these "benefits", of which people are so proud, very largely illusory? Our contemporaries claim they increase their "welfare" by this means; in our opinion, the end they set themselves, even if it were really attained, is hardly worth the expenditure of so much effort; but what is more, it seems a very debatable question whether they do attain it. In the first place, the fact should be taken into account that not all men have the same tastes or the same needs, and that there are still some who would wish to avoid modern commotion and the craving for speed, but who can no longer do so. Could anyone presume to maintain that it is a "benefit" to these people to have thrust on them what is most contrary to their nature? It will be said in reply that there are few such men today, and this is considered a justification for treating them as a negligible quantity; in this, as in the field of politics, the majority arrogates to itself the right to crush minorities, which, in its eyes, evidently have no right to exist, since their very existence defies the egalitarian mania for uniformity. But if the whole of mankind be taken into consideration, instead of merely the Western world, the question bears a different aspect: the majority we have just spoken of then becomes a minority. A different argument is therefore used in this case, and by a strange contradiction it is in the name of their "superiority" that these "egalitarians" seek to impose their civilization on the rest of the world, and that they bring trouble to people who have never asked them for anything; and, since this "superiority" exists only from the material point of view, it is quite natural that the most brutal means are used to assert it. Let there be no confusion on this point: if the general public accepts the pretext of "civilization" in all good faith, there are those for whom it is no more than mere moralistic hypocrisy, serving as a mask for designs of conquest or economic ambitions. It is really an extraordinary epoch in which so many men can be made to believe that a people is being given happiness by being reduced to subjection, by being robbed of all that is most precious to it, that is to say of its own civilization, by being forced to adopt manners and institutions that were made for a different race, and by being constrained to the most distasteful kinds of work, in order to make it acquire things for which it has not the slightest use. For that is what is taking place: the modern West cannot tolerate that men should prefer to work less and be content to live on little; as it is only quantity that counts, and as everything that escapes the senses is held to be nonexistent, it is taken for granted that anyone who is not in a state of agitation and who does not produce much in a material way must be "lazy". In evidence of this and without speaking of the opinions commonly expressed about Eastern peoples, it is enough to note how the contemplative orders are viewed, even in circles that consider themselves religious. In such a world, there is no longer any place for intelligence, or anything else that is purely inward, for these are things that can neither be seen nor touched, that can neither be counted nor weighed; there is a place only for outward action in all its forms, even those that are the most completely mean-ingless. For this reason it should not be a matter for surprise that the Anglo-Saxon mania for sport gains ground day by day: the ideal of the modern world is the "human animal" who has developed his muscular strength to the highest pitch; its heroes are athletes, even though they be mere brutes; it is they who awaken popular enthusiasm, and it is their exploits that command the passionate interest of the crowd. A world in which such things are seen has indeed sunk low and seems near its end.

However, let us consider things for a moment from the standpoint of those whose ideal is material "welfare", and who therefore rejoice at all the improvements to life furnished by modern "progress"; are they quite sure they are not being duped? Is it true that, because they dispose of swifter means of communication and other things of the kind, and because of their more agitated and complicated manner of life, men are happier today than they were formerly? The very opposite seems to us to be true: disequilibrium cannot be a condition of real happiness. Moreover, the more needs a man has, the greater the likelihood that he will lack something, and thereby be unhappy; modern civilization aims at creating more and more artificial needs, and as we have already said, it will always create more needs than it can satisfy, for once one has started on this path, it is very hard to stop, and, indeed, there is no reason for stopping at any particular point. It was no hardship for men to do without things that did not exist and of which they had never dreamed; now, on the contrary, they are bound to suffer if they lack these things, since they have become accustomed to consider them as necessities, with the result that they have, in fact, really become necessary to them. Therefore men struggle in every possible way to obtain the means of procuring material satisfactions, the only ones that they are capable of appreciating: they are interested only in "making money", because it is money that enables them to obtain these things, the more of which they have, the more they wish to have, as they go on discovering fresh needs; and this passion becomes for them the sole end in life. Hence the savage competition certain evolutionists have raised to the dignity of a scientific law under the name of "the struggle for existence", whose logical consequence is that only the strongest, in the narrowly material sense of the word, have a right to exist. Hence also the envy and even hatred felt toward those who possess wealth by those who do not; how could men to whom egalitarian theories have been preached fail to revolt when they see all around them inequality in the most material order of things, the order to which they are bound to be the most sensitive? If modern civilization should some day be destroyed by the disordered appetites that it has awakened in the masses, one would have to be very blind not to see in this the just punishment of its basic vice—or, without resorting to the language of morality, the repercussion of its own action in the same domain in which this action has taken place. The Gospel says "all they that take the sword shall perish by the sword"; those who unchain the brute forces of matter will perish, crushed by these same forces, of which they will no longer be masters; having once imprudently set them in motion, they cannot hope to hold back indefinitely their fatal course. It is of little consequence whether it be the forces of nature or the forces of the human mob, or both together; in any case it is the laws of matter that are called into play, and that will inexorably destroy him who has aspired to dominate them without raising himself above matter. The Gospel also says: "If a house be divided against itself, that house cannot stand"; this saying also applies fully to the modern world with its material civilization, which cannot fail, by its very nature, to cause strife and division everywhere. The conclusion is obvious and, even without appealing to other considerations, it is possible to predict with all certainty that this world will come to a tragic end, unless a change as radical as to amount to a complete reversal of direction should intervene, and that very soon.

In speaking as we have done of the materialism of modern civilization, we are aware that some will reproach us for having overlooked certain elements that seem at least to alleviate this materialism; and indeed, if there were none such, one could truly say that this civilization would most probably have already perished miserably. We do not, therefore, in the least dispute that there are such elements, but on the other hand there should be no illusions on this subject: in the first place, the various philosophical movements that assume labels such as "spiritualism" and "idealism" are not to be counted among them, any more than are the contemporary tendencies that take the form of moralism and sentimentalism. We have already explained the reasons for this, and wish merely to recall that for us these points of view are no less "profane" than theoretical or practical materialism, and far less remote from it in reality than in appearance. In the second place, if there are still remnants of real spirituality, it is in spite of the modern outlook and in opposition to it that they have persisted. Such remnants of spirituality, insofar as they are really Western, are to be found only in religion; but we have already remarked how shrunken religion is today, what a narrow and mediocre conception of it even believers hold, and to what point it has been deprived of intellectuality, which is one with true spirituality; under such conditions, if certain possibilities still remain, it is merely in a latent state, and their effective influence amounts to very little. It is nonetheless remarkable to see the vitality of a religious tradition that, even though sunk thus into a sort of virtual state, still endures despite all the attempts made in the course of several centuries to crush and destroy it. Those who are capable of reflection must see in this resistance signs of a more than human power; but we must repeat once more that this tradition does not belong to the modern world, nor is it one of its component elements, but is the direct opposite of its tendencies and aspirations. This should be admitted frankly, instead of seeking for a vain conciliation: there can be nothing but antagonism between the religious spirit, in the true sense of the word, and the modern mentality, and any compromise is bound to weaken the former and favor the latter, whose hostility moreover will not be placated thereby, since it can only aim at the utter destruction of everything that reflects in mankind a reality higher than the human.

The modern West is said to be Christian, but this is untrue: the modern outlook is anti-Christian, because it is essentially anti-religious; and it is anti-religious because, still more generally, it is anti-traditional; this is its distinguishing characteristic and this is what makes it what it is. Undoubtedly, something of Christianity has passed even into the anti-Christian civilization of our time, even the most "advanced" of whose representatives, to use their own jargon, cannot help, involuntarily and perhaps unconsciously, having undergone and still undergoing a certain Christian influence, though an indirect one; however radical a breach with the past may be, it can never be quite complete and such as to break all continuity. More than this: we even assert that everything of value that there may be in the modern world has come to it from Christianity, or at any rate through Christianity, for Christianity has brought with it the whole heritage of former traditions, has kept this heritage alive so far as the state of things in the West made it possible, and still contains its latent possibilities. But is there anyone today, even among those calling themselves Christians, who has any real consciousness of these possibilities? Where are to be found, even in Catholicism, the men who know the deeper meaning of the doctrine that they profess outwardly, and who, not content with "believing" in a more or less superficial way—and more through sentiment than intelligence—really "know" the truth of the tradition they hold to be theirs? We would wish to see proof that there are at least a few such men, for this would be the greatest and perhaps the sole hope of salvation for the West; but we have to admit that, up to the present, we have not encountered any: is one to suppose that they live in hiding, like certain Eastern sages, in some almost inaccessible retreat, or must this last hope be definitely abandoned? The West was Christian in the Middle Ages, but is so no longer; if anyone should reply that it may again become so, we will rejoinder that no one desires this more than we do, and may it come about sooner than all we see round about us would lead us to expect. But let no one delude himself on this point: if this should happen, the modern world will have lived its day.

4

Introduction to
The Reign of Quantity *and the Signs of the Times*

Since the time when *The Crisis of the Modern World* was written [in 1927], the march of events has only served to confirm, all too completely and all too quickly, the validity of the outlook on the present situation that was adopted in that book, although the subject matter was then dealt with independently of all preoccupation with immediate "actuality" as well as of any intention toward a vain and barren "critique". Indeed, it goes without saying that considerations of that order are worth nothing except insofar as they represent an application of principles to certain particular circumstances; and it may also be noted in passing that if those who have formed the truest judgment of the errors and insufficiencies of the mentality of our times have generally maintained toward them a purely negative attitude, or have only departed from that attitude to propose virtually insignificant remedies quite inadequate to cope with the growing disorder in all domains, it is because a knowledge of true principles has been just as lacking in their case as it has been in the case of those who have persisted in admiring a so-called "progress" and in deluding themselves as to its fatal outcome.

Besides, even from a purely disinterested and "theoretical" point of view, it is not enough to denounce errors and to show them up for what they really are; useful though that may be, it is still more interesting and instructive to explain them, that is to say to investigate how and why they have come about; for everything that has any kind of existence, even error, has necessarily its reason for existence, and disorder itself must in the end find its place among the elements of universal order. Thus, whereas the modern world considered in itself is an anomaly and even a sort of monstrosity, it is no less true that, when viewed in relation to the whole historical cycle of which it is a part, it corresponds exactly to the conditions pertaining to a certain phase of that cycle, the phase that the Hindu tradition specifies as the final period of the *Kali-Yuga*. It is these conditions, arising as a consequence of the development of the cycle's manifestation, that have determined its peculiar characteristics, and from this point of view it is clear that the present times could not be otherwise than they actually are. Nonetheless, it is evident that if disorder is to be seen as an element of order, or if error is to be reduced to a partial and distorted aspect of some truth, it is necessary to place oneself above the level of the contingencies of the domain to which that disorder and those errors as such belong; similarly, in order to grasp the true significance of the modern world in the light of the cyclical laws governing the development of the present terrestrial humanity, it is necessary to be entirely detached from the mentality that is its special characteristic and to avoid being affected by it in the least degree. This is the more evident in that the said mentality implies of necessity, and as it were by definition, a complete ignorance of the laws in question, as well as of all other truths which, being more or less directly derived from transcendent principles, are essentially part of traditional knowledge; all characteristically modern conceptions are, consciously or unconsciously, a direct and unqualified denial of that knowledge.

For some time past the author has had it in mind to follow up *The Crisis of the Modern World* with a work of a more strictly "doctrinal" character, in order to set out with more precision certain aspects of the explanation of the present period given in the earlier book, in conformity with the strictly traditional point of view, which will always be adhered to; in the present case it is, for the very reasons already given, not merely the only valid point of view, but it might even be said to be the only point of view possible, since no such explanation could be imagined apart from it. Various circumstances have delayed the realization of that project up till now, but this is beside the point for anyone who is sure that everything that must happen necessarily happens in its due time, and often in ways both unforeseen and completely independent of our will. The feverish haste with which our contemporaries approach everything they do is powerless against this law and can produce only agitation and disorder, that is to say effects which are wholly negative; but would these people still be "moderns" if they were capable of understanding the advantages of following the indications given by circumstances that, far from being "fortuitous"— as their ignorance leads them to suppose—are basically nothing but more or less particularized expressions of the general order, an order at the same time both human and cosmic, with which we are compelled to integrate ourselves either voluntarily or involuntarily?

Among the features characteristic of the modern mentality, the tendency to bring everything down to an exclusively quantitative point of view will be taken from now on as the central theme of this study. This tendency is most marked in the "scientific" conceptions of recent centuries; but it is almost as conspicuous in other domains, notably in that of social organization—so much so that, with one reservation the nature and necessity of which will appear hereafter, our period could almost be defined as being essentially and primarily the "reign of quantity". This characteristic is chosen in preference to any other, not solely nor even principally because it is one of the most evident and least contestable, but above all because of its truly fundamental nature, for reduction to the quantitative is strictly in conformity with the conditions of the cyclic phase at which humanity has now arrived; and also because it is the particular tendency in question that leads logically to the lowest point of the "descent" that proceeds continuously and with ever-increasing speed from the beginning to the end of a *Manvantara*, that is to say throughout the whole course of the manifestation of a humanity such as ours. This "descent", as has often been pointed out on previous occasions, is but a gradual movement away from the principle, which is necessarily inherent in any process of manifestation; in our world, by reason of the special conditions of existence to which it is subject, the lowest point takes on the aspect of pure quantity, deprived of every qualitative distinction; it goes without saying that this point represents strictly speaking a limit, and that is why it is not legitimate to speak otherwise than of a "tendency", for, during the actual course of the cycle, the limit can never be reached since it is as it were outside and beneath any existence, either realized or even realizable.

We come now to a matter of particular importance which must be established from the outset, both in order to avoid possible misconceptions and in order to dispose in advance of a possible source of delusion, namely the fact that, by virtue of the law of analogy, the lowest point is as it were the obscure reflection or the inverted image of the highest point, from which follows the consequence, paradoxical only in appearance, that the most complete absence of all principle implies a sort of "counterfeit" of the principle itself, something that has been expressed in a "theological" form in the words "Satan is the ape of God". A proper appreciation of this fact can help greatly toward the understanding of some of the darkest enigmas of the modern world, enigmas which that world itself denies because though it carries them in itself it is incapable of perceiving them, and because this denial is an indispensable condition for the maintenance of the special mentality whereby it exists. If our contemporaries as a whole could see what it is that is guiding them and where they are really going, the modern world would at once cease to exist as such, for the "rectification" that has often been alluded to in the author's other works could not fail to come about through that very circumstance; on the other hand, since this "rectification" presupposes arrival at the point at which the "descent" is completely accomplished, where "the wheel stops turning"—at least for the instant marking the passage from one cycle to another—it is necessary to conclude that, until this point is actually attained, it is impossible that these things should be understood by men in general, but only by the small number of those who are destined to prepare, in one way or in another, the germs of the future cycle. It is scarcely necessary to say that everything that the author has set out in this book and elsewhere is intended to be addressed exclusively to these few, without any concern for the inevitable incomprehension of the others; it is true that these others are, and still must be for a certain time to come, an immense majority, but then it is precisely in the "reign of quantity", and only then, that the opinion of the majority can claim to be taken into consideration at all.

However that may be, it is particularly desirable before going any further to apply the principle outlined above to a more limited sphere than that to which it has just been applied. It must serve to dispel any confusion between the point of view of traditional science and that of profane science, especially as certain outward similarities may appear to lend themselves to such confusion. These similarities often arise only from inverted correspondences; for whereas traditional science envisages essentially the higher of the corresponding terms and allows no more than a relative value to the lower term, and then only by virtue of its correspondence with the higher term, profane science on the other hand only takes account of the lower term, and being incapable of passing beyond the domain to which it is related, claims to reduce all reality to it. Thus, to take an example directly connected with the subject of this book, the Pythagorean numbers, envisaged as the principles of things, are by no means numbers as understood by the moderns, whether mathematicians or physicists, just as principial immutability is by no means the immobility of a stone, nor true unity the uniformity of beings denuded of all their qualities; nonetheless, because numbers are in question in both cases, the partisans of an exclusively quantitative science have not failed to reckon the Pythagoreans as among their "precursors". So as not unduly to anticipate developments to follow, only this much need be said here, namely that this is but one more instance of the fact that the profane sciences of which the modern world is so proud are really and truly only the degenerate "residues" of the ancient traditional sciences, just as quantity itself, to which they strive to reduce everything, is, when considered from their special point of view, no more than the "residue" of an existence emptied of everything that constituted its essence; thus these pretended sciences, by leaving aside or even intentionally eliminating all that is truly essential, clearly prove themselves incapable of furnishing the explanation of anything whatsoever.

Just as the traditional science of numbers is quite a different thing from the profane arithmetic of the moderns, including all the algebraic or other extensions of which the latter is capable, so there is also a "sacred geometry" no less profoundly different from the "academic" science nowadays designated by the same name. There is no need to insist at length on this point, for those who have read the author's earlier works, in particular *The Symbolism of the Cross*, will call to mind many references to the symbolical geometry in question, and they will have been able to see for themselves how far it lends itself to the representation of realities of a higher order, at least to the extent that those realities are capable of being represented in a form accessible to the senses; and besides, are not geometrical forms fundamentally and necessarily the very basis of all figured or "graphic" symbolism, from that of the alphabetical and numerical characters of all languages to that of the most complex and apparently strange initiatic *yantras*? It is easy to understand that this kind of symbolism can give rise to an indefinite multiplicity of applications; and it should be equally clear that such a geometry, very far from being related only to pure quantity, is on the contrary essentially qualitative. The same can be said of the true science of numbers, for the principial numbers, though they must be referred to as numbers by analogy, are situated relatively to our world at the pole opposite to that at which are situated the numbers of common arithmetic; the latter are the only numbers the moderns know, and on them they turn all their attention, thus taking the shadow for the reality, like the prisoners in Plato's cave.

The present study is designed to provide a further and more complete demonstration of what, in a very general sense, is the true nature of these traditional sciences, thus bringing into prominence the abyss separating them from the profane sciences, which are something like a caricature or parody of them. This in turn will make it possible to measure the extent of the decadence undergone by the modern mentality in passing from one to the other; it will also indicate, by correctly situating the objects taken into account by each science, how this decadence follows strictly the downward movement of the cycle now being passed through by our humanity. Let it be clear however that these are questions nobody can ever claim to treat completely, for they are by their very nature inexhaustible; but an attempt will be made to say enough to enable anyone to draw the necessary con-clusions so far as the determination of the "cosmic moment" corre-sponding to the present period is concerned. If, however, a proportion of the matters to be dealt with nevertheless continues to appear obscure to some people, that will only be because the point of view adopted fails to conform to their mental habits, and is too foreign to everything that has been inculcated into them by the education they have received and by the environment in which they live; nothing can be done about this, for there are things for which a symbolical mode of expression properly so called is the only one possible, and which will consequently never be understood by those for whom symbolism is a dead letter. It must also be remembered that a symbolical mode of expression is the indispensable vehicle of all teaching of an initiatic character; but, without even considering the profane world and its evident and in a sense natural lack of comprehension, it is enough to glance at the vestiges of initiation that still persist in the West in order to see what some people, for lack of intellectual "qualification", make of the symbols proffered for their meditation. One may be quite sure that these people, with whatever titles they may be endowed and whatever initiatic degrees they may have received "virtually", will never get so far as to penetrate to the real meaning of the smallest fragment of the mysterious geometry of "the Great Architects of the Orient and of the Occident".

As the West has just been alluded to, one further remark is called for: however far afield the state of mind that has been specifically designated as "modern" may have spread, especially in recent years, and however strong may be the hold it has taken and that it exercises ever more completely—at least externally—over the whole world, this state of mind remains nevertheless purely Western in origin: in the West it had its birth, and the West was for a long time its exclusive domain; in the East its influence will never be anything but a Westernization. However far that influence may extend in the course of events still to be unfolded, its extension can never be held to contradict what has been said about the difference between the spirit of the East and that of the West, and this difference is none other than that between the traditional spirit and the modern spirit; for it is all too clear that to the extent that a man "Westernizes" himself, whatever may be his race or country, to that extent he ceases to be an Easterner spiritually and intellectually, that is to say from the one point of view that really holds any interest. This is not a simple question of geography, unless that word be understood in a sense other than its modern one, for there is also a symbolical geography; indeed, in this connection, there is a very significant correspondence between the domination of the West and the end of a cycle, for the West is the place where the sun sets, that is to say where it arrives at the end of its daily journey, and where, according to Chinese symbolism, "the ripe fruit falls to the foot of the tree". As to the means whereby the West has come to establish that domination, of which the "modernization" of a more or less considerable number of Easterners is only the latest and most vexing consequence, it has been made sufficiently clear in the author's other works that these means are based on material strength alone, which amounts to saying that Western domination is itself no more than an expression of the "reign of quantity".

Thus, from whatever side one looks at things, one is always brought back to the same considerations and constantly sees them verified in all possible applications. There ought not to be anything surprising in this, for truth is necessarily coherent; but that certainly does not mean that truth is "systematic", as profane philosophers and scholars all too readily imagine, confined as they are within narrowly limited conceptions to which alone the word "systems" can properly be applied, and which merely reflect the insufficiency of individual minds left to their own devices; this is so even when the minds in question belong to those conventionally called "men of genius", for all the most vaunted speculations of such people are certainly not equal in value to a knowledge of the smallest traditional truth. Enough has been said on that subject in another place, for it has previously been found necessary to denounce the errors of "individualism", for that again is one of the characteristics of the modern spirit; here it may be added that the false unity of the individual, conceived as constituting in himself a complete whole, corresponds in the human order to the false unity of the so-called "atom" in the cosmic order: both the one and the other are merely elements that are regarded as "simple" from a purely quantitative point of view, and as such are supposed to be capable of a sort of indefinite repetition, which is strictly speaking an impossibility since it is essentially incompatible with the very nature of things; in fact, this indefinite repetition is nothing but the pure multiplicity toward which the present world is straining with all its might, without however being able ever to lose itself entirely therein, because pure multiplicity is situated beneath the level of manifested existence, and represents the extreme opposite of principial unity. The descending cyclic movement must therefore be considered as taking place between these two poles, starting from unity, or rather from the point closest to unity in the domain of manifestation, relatively to the state of existence envisaged, and gradually tending toward multiplicity, that is to say toward multiplicity considered analytically and without reference to any principle, for it goes without saying that in the principial order all multiplicity is synthetically comprehended in unity itself. It might appear that there is, in a sense, multiplicity at the two extreme points, in the same way as there is correlatively, as has just been pointed out, unity on the one side and "units" on the other; but the notion of inverse analogy applies strictly here too, so that while the principial multiplicity is contained in metaphysical unity, arithmetical or quantitative "units" are on the other hand contained in the other and inferior multiplicity. Incidentally, does not the mere possibility of speaking of "units" in the plural show clearly enough how far removed the thing so spoken of is from true unity? The multiplicity of the lower order is by definition purely quantitative, it could be said to be quantity itself, deprived of all quality; on the other hand the multiplicity of the higher order, or that which can be called so analogically, is really a qualitative multiplicity, that is to say the integrality of the qualities or attributes that constitute the essence of beings and of things. So it can be said that the descent referred to tends away from pure quality toward pure quantity, both the one and the other being limits situated outside manifestation, the one above it and the other beneath. In relation to the special conditions of our world or of our state of existence, these limits are an expression of the two universal principles that have elsewhere been referred to as "essence" and "substance", and they are the two poles between which all manifestation is produced. This is a point that must be explained more fully before going any further, for it provides an indispensable key to the better understanding of the considerations to be developed later in this study.

5

Quality and Quantity

Quality and quantity are fairly generally regarded as complementary terms, although the profound reason for their complementarism is often far from being understood, this reason lying in the "polar" correspondence referred to toward the end of the introduction to this book.[1] This, the first of all cosmic dualities, is a starting-point, for it is situated at the very principle of existence or of universal manifestation, and without it no manifestation would be possible in any mode whatsoever: it is the duality of *Purusha* and *Prakriti* according to the Hindu doctrine, or to use another terminology, that of "essence" and "substance". Its two terms must be envisaged as universal principles, and as being the two poles of all manifestation; but, at another level, or rather at a number of different levels (for there are many levels, corresponding to the more or less particularized domains that can be envisaged in the interior of universal manifestation), these two terms can also be used analogically and in a relative sense to designate that which corresponds to the two principles, or most directly represents them with reference to a particular more or less limited mode of manifestation. Thus it is that essence and substance can be spoken of in relation either to a world, that is to say to a state of existence determined by certain special conditions, or in relation to a being considered as a separate entity, or even to each of the states of that being, that is to say, to its manifestation in each of the degrees of existence; in this last case, there is naturally a correspondence between what essence and substance represent in the microcosm and what they represent, considered from a macrocosmic point of view, in the world in which the manifestation of the being is situated; in other words, they are then only particularizations of the relative principles that are the determinations of universal essence and substance in relation to the conditions of the world in question.

Understood in this relative sense, and especially with reference to particular beings, essence and substance are in effect the same as the

---

[1] *The Reign of Quantity and the Signs of the Times.* ED

"form" and "matter" of the scholastic philosophers; but it is better to avoid the use of these latter terms because, doubtless owing to an imperfection of the Latin language in this connection, they only convey rather inaccurately the ideas they ought to express,[2] and also because they have lately become even more equivocal by reason of the quite different meaning commonly assigned to them in current speech. However that may be, to say that every manifested being is a composite of "form" and "matter" amounts to saying that its existence necessarily proceeds simultaneously from both essence and substance, and consequently that there is in each being something corresponding both to the one and to the other of these two principles, in such a way that the being is as it were a resultant of their union, or to speak more exactly, a resultant of the action exercised by the active principle, Essence, on the passive principle, Substance; and if consideration is confined to the special case of individual beings, the "form" and the "matter" that constitute those beings are respectively identical with what the Hindu tradition designates as *nāma* and *rupa*. While on the subject of concordances between different terminologies, thus perhaps incidentally enabling some people to translate the explanations given into a language to which they are more accustomed, it may be added that the Aristotelian designations "act" and "potency" also correspond to essence and substance. Aristotle's terms are susceptible of a more extended application than are the terms "form" and "matter", but to say that there is in every being a mixture of act and potency comes back to the same thing in the end, for act is that in him by which he participates in essence, and potency is that in him by which he participates in substance; pure act and pure potency could not exist anywhere in manifestation, since they are true equivalents of universal essence and substance.

Provided that this is clearly understood, it is possible to speak of the Essence and of the Substance of our world, that is, of the world that is the domain of the individual human being, and it can be said that in conformity with the particular conditions that define this world as such, these two principles appear in it under the aspects of quality and of quantity respectively. This may appear evident at first

---

[2] These words translate in a rather unsatisfactory way the Greek terms εἶδος and ὕλη, employed in the same sense by Aristotle. These terms will be referred to again later.

sight so far as quality is concerned, since essence is the principial synthesis of all the attributes that belong to a being and make that being
what it is, and since attributes and qualities are really synonymous: and
it may be observed that quality, considered as the content of Essence,
if such an expression be allowable, is not exclusively confined to our
world, but is susceptible of a transposition that universalizes its significance. There is nothing remarkable in this, since Essence represents
the superior principle; but in any such universalization quality ceases
to be the correlative of quantity, for quantity, unlike quality, is strictly
linked up with the special conditions of our world; furthermore, from
a theological point of view, is not quality in some way brought into
relation with God himself when his attributes are spoken of, whereas
it would be manifestly inconceivable to pretend to assign to him
any sort of corresponding quantitative determination.[3] To this the
objection might perhaps be raised that Aristotle ranks quality as well
as quantity among his "categories", which are only special modes of
the being and not co-extensive with it; he does so however without
effecting the transposition previously mentioned, indeed he has no
need to effect it, for the enumeration of his "categories" relates only
to our world and to its conditions, in such a way that quality cannot
be and is not really meant to be understood otherwise than in a sense
that is more immediate for us in our state as individuals, the sense in
which, as explained earlier, it appears as a correlative of quantity.

It is of interest to note on the other hand that the "form" of the
scholastics is what Aristotle calls εἶδος, and that this latter word is
also used to mean "species", which is properly speaking a nature or
an essence common to an indefinite multitude of individuals. Specific
nature is of a purely qualitative order, for it is truly "innumerable"
in the strict sense of the word, that is to say it is independent of
quantity, being indivisible and entire in every individual belonging
to the species, so that it is quite unaffected by the number of those
individuals, "plus" or "minus" not being applicable to it. Moreover,
εἶδος is etymologically the "idea", not only in the modern psychological sense, but also in an ontological sense nearer than is ordinarily
supposed to the sense in which Plato uses it, for whatever may be the

---

[3] It is possible to speak of *Brahma saguṇa* or "qualified", but there can be no possible
question of *Brahma* "quantified".

real differences in this connection between the conceptions of Plato and of Aristotle, as so often happens they have been greatly exaggerated by disciples and commentators. The Platonic ideas are also essences; Plato gives expression chiefly to the transcendent aspect and Aristotle to the immanent aspect, but this does not imply incompatibility; independently of any conclusions to which the "systematic" spirit may lead, it is only a matter of a difference of level; in any case, they are always considering "archetypes" or the essential principles of things, such principles representing what may be called the qualitative side of manifestation. Furthermore, the Platonic ideas, under another name and by direct filiation, are the same thing as the Pythagorean numbers; and this shows clearly that although the Pythagorean numbers are, as already indicated, called numbers analogically, they are in no way numbers in the ordinary quantitative sense of the word; they are on the contrary purely qualitative, corresponding inversely on the side of essence to what the quantitative numbers are on the side of substance.[4]

On the other hand, when Saint Thomas Aquinas says that *numerus stat ex parte materiae* he is speaking of quantitative number, thereby affirming decisively that quantity has an immediate connection with the substantial side of manifestation. The word "substantial" is used here because *materia* in the scholastic sense is not by any means the same as "matter" as understood by modern physicists, but is properly "substance", whether that word be taken in its relative meaning, as when it is put into correlation with *forma* and referred to particular beings, or whether it be taken, when *materia prima* is in question, as the passive principle of universal manifestation, that is, as pure potentiality, and so as the equivalent of *Prakriti* in the Hindu doctrine. However, as soon as "matter" is in question, in whatever sense the word be taken, everything becomes particularly obscure and confused, and doubtless not without reason. . . .[5]

---

[4] It may be observed that the name of a being, insofar as it is an expression of its essence, is properly speaking a number understood in this qualitative sense; and this establishes a close link between the conception of the Pythagorean numbers—and consequently that of the Platonic ideas—and the use of the Sanskrit word *nāma* to denote the essential side of a being.

[5] It must be pointed out, in connection with essence and substance, that the scholastics

often translate as *substantia* from the Greek, which on the contrary means properly and literally "essence", and this contributes not a little to the growth of linguistic confusion; hence such expressions as "substantial form" for instance, this expression being very ill adapted to convey the idea of that which really constitutes the essential side of a being and not its substantial side.

6

The Postulates of Rationalism

. . . The moderns claim to exclude all "mystery" from the world as they see it, in the name of a science and a philosophy characterized as "rational", and it might well be said in addition that the more narrowly limited a conception becomes the more it is looked upon as strictly "rational"; moreover it is well enough known that, since the time of encyclopaedists of the eighteenth century, the most fanatical deniers of all supra-sensible reality have been particularly fond of invoking "reason" on all occasions, and of proclaiming themselves to be "rationalists". Whatever difference there may be between this popular "rationalism" and a real philosophic "rationalism", it is at any rate only a difference of degree, both the one and the other corresponding fully to the same tendencies, which have become more and more exaggerated and at the same time more "popular" throughout the course of modern times. "Rationalism" has so frequently been spoken of in the author's earlier works, and its main characteristics have been so fully defined, that it might well suffice to refer the reader to those works;[1] nevertheless, it is so closely bound up with the very conception of a quantitative science that a few more words here and now cannot well be dispensed with.

Let it be recalled, then, that rationalism properly so called goes back to the time of Descartes, and it is worthy of note that it can thus be seen to be directly associated right from its beginnings with the idea of a "mechanistic" physics; Protestantism had prepared the way for this, by introducing into religion, together with "free enquiry", a sort of rationalism, although the word itself was not then in existence, but was only invented when the same tendency asserted itself more explicitly in the domain of philosophy. Rationalism in all its forms is essentially defined by a belief in the supremacy of reason, proclaimed as a veritable "dogma", and implying the denial of everything that is of a supra-individual order, notably of pure intellectual intuition, and this carries with it logically the exclusion of all true metaphysical knowl-

---

[1] In particular to *East and West* and to *The Crisis of the Modern World.*

edge. This same denial has also as a consequence, in another field, the rejection of all spiritual authority, which is necessarily derived from a "supra-human" source; rationalism and individualism are thus so closely linked together that they are usually confused, except in the case of certain recent philosophical theories which though not rationalistic are nonetheless exclusively individualistic. It may be noted at this point how well rationalism fits in with the modern tendency to simplification: the latter naturally always operates by the reduction of things to their most inferior elements, and so asserts itself chiefly by the suppression of the entire supra-individual domain, in anticipation of being able later on to bring everything that is left, that is to say everything in the individual order, down to the sensible or corporeal modality alone, and finally that modality itself to a mere aggregation of quantitative determinations. It is easy to see how rigorously these steps are linked together, so as to constitute as it were so many necessary stages in a continuous "degradation" of the conceptions that man forms of himself and of the world.

There is yet another kind of simplification inherent in Cartesian rationalism, and it is manifested in the first place by the reduction of the whole nature of the spirit to "thought" and that of the body to "extension"; this reduction of bodies to extension is, as pointed out earlier, the very foundation of "mechanistic" physics, and it can be regarded as the starting-point of a fully quantitative science.[2] But this is not all: in relation to "thought" another mischievous simplification arises from the way in which Descartes actually conceives of reason, which he also calls "good sense" (and if one thinks of the meaning currently assigned to that expression, it suggests something situated at a singularly mediocre level); he declares too that reason is "the most widely shared thing in the world", which at once suggests some sort of "egalitarian" idea, besides being quite obviously wrong; in all this he is only confusing completely reason "in act" with "rationality", insofar as the latter is in itself a character specific to the human being

---

[2] As for Descartes' own conception of science, it should be noted that he claims that it is possible to reach the stage of having "clear and distinct" ideas about everything, that is, ideas like those of mathematics, thus obtaining the sort of "evidence" that can actually be obtained in mathematics alone.

as such.[3] Human nature is of course present in its entirety in every individual, but it is manifested there in very diverse ways, according to the inherent qualities belonging to each individual; in each the inherent qualities are united with the specific nature so as to constitute the integrality of their essence; to think otherwise would be to think that human individuals are all alike and scarcely differ among themselves otherwise than *solo numero*. Yet from thinking of that kind all those notions about the "unity of the human spirit" are directly derived: they are continually invoked to explain all sorts of things, some of which in no way belong to the "psychological" order, as for example the fact that the same traditional symbols are met with at all times and in all places. Apart from the fact that these notions do not really concern the "spirit" but simply the "mind", the alleged unity must be false, for true unity cannot belong to the individual domain, which alone is within the purview of people who talk in this way, as it is also, and more generally, of those who think it legitimate to speak of the "human spirit", as if the spirit could be modified by any specific character. In any case, the community of nature of the individuals within the species can only produce manifestations of a very generalized kind, and is quite inadequate to account for concordances in matters that are, on the contrary, of a very detailed precision; but how could these moderns be brought to understand that the fundamental unity of all the traditions is explained solely by the fact that there is in them something "supra-human"? On the other hand, to return to things that actually are purely human, Locke, the founder of modern psychology, was evidently inspired by the Cartesian conception when he thought fit to announce that, in order to know what the Greeks and Romans thought in days gone by (for his horizon did not extend beyond Western "classical" antiquity) it is enough to find out

---

[3] In the classical definition of the human being as a "reasonable animal", "rationality" represents the "specific difference" by which man is distinguished from all other species in the animal kingdom; it is not applicable outside that kingdom, or in other words, is properly speaking only what the scholastics called a *differentia animalis*; "rationality" cannot therefore be spoken of in relation to beings belonging to other states of existence, in particular to supra-individual states, those of the angels, for example; and this is quite in agreement with the fact that reason is a faculty of an exclusively individual order, and one that can in no way overstep the boundaries of the human domain.

what Englishmen and Frenchmen are thinking today, for "man is everywhere and always the same". Nothing could possibly be more false,
yet the psychologists have never got beyond that point, for, while
they imagine that they are talking of man in general, the greater part
of what they say really only applies to the modern European; does it
not look as if they believe that the uniformity that is being imposed
gradually on all human individuals has already been realized? It is true
that, by reason of the efforts that are being made to that end, differences are becoming fewer and fewer, and therefore that the psychological hypothesis is less completely false today than it was in the time
of Locke (always on condition that any attempt to apply it, as he did,
to past times is carefully guarded against); but nonetheless the limit
can never be reached, as was explained earlier, and for as long as the
world endures there will always be irreducible differences. Finally, to
crown all this, how can a true knowledge of human nature possibly
be gained by taking as typical of it an "ideal" that in all strictness can
only be described as "infra-human"?

That much being established, it still remains to explain why rationalism is linked to the idea of an exclusively quantitative science, or
more accurately, why the latter proceeds from the former; and in this
connection it must be recognized that there is a considerable element
of truth in the analysis which Bergson applies to what he wrongly calls
"intelligence", though it is really only reason, or more correctly a particular way of using reason based on the Cartesian conception, there
being no doubt that all the forms of modern rationalism arose out of
that conception. It may be remarked incidentally that the contentions
of philosophers are often much more justifiable when they are arguing
against other philosophers than when they pass on to expound their
own views, and as each one generally sees fairly clearly the defects
of the others, they more or less destroy one another mutually. Thus
it is that Bergson, if one takes the trouble to rectify his mistakes in
terminology, gives a good demonstration of the faults of rationalism
(which, so far from being one with "intellectualism", is on the contrary its negation) and of the insufficiencies of reason, but he is no less
wrong in his own turn when, to fill the gap thus created, he probes the
"infra-rational" instead of lifting his gaze toward the "supra-rational"
(and this is why his philosophy is just as individualistic and ignores
the supra-individual order just as completely as that of his rivals). And
so, when he reproaches reason, to which it is only necessary here to

restore its rightful name, for "artificially clipping reality", there is no need to adopt his special notion of "reality", even purely hypothetically and provisionally, in order fully to understand his meaning: he is evidently thinking in terms of the reduction of all things to elements supposed to be homogeneous or identical one with another, which amounts to nothing but a reduction to the quantitative, for elements of that kind can only be conceived from a quantitative point of view; and the idea of "clipping" itself suggests fairly clearly the efforts that are made to introduce a discontinuity rightly belonging only to pure or numerical quantity, or broadly speaking to the tendency referred to earlier, namely, that of refusing to recognize as "scientific" anything that cannot be "put into figures".[4] In the same way, when he says that reason is not at ease except when it applies itself to something "solid", wherein it finds its own true domain, he seems to be aware of the inevitable tendency of reason, when reduced to itself alone, to "materialize" everything in the ordinary sense of the word, that is, to consider in all things only their grossest modalities, because quality is then at a minimum in relation to quantity; only he seems to be considering the end-point of this tendency rather than its starting-point, which renders him liable to the accusation of exaggeration, for there are evidently degrees of "materialization". Nevertheless, if one looks at the existing state of scientific conceptions . . . it is quite certain that they represent as nearly as is possible the last or lowest degree of materialization, the degree in which "solidity" understood in its material sense has reached its maximum, and that in itself is a particularly characteristic mark of the period at which we have arrived. There is evidently no need to suppose that Bergson himself understood these matters in as clear a light as is shed by the above "translation" of his language, indeed it seems very unlikely that he did, considering the multiple confusions he is constantly perpetrating; but it is nonetheless true that these views were in fact suggested to him by his estimation of what present-day science is, and on that account the testimony of a man who is incontestably a representative of the modern spirit cannot be regarded as negligible. . . .

---

[4] It can be said in this connection that of all the meanings that were comprised in the Latin word *ratio* one alone has been retained, that of "calculation", in the use to which reason is now put in the realm of "science".

To summarize the foregoing, this much can be said: rationalism, being the denial of every principle superior to reason, brings with it as a "practical" consequence the exclusive use of reason, but of reason blinded, so to speak, by the very fact that it has been isolated from the pure and transcendent intellect, of which, normally and legitimately, it can only reflect the light in the individual domain. As soon as it has lost all effective communication with the supra-individual intellect, reason cannot but tend more and more toward the lowest level, toward the inferior pole of existence, plunging ever more deeply into "materiality"; as this tendency grows, it gradually loses hold of the very idea of truth, and arrives at the point of seeking no goal other than that of making things as easy as possible for its own limited comprehension, and in this it finds an immediate satisfaction in the very fact that its own downward tendency leads it in the direction of the simplification and uniformization of all things; it submits all the more readily and speedily to this tendency because the results of this submission conform to its desires, and its ever more rapid descent cannot fail to lead at last to what has been called the "reign of quantity".

7

The End of a World

The various matters dealt with in the course of this study together
constitute what may, in a general way, be called the "signs of the
times" in the Gospel sense, in other words, the precursory signs of the
"end of a world" or of a cycle. This end only appears to be the "end
of the world", without any reservation or specification of any kind, to
those who see nothing beyond the limits of this particular cycle; a very
excusable error of perspective it is true, but one that has nonetheless
some regrettable consequences in the excessive and unjustified terrors
to which it gives rise in those who are not sufficiently detached from
terrestrial existence; and naturally they are the very people who form
this erroneous conception most easily, just because of the narrowness
of their point of view. In truth there can be many "ends of the world",
because there are cycles of very varied duration, contained as it were
one within another, and also because this same notion can always be
applied analogically at all degrees and at all levels; but it is obvious
that these "ends" are of very unequal importance, as are the cycles
themselves to which they belong; and in this connection it must be
acknowledged that the end now under consideration is undeniably of
considerably greater importance than many others, for it is the end of
a whole *Manvantara,* and so of the temporal existence of what may
rightly be called a humanity, but this, it must be said once more, in no
way implies that it is the end of the terrestrial world itself, because,
through the "rectification" that takes place at the final instant, this
end will itself immediately become the beginning of another *Manvantara.*

    While on this subject, there is yet one more point needing to be
explained more precisely: the partisans of "progress" have a habit of
saying that the "golden age" is not in the past but in the future; nevertheless the truth is that so far as our own *Manvantara* is concerned
it is in the past, for it is nothing other than the "primordial state"
itself. There is a sense however in which it is both in the past and
in the future, but only on condition that attention is not confined to
the present *Manvantara* but is extended to include the succession of
terrestrial cycles, for insofar as the future is concerned nothing but

the "golden age" of another *Manvantara* can possibly be in question; it is therefore separated from our period by a "barrier" completely insurmountable to the profane people who say that sort of thing, and they have no idea what they are talking about when they announce the near approach of a "new age" as being one with which the existing humanity will be concerned. Their error, in its most extreme form, will be that of the Antichrist himself when he claims to bring the "golden age" into being through the reign of the "counter-tradition", and when he even gives it an appearance of authenticity, purely deceitful and ephemeral though it be, by means of a counterfeit of the traditional idea of the *Sanctum Regnum;* this makes clear the reason for the afore-said preponderant part played by "evolutionist" conceptions in all the "pseudo-traditions", and although these "pseudo-traditions" are still but very partial and very feeble "prefigurations" of the "counter-tradition", yet they are no doubt unconsciously contributing more directly than anything else to the preparations for its arrival. The "barrier" recently alluded to, which in a sense compels those for whom it exists to confine themselves entirely to the interior of the present cycle, is of course a still more insuperable obstacle to the representatives of the "counter-initiation" than it is to those who are merely profane, for the former are oriented wholly toward dissolution, and so they above all are those for whom nothing can exist outside the present cycle, and it is therefore more particularly for them that the end of the cycle must really be the "end of the world" in the most complete sense that the expression can bear.

This raises another related question on which a few words should be said, although an answer is really contained implicitly in some of the considerations previously dealt with, and it is this: to what extent are the people who most fully represent the "counter-initiation" effectively conscious of the part they are playing, and to what extent are they on the other hand but the tools of a will surpassing their own and therefore hidden from them, though they be inescapably subor-dinated to it? In accordance with what has been said above, the limits between the two points of view from which their action can be envis-aged is necessarily determined by the limits of the spiritual world, into which they can in no way penetrate; they may possess a knowledge of the possibilities of the "intermediary world" as extensive as anyone cares to think, but this knowledge will nevertheless always be irreme-diably falsified by the absence of the spirit, which alone could give it its true meaning. Obviously such beings can never be mechanists or materialists, nor even partisans of "progress" or "evolutionists" in the popular sense of the words, and when they promulgate in the world the ideas which these words express, they are practicing a conscious deceit; but these ideas concern only the merely negative "anti-tradition", which for them is but a means and not an end, and they could, just like anyone else, seek to excuse their deception by saying that "the end justifies the means". Their error is of a much more profound order than that of the men whom they influence and to whom they apply "suggestion" by means of those ideas, for it arises in no other way than as the consequence of their total and invincible ignorance of the true nature of all spirituality; this makes it much more difficult to say exactly up to what point they may be conscious of the falsity of the "counter-tradition" they aim at setting up, for they may really believe that in doing so they are opposing the spirit as manifested in every normal and regular tradition, and that they are situated on the same level as those who represent it in this world; and in this sense the Antichrist must surely be the most "deluded" of all beings. This delusion has its root in the "dualist" error . . . ; dualism is found in one form or another in all beings whose horizon does not extend beyond certain limits even if the limits are those of the entire manifested world; such people cannot resolve the duality they see in all things lying within those limits by referring it to a superior principle, and so they think that it is really irreducible and are thereby led to a denial of the Supreme Unity, which indeed for them is as if it were not. For this reason it has been possible to say that the representatives of the "counter-initiation" are in the end the dupes of the part they themselves are playing, and that their delusion is in truth the worst delusion of all, since it is positively the only one whereby a being can be not merely led more or less seriously astray, but actually irremediably lost; nonetheless, if they were not so deluded they would clearly not be fulfilling a function that must be fulfilled, like every other function, so that the Divine plan may be accomplished in this world.

This leads back to the consideration of the twofold, or "benefic" and "malefic" aspect of the whole history of the world, seen as a cyclic manifestation; and this is really the "key" to all traditional explanations of the conditions under which this manifestation is developed, especially when it is being considered, as at present, in the period leading directly to its end. On the one hand, if this manifestation is simply taken by itself, without relating it to a much greater whole, the entire process from its beginning to its end is clearly a progressive "descent" or "degradation", and this is what may be called its "malefic" aspect; but, on the other hand, the same manifestation, when put back into the whole of which it is a part, produces results that have a truly "positive" result in universal existence; and its development must be carried right to the end, so as to include a development of the inferior possibilities of the "dark age", in order that the "integration" of those results may become possible and may become the immediate principle of another cycle of manifestation; this is what constitutes its "benefic" aspect. The same applies when the very end of the cycle is considered: from the special point of view of that which must then be destroyed because its manifestation is finished and as it were exhausted, the end is naturally "catastrophic" in the etymological sense, in which the word evokes the idea of a sudden and irretrievable "fall"; but, on the other hand, from the point of view according to which manifestation, in disappearing as such, is brought back to its principle so far as all that is positive in its existence is concerned, this same end appears on the contrary as the "rectification" whereby, as explained, all things are no less suddenly re-established in their "primordial state". Moreover this can be applied analogically to all degrees, whether a being or a world is in question: in short, it is always the partial point of view that is "malefic", and the point of view that is total, or relatively total with respect to the other, that is "benefic", because all possible disorders are only disorders when they are considered in themselves and "separatively", and because these partial disorders are completely effaced in the presence of the total order into which they are finally merged, constituting, when stripped of their "negative" aspect, elements in that order comparable to all others; there is indeed nothing that is "malefic" except the limitation that necessarily conditions all contingent existence, and this limitation as such has in reality but a purely negative existence. The two points of view, respectively "benefic" and "malefic", have been spoken of earlier as if they were in some way symmetrical; but it is easy to understand that they are nothing of the kind, and that the second signifies only something that is unstable and transitory, whereas only that which the first represents has a permanent and positive character, so that the "benefic" aspect cannot but prevail in the end, while the "malefic" aspect vanishes completely because it was in reality only an illusion inherent in "separativity".

Nevertheless, the truth is that it then becomes no longer proper to use the word "benefic" any more than the word "malefic", for the two terms are essentially correlative and cannot properly be used to indicate an opposition when it no longer exists, for it belongs, like all oppositions, exclusively to a particular relative and limited domain; as soon as the limits of that domain are overstepped, there is only that which is, and which cannot not be, or be other than it is; and so it comes about that, if one does not stop short of the most profound order of reality, it can be said in all truth that the "end of a world" never is and never can be anything but the end of an illusion.

8

Civilization and Progress

The civilization of the modern West appears in history as a veritable anomaly: among all those which are known to us more or less completely, this civilization is the only one that has developed along purely material lines, and this monstrous development, whose beginning coincides with the so-called Renaissance, has been accompanied, as indeed it was fated to be, by a corresponding intellectual regress; we say corresponding and not equivalent, because here are two orders of things between which there can be no common measure. This regress has reached such a point that the Westerners of today no longer know what pure intellect is; in fact they do not even suspect that anything of the kind can exist; hence their disdain, not only for Eastern civilization, but also for the Middle Ages of Europe, whose spirit escapes them scarcely less completely. How is the interest of a purely speculative knowledge to be brought home to people for whom intelligence is nothing but a means of acting on matter and turning it to practical ends, and for whom science, in their limited understanding of it, is above all important insofar as it may be applied to industrial purposes? We exaggerate nothing; it only needs a glance at one's surroundings to realize that this is indeed the mentality of the vast majority of our contemporaries; and another glance, this time at philosophy from Francis Bacon and Descartes onward, could only confirm this impression still further. We will mention, by way of reminder, that Descartes limited intelligence to reason, that he granted to what he thought might be called "metaphysics" the mere function of serving as a basis for physics, and that this physics itself was by its very nature destined, in his eyes, to pave the way for the applied sciences, mechanical, medicinal, and moral—the final limit of human knowledge as he conceived it. Are not the tendencies which he so affirmed just those that at the first glance may be seen to characterize the whole development of the modern world? To deny or to ignore all pure and supra-rational knowledge was to open up the path which logically could only lead on the one hand to positivism and agnosticism, which resign themselves to the narrowest limitations of intelligence and of its object, and on the other hand to all those sentimental and "voluntarist" theories that feverishly seek in the infra-rational for what reason cannot give them. Indeed, those of our contemporaries who wish to react against rationalism accept nonetheless the complete identification of intelligence with mere reason, and they believe that it is nothing more than a purely practical faculty, incapable of going beyond the realm of matter. Bergson has written as follows: "Intelligence, considered in what seems to be its original feature, is the faculty of manufacturing artificial objects, in particular tools to make tools [*sic*], and of indefinitely varying the manufacture."[1] And again: "Intelligence, even when it no longer operates upon its own object (i.e., brute matter), follows habits it has contracted in that operation: it applies forms that are indeed those of unorganized matter. It is made for this kind of work. With this kind of work alone is it fully satisfied. And that is what intelligence expresses by saying that thus only it arrives at distinctness and clearness."[2] From these last features it becomes obvious that there is no question here of intelligence itself, but quite simply of the Cartesian conception of intelligence, which is very different: and the "new philosophy", as its adherents call it, substitutes for the superstition of reason another that is in some respects still grosser, namely, the superstition of life. Rationalism, though powerless to attain to absolute truth, at least allowed relative truth to subsist; the intuitionism of today lowers that truth to be nothing more than a representation of sensible reality, in all its inconsistency and ceaseless change; finally, pragmatism succeeds in blotting out altogether the very notion of truth by identifying it with that of utility, which amounts to suppressing it purely and simply. We may have schematized things a little here, but we have not falsified them in the least, and whatever may have been the intermediate stages, the fundamental tendencies are indeed those we have just stated; the pragmatists, in going to the limit, show themselves to be the most authentic representatives of modern Western thought: what does the truth matter in a world whose aspirations, being solely material and sentimental and not intellectual, find complete satisfaction in industry and morality, two spheres where indeed one can very well do without conceiving the truth? To be sure, this extremity was not

---

[1] *Creative Evolution*, p. 146, in the English translation of Arthur Mitchell.

[2] Ibid., p. 169.

reached at a single stride, and many Europeans will protest that they have not reached it yet; but we are thinking particularly of the Americans, who are at a more "advanced" stage of the same civilization. Mentally as well as geographically, modern America is indeed the "Far West"; and Europe will follow, without any doubt, if nothing comes to stop the development of the consequences implied in the present state of things.

. . . These two ideas, then, of "civilization" and "progress", which are very closely connected, both date only from the second half of the eighteenth century, that is to say from the epoch which saw, among other things, the birth of materialism;[3] and they were propagated and popularized especially by the socialist dreamers of the beginning of the nineteenth century. It cannot be denied that the history of ideas leads sometimes to rather surprising observations, and helps to reduce certain fantastic ideas to their proper value; it would do so more than ever if it were not, as is moreover the case with ordinary history, falsified by biased interpretations, or limited to efforts of mere scholarship and to pointless research into questions of detail. True history might endanger certain political interests; and it may be wondered if this is not the reason, where education is concerned, why certain methods are officially imposed to the exclusion of all others: consciously or not, they begin by removing everything that might make it possible to see certain things clearly, and that is how "public opinion" is formed. But to go back to the two ideas that we have just been speaking of, let us make it quite clear that in giving them so close an origin we have in mind simply this absolute and, as we think, illusory interpretation, which is the one most usually given them today. As for the relative meaning in which the same words may be used, that is quite another question, and as this meaning is very legitimate, there can be no question here of ideas that originated at some definite moment; it matters little that they may have been expressed in one way or another and, if a term is convenient, it is not because of its recent creation that we

---

[3] The word "materialism" was invented by Berkeley, who only used it to designate belief in the reality of matter; materialism in its modern sense, that is to say the theory that nothing exists but matter, originates only with La Mettrie and Holbach; it should not be confused with mechanism, several examples of which are to be found even among the ancients.

see disadvantages in using it. Thus we do not hesitate to say that there have been and still are many different "civilizations"; it would be rather hard to define exactly this complex assemblage of elements of different orders which make up what is called a civilization, but even so everyone knows fairly well what is to be understood by it. We do not even think it necessary to try to enclose in a rigid formula either the general characteristics of civilization as a whole, or the special characteristics of some particular civilization; that is a somewhat artificial process, and we greatly distrust these narrow "pigeon-holes" that the systematic turn of mind delights in. Just as there are "civilizations", there are also, during the development of each of them, or for certain more or less limited periods of this development, "progresses" which, far from influencing everything indiscriminately, affect only this or that particular domain; in fact this is only another way of saying that a civilization develops along certain lines and in a certain direction; but just as there are progresses, there are also regresses, and sometimes the two are brought about at one and the same time in different domains. We insist, then, that all this is eminently relative; if the same words are accepted in an absolute sense they no longer correspond to any reality, and it is then that they come to represent these new ideas which have existed for barely a century and a half, and then only in the West. Certainly "Progress" and "Civilization", with capital letters, may be very effective in certain sentences, as hollow as they are rhetorical, most suitable for imposing on a mob, for which words are rather a substitute for thought than a means of expressing it, thus it is that these two words play one of the most important parts in the battery of formulas which those "in control" today use to accomplish their strange task of collective suggestion without which the mentality that is characteristic of modern times would indeed be short-lived. In this respect we doubt whether enough notice has ever been given to the analogy, which is nonetheless striking, between, for example, the actions of the orator and the hypnotist (and that of the animal-tamer belongs equally to the same class); here is another subject for the psychologists to study, and we call their attention to it in passing. No doubt the power of words has been more or less made use of in other times than ours; but what has no parallel is this gigantic collective hallucination by which a whole section of humanity has come to take the vainest fantasies for incontestable realities; and, among these idols of modern worship, the two which we are at the moment denouncing are perhaps the most pernicious of all.

As for the conception of "moral progress", it represents the other predominant factor in the modern mentality, that is, sentimentality. The presence of this element does not serve in the least to make us modify the judgment which we formulated in saying that the Western civilization is altogether material. We are well aware that some people seek to oppose the domain of sentiment to that of matter, to make the development of the one a sort of counterbalance against the spread of the other, and to take for their ideal an equilibrium as settled as possible between these two complementary elements. Such is perhaps, when all is said and done, the thought of the intuitionists who, associating intelligence inseparably with matter, hope to deliver themselves from it with the help of a rather vaguely defined instinct. Such is still more certainly the thought of the pragmatists, who make utility a substitute for truth and consider it at one and the same time under its material and moral aspects; and we see here too how fully pragmatism expresses the particular tendencies of the modern world, and above all of the Anglo-Saxon world, which is one of its most typical portions. Indeed, materialism and sentimentality, far from being in opposition, can scarcely exist one without the other, and they both attain side by side to their maximum development; the proof of this lies in America, where, as we have had occasion to remark in our books on Theosophism and Spiritualism, the worst pseudo-mystical extravagances come to birth and spread with incredible ease at the very time when industrialism and the passion for "business" are being carried to a pitch that borders on madness; when things have reached this state it is no longer an equilibrium which is set up between the two tendencies, but two disequilibriums side by side which aggravate each other, instead of counterbalancing. It is easy to see the cause of this phenomenon: where intellectuality is reduced to a minimum, it is quite natural that sentiment should assume the mastery; and sentiment, in itself, is very close to the material order of things: there is nothing, in all that concerns psychology, more narrowly dependent on organism, and, in spite of Bergson, it is obviously sentiment and not intellect that is bound up with matter. The intuitionists may reply, as we are well aware, that intelligence, such as they conceive it, is bound up with inorganic matter (it is always Cartesian mechanics and its derivations that they have in mind) and sentiment with living matter, which seems to them to rank higher in the scale of existences. But whether inorganic or living, it is always matter, and in its domain there can never be any but sensible things; it is indeed impossible for the modern mentality, and for the philosophers who represent it, to escape from this limitation. Strictly speaking, if it be insisted that there are two different tendencies here, then one must be assigned to matter and one to life, and this distinction may serve as a fairly satisfactory way of classing the great superstitions of our epoch; but we repeat, they both belong to the same order of things and cannot really be dissociated from each other; they are on one same plane, and not superposed in hierarchy. It follows then that the "moralism" of our contemporaries is really nothing but the necessary complement of their practical materialism;[4] and it would be an utter illusion to seek to exalt one to the detriment of the other because, going necessarily together, they both develop simultaneously along the same lines, which are those of what is termed, by common accord, "civilization".

We have just seen why the conceptions of "material progress" and "moral progress" are inseparable, and why our contemporaries are almost as indefatigably engrossed with the latter as they are with the former. We have in no way contested the existence of "material progress", but only its importance: we maintain that it is not worth the intellectual loss which it causes, and it is impossible to think differently without being altogether ignorant of true intellectuality. Now, what is to be thought of the reality of "moral progress"? That is a question which it is scarcely possible to discuss seriously, because, in this realm of sentiment, everything depends on individual appreciation and preferences; everyone gives the name "progress" to what is in conformity with his own inclinations, and, in a word, it is impossible to say that one is right any more than another. Those whose tendencies are in harmony with those of their time cannot be other than satisfied with the present state of things, and this is what they express after their fashion when they say that this epoch marks a progress over those that preceded it; but often this satisfaction of their sentimental aspirations is only relative, because the sequence of events is not always what they would have wished, and that is why they suppose that the progress will be continued during future epochs. The

---

[4] We say practical materialism to denote a tendency and to distinguish it from philosophic materialism, which is a theory, and on which this tendency is not necessarily dependent.

facts come sometimes to belie those who are convinced of the present reality of "moral progress", according to the most usual conception of it; but all they do is modify their ideas a little in this respect, or refer the realization of their ideal to a more or less remote future, and they, too, might crawl out of their difficulties by talking about a "rhythm of progress". Besides this, by a much simpler solution, they usually strive to forget the lesson of experience: such are the incorrigible dreamers who, at each new war, do not fail to prophesy that it will be the last. The belief in indefinite progress is, all told, nothing more than the most ingenuous and the grossest of all kinds of "optimism"; whatever forms this belief may take, it is always sentimental in essence, even when it is concerned with "material progress". If it be objected that we ourselves have recognized the existence of this progress, we reply that we have only done so as far as the facts warrant, which does not in the least imply an admission that it should, or even that it can, continue its course indefinitely; furthermore, as we are far from thinking it the best thing in the world, instead of calling it progress we would rather call it quite simply development; it is not in itself that the word progress offends us, but because of the idea of "value" that has come almost invariably to be attached to it. This brings us to another point: there is indeed also a reality which cloaks itself under the so-called "moral progress", or which, in other words, keeps up the illusion of it; this reality is the development of sentimentalism, which, whether one likes it or not, does actually exist in the modern world, just as incontestably as does the development of industry and commerce (and we have said why one does not go without the other). This development, in our eyes excessive and abnormal, cannot fail to seem a progress to those who put feelings above everything; and it may perhaps be said that in speaking of mere preferences, as we did not long ago, we have robbed ourselves in advance of the right to confute them. But we have done nothing of the kind: what we said then applies to sentiment, and to sentiment taken alone, in its variations from one individual to another: if sentiment, considered in general, is to be put into its proper place in relation to intelligence, the case is quite different, because then there is a hierarchy to be observed. The modern world has precisely reversed the natural relations between the different orders of things: once again, it is depreciation of the intellectual order (and even absence of pure intellectuality), and exaggeration of the material and the sentimental orders, which all go together to make the Western civilization of today an anomaly, not to say a monstrosity. . . .

PART TWO

THE METAPHYSICAL WORLD

True metaphysics represents spiritual knowledge of a higher order, which Guénon considered the most primordial and comprehensive body of knowledge possessed by the human race. Beyond the purely rational knowledge of science lies the knowledge of universal principles, apprehended by the pure intellect, which leads to an "effective awareness of the supra-individual states of being". That is the "real object of metaphysics".

9

Eastern Metaphysics

I have taken Eastern metaphysics as the subject of this essay. It would perhaps have been better simply to say metaphysics unqualified, for in truth pure metaphysics is neither Eastern nor Western, but universal, being in essence above and beyond all forms and all contingencies. It is only the exterior forms in which it is clothed in order to serve the necessities of exposition, so as to express whatever is expressible, that can be either Eastern or Western; but beneath their diversity there is always and everywhere a selfsame basis, at least wherever true metaphysics exists, and this for the simple reason that truth is one.

If this be so, what need is there to speak specifically of Eastern metaphysics? The reason is that in the present intellectual state of the Western world metaphysics is a thing forgotten, generally unknown and more or less entirely lost, whereas in the East it still remains the object of an effective knowledge. If one wishes to know metaphysics, therefore, one must turn to the East; and even if one's wish is to recover some of the metaphysical traditions that may once have existed in the West, a West that was in many respects much closer to the East than it is today, it is above all with the help of Eastern doctrines and by comparison with them that one may succeed, because these are the only teachings in the domain of metaphysics that can still be studied directly. But in order to do so, it is quite clear that they must be studied as the Easterners themselves study them, and not in giving oneself over to more or less hypothetical and occasionally wholly fantastical interpretations. It is also too often forgotten that the Eastern civilizations still exist and that they still have qualified representatives to whom one need only apply in order to learn the true nature of the subject.

I have said "Eastern metaphysics" and not exclusively Hindu metaphysics, for doctrines of this order, with all they imply, are not to be found only in India, contrary to what some people believe, who in any case have but a poor understanding of their true nature. The case of India is by no means exceptional in this respect—it is precisely that of all civilizations that possess what might be called a traditional foundation. What is exceptional and abnormal, rather, are those civilizations which lack such a foundation; and in all truth, the only one known to us is that of the modern West. To take only the principal Eastern civilizations, in China the equivalent of Hindu metaphysics can be found in Taoism; elsewhere it can be found in certain esoteric schools of Islam (it should be understood, furthermore, that this Islamic esoterism has nothing in common with the overt philosophy of the Arabs, which is for the most part of Greek inspiration). The only difference is that everywhere but in India these doctrines are reserved for a relatively restricted and insular elite. This was also the case in the West during the Middle Ages, for an esoterism similar in many respects to that of Islam, and just as purely metaphysical, but of which the moderns for the most part do not even suspect the existence. In India it is not possible to speak of esoterism in the strict sense of the word because there one does not find doctrine with the two aspects, exoteric and esoteric. One can only speak of a natural esoterism, in the sense that each individual will reach just those depths or go just so far into the doctrine as his own intellectual capacities allow, because for certain human individuals there are limitations inherent in their very nature that are impossible for them to overcome.

Naturally, forms differ from one civilization to another since they must adapt to different conditions. Although more familiar myself with the Hindu forms, I have no qualms in employing others as need arises if they can further the understanding of certain points. There is nothing problematic in this, since they are only different expressions of the same thing. Once again, truth is one, and it is the same for all who, by whatever way, come to know it.

This being said, it should now be made clear just what is meant by the word "metaphysics", and all the more so since I have frequently had occasion to note that everyone does not understand it in quite the same way. I think the best course to take in dealing with words that might give rise to ambiguity is to restore to them as much as possible their primal and etymological meaning. Now, according to its composition, the word "metaphysics" means literally "beyond physics", taking the word "physics" in the accepted sense it always had for the ancients, that is to say as "knowledge of nature" in its widest sense. Physics is the study of all that pertains to the domain of nature; metaphysics, on the other hand, is the study of what lies beyond nature. How, then, can some people claim that metaphysical knowledge is natural knowledge, either in respect of its object or with regard to the faculties by which it is obtained? Here we have a complete misconception, a contradiction in terms; and yet what is more amazing is that this confusion affects even those who should preserve some idea of true metaphysics and know how to distinguish it clearly from the pseudo-metaphysics of modern philosophers.

But perhaps one might say that if the word "metaphysics" gives rise to such confusion, would it not be better to abandon it and replace it with something more suitable? In reality this would cause problems, since by its formation this word is perfectly suited for that to which it refers; moreover, it would hardly be possible, seeing that Western languages posses no other word equally well adapted to this usage. It is out of the question to use the word "knowledge" pure and simple, as is done in India, although this is indeed knowledge par excellence, the only kind truly worthy of the name, because it would only make things more confusing for Westerners who habitually associate knowledge with nothing outside the scientific and rational domain. And in any event, is it necessary to be so concerned over the abuse made of one word? If all such words had to be rejected, how many would remain at our disposal? Is it not sufficient to take precautions to avoid misunderstandings and misrepresentations? We are no more attached to the word "metaphysics" than to any other, but until a better term is suggested to take its place, we will continue to use it as before.

Unfortunately, there are people who think they can "judge" that of which they are ignorant, and who, because they apply the name "metaphysics" to a purely human and rational knowledge (which for us is merely science or philosophy), imagine that Eastern metaphysics is nothing more nor other than that, whence they draw the logical conclusion that this metaphysics cannot truly lead to any particular results. Yet it does indeed lead to such results, but only because it is something quite other than they supposed. Now what they envisage really has nothing to do with metaphysics, since it is only knowledge of a natural order, a knowledge that is profane and superficial; this is definitely not what we wish to discuss. Do we then make "metaphysical" synonymous with "supernatural"? We would willingly accept such an assimilation, since, as long as we do not go beyond nature, that is to say the manifest world in all its extension (and not only the perceptible world, which is but one infinitesimal element of it), we remain in the realm of the physical. What is metaphysical, as we have already said, is that which lies beyond and above nature, and is thus properly speaking "supernatural".

But here an objection will undoubtedly be raised: is it possible, then, to go beyond nature? We do not hesitate to answer plainly: not only is it possible, but it is done. But those are just words, it will be said; what proofs can you give us? It is truly strange that people ask for proof concerning the possibility of a kind of knowledge instead of searching for it and verifying it for themselves by undertaking the work necessary to acquire it. For those who possess this knowledge, what interest can there be in all this discussion? Substituting a "theory of knowledge" for knowledge itself is perhaps the greatest admission of impotence in modern philosophy.

Moreover, all certitude contains something incommunicable; no one can truly attain to any knowledge other than through a strictly personal effort, and all that one can do for another is to provide an opportunity and indicate the means by which to attain it. That is why it would be vain to attempt to impose any belief in the purely intellectual realm; in this respect the best argument in the world cannot replace direct and effective knowledge.

Now, can metaphysics as we understand it be defined? No, for to define is always to limit, and what is under consideration is, in and of itself, truly and absolutely limitless and thus cannot be confined to any formula or any system whatsoever. Metaphysics might be partially characterized, for example, by saying that it is the knowledge of universal principles, but this is not a definition in the proper sense and in any case only conveys a fairly vague notion. Something can be added by saying that the scope of these principles is far greater than was thought by some Westerners, who, although really studying metaphysics, did so in a partial and incomplete way. Thus, when Aristotle considered metaphysics as a knowledge of being as being, he identified it with ontology, which is to say that he took the part for the whole. For Eastern metaphysics, pure being is neither the first nor the most universal of principles, for it is already a determination. It is thus necessary to go beyond being, and it is this that is of the greatest importance. This is why in all truly metaphysical conceptions, allowance must always be made for the inexpressible; and just as everything that can be expressed is literally nothing in comparison with that which surpasses expression, so the finite, whatever its magnitude, is as nothing to the infinite. One can intimate much more than one can express, and ultimately, this is the part played by exterior forms; all such forms, whether words or symbols, merely constitute supports, footholds from which to rise to possibilities of conception that transcend them immeasurably. We will return to this point later.

We speak of metaphysical conceptions for lack of any other term whereby to make ourselves understood, but this should not be taken to mean that here is something comparable to scientific or philosophic conceptions; it is not a question of effecting some sort of "abstraction", but of attaining direct knowledge of reality as it is. Science is rational, discursive knowledge, always indirect, a knowledge by reflection; metaphysics is a supra-rational, intuitive, and unmediated knowledge. Moreover, this pure intellectual intuition, without which there is no true metaphysics, has no connection with the intuition spoken of by certain contemporary philosophers, which is, on the contrary, infra-rational. There is an intellectual intuition and a sensible intuition; the one is beyond reason, but the other is within it; the latter can know only the world of change and becoming, that is to say of nature, or rather of a minute part of nature. The realm of intuition, on the contrary, is that of eternal and immutable principles—the metaphysical realm.

To comprehend universal principles directly, the transcendent intellect must itself be of a universal order; it is no longer an individual faculty, and to consider it as such would be contradictory, because it is not within the power of the individual to go beyond its own limits or to step outside the conditions that limit it as an individual. Reason is wholly and specifically a human faculty, but what lies beyond reason is truly "nonhuman"; it is what makes metaphysical knowledge possible, and this knowledge, it must be reaffirmed, is not a human knowledge. In other words, it is not as man that man can attain it, but as that being which is human in one of its aspects and at the same time is something other, more than a human being; and it is the attainment of effective awareness of supra-individual states that is the real object of metaphysics, or better still, of metaphysical knowledge itself. Thus, we arrive at one of the most essential points, which it is necessary to stress: if the individual were a complete being, if it constituted a closed system in the manner of Leibnitz's monad, metaphysics would not be possible; irremediably closed in on itself, such a being would have no means of becoming aware of anything outside its own order of existence. But such is not the case: in reality, the individual represents but one transitory and contingent manifestation of the true being; it is but one specific state among an indefinite multitude of states of the same being, and that being is in itself absolutely independent of all its manifestations, just as, to use an analogy that appears frequently in Hindu texts, the sun is absolutely independent of the many images in which it is reflected. Such is the fundamental distinction between "Self" and "ego", the personality and the individuality; and, just as the images are connected by the luminous rays to the solar source without which they would have neither existence nor reality, so the individuality, either of the human individual or of any analogous state of manifestation, is bound by the personality to the principial center of being by this transcendent intellect of which we have just spoken. Within the limits of this exposition it is impossible to develop such considerations more fully, or to give a more exact idea of the theory of the multiple states of being, but I think I have said enough to give at least a sense of the paramount importance of any truly metaphysical doctrine.

I said "theory", but it is not only a question of theory, and this is yet another point that requires clarification. Theoretical knowledge, which is still only indirect and in some way symbolic, is merely a preparation—although indispensable—for true knowledge. It is, moreover, the only knowledge that is in any way communicable, and this is why all exposition is but a means of approaching knowledge, which, being only virtual in the beginning, must later be effectively realized. Here we find another difference from the more limited metaphysics to which we referred earlier, that of Aristotle for instance, which remains theoretically inadequate in that it limits itself to being, and in which, moreover, theory seems to be presented as self-sufficient rather than expressly bound up with a corresponding realization, as is the case in all Eastern doctrines. And yet, even in this imperfect metaphysics—we might be tempted to call it a demi-metaphysics—statements sometimes are encountered which, had they been properly understood, should have led to entirely different conclusions. Thus, did not Aristotle specifically state that a being is all that it knows? This affirmation of identification through knowledge is the very principle of metaphysical realization; but here the principle remains isolated, its value merely that of a wholly theoretical statement; it carries no weight, and it seems that, after having been propounded, it is no longer even thought of. How was it that Aristotle himself and his followers failed to see all that was implied therein? Admittedly, the same holds true in many other cases, where they seem to have forgotten other equally essential things, such as the distinction between pure intellect and reason, even after having defined them no less explicitly. Such lapses are strange indeed. Should one see in this the effect of certain limitations inherent in the Western mind, apart from some rare but always possible exceptions? This might be true to a certain extent, yet it is not necessary to believe that Western intellectuality has always been as narrowly limited as it is in the present age. However, such doctrines are only outward, after all, although certainly superior to many others since in spite of everything they incorporate a part of true metaphysics, even if always in conjunction with considerations of another order that have nothing to do with metaphysics. For our part, we are certain that there was in antiquity and in the Middle Ages more than this in the West, that there were available to the elite doctrines of a purely metaphysical nature that could be called complete, including that realization which for most moderns is certainly a thing barely conceivable. If the West has lost its memory of such teachings so completely, it is because it has broken with its own tradition, and this is why modern civilization is an abnormal and deviant one.

If purely theoretical knowledge were itself its own end, and if metaphysics went no further, it would still assuredly be worth something, but it would be altogether insufficient. In spite of conferring the genuine certainty, even greater than mathematical certainty, that belongs to such knowledge, it would remain analogous to that certainty which at an inferior level constitutes terrestrial and human, scientific and philosophical, speculation, although in an incomparably superior order. That is not what metaphysics should be. Let others dabble in "mental sport", or in what passes for such; that is their affair. But such things as these are of no interest to us, and we think moreover that the inquisitiveness of the psychologist must remain entirely alien to the metaphysician. For the latter, what matters is to know what is, and to know it in such a manner that one is truly and effectively the sum-total of what one knows.

As for the means of metaphysical realization, we are well aware of such objections as can be made by those who believe it their duty to contest the possibility of such realization. These means, indeed, must be within man's reach; they must, in the first stages at least, be adapted to the conditions of the human state, since this is the state in which the being actually finds itself and from which it must subsequently take possession of the higher states. Thus it is the forms belonging to the world in which its current manifestation is situated that the being will use as a support to raise itself above this very world. Words, symbolic signs, rites, or preparatory methods of various kinds, have no other *raison d'être* or function; as we have already said, they are supports and nothing else. But, some will ask, how is it possible that merely contingent means produce effects that immeasurably surpass them, effects of a wholly different order than that to which they themselves belong? We should first point out that in reality these are only accidental means, and that the results they help to obtain are in no way effected by them; they place the being in the desired frame of mind to achieve these results more easily, and that is all. If this objection were valid in the present case, it would be equally valid for religious rites, the sacraments for example, in which the disparity between means and end is no less disproportionate. Perhaps some of those who raise such objections have not considered them sufficiently. As for us, we do not confuse a simple means with a cause in the true sense of the word, and we do not regard metaphysical realization as an effect of anything at all, because it is not the production of something that does not yet exist, but the awareness of that which is, permanently and immutably, beyond all succession, temporal or otherwise, since all states of the being considered in their principle exist in perfect simultaneity in the eternal present.

Thus we see no difficulty in recognizing that there is no common measure between metaphysical realization and the means leading to it, or, if one prefers, that prepare for it. Furthermore, that is why none of these means are strictly or absolutely necessary, or at least there is only one truly indispensable preparation, and that is theoretical knowledge. On the other hand, the latter could not go very far without a means that should thus be considered as playing the most important and constant part, which means is concentration, something completely foreign, even contrary, to the mental habits of the modern West, where everything tends toward dispersion and incessant change. All other means are secondary in relation to this one; they serve above all to promote concentration and to harmonize the diverse elements of human individuality in order to facilitate effective communication between this individuality and the higher states of the being.

From the very start, moreover, these means can be almost indefinitely varied, for they have to be adapted to the temperament of each individual and to his particular aptitudes and dispositions. Thereafter, the differences diminish, for it is a case of multiple paths all leading to the same end. At a certain stage all multiplicity disappears, but at that stage the individual and contingent means will have played their part. This part, which it is unnecessary to enlarge upon, is compared in certain Hindu writings to a horse that helps a man to reach the end of his journey more quickly and easily, but without which he could still reach it. Rites and various methods point the way to metaphysical realization, but one could nevertheless set them aside, and by unswervingly setting the mind and all powers of the being on the aim of this realization, could finally attain the supreme goal. But if there are means that make the effort less laborious, why choose to neglect them? Is it confusing the contingent and the absolute to take into account the conditions of our human state, since it is from this state, itself contingent, that we are at present obliged to set forth in conquest of the higher states, and finally of the supreme and unconditioned state?

Having considered the teachings common to all traditional doctrines, let us now turn to the principal stages of metaphysical realization. The first, which to a certain extent is merely preliminary, operates in the human domain and does not extend beyond the limits of the individuality. It consists of an indefinite extension of that individuality of which the corporeal modality, the only modality developed in the ordinary man, represents but the smallest portion. In fact one must start from the corporeal modality, whence the use in the beginning of means borrowed from the sensible order, which means must have repercussions throughout the other modalities of the human being. In short, the phase in question is the realization or development of all the potentialities contained virtually within the human individuality, constituting multiple prolongations thereof that reach out in diverse directions beyond the corporeal and sensible realm; and it is by means of these prolongations that it is possible to establish communication with the other states.

This realization of the integral individuality is described by all traditions as the restoration of what is called the "primordial state", which is regarded as the state of true man and which already escapes some of the limitations characteristic of the ordinary state, notably those due to the temporal condition. The being that has attained this "primordial state" is still only a human individual and is without effective possession of any supra-individual states. Nevertheless he is henceforth liberated from time, the apparent succession of things having been transmuted for him into simultaneity; he is in conscious possession of a faculty unknown to the ordinary man, which might be called the "sense of eternity". This is of extreme importance, for he who cannot rise above the vantage-point of temporal succession and envisage all things in simultaneous mode is incapable of the least conception of the metaphysical order. The first thing to be done by those who wish to achieve true metaphysical understanding is to step outside time—we would willingly say into "non-time", if such an expression did not seem too peculiar and unusual. This knowledge of the intemporal can, moreover, be achieved in some real measure, if incompletely, before one has attained the fullness of the "primordial state" of which we have just spoken.

Perhaps it will be asked why this designation "primordial state"? It is because all traditions, including that of the West (for the Bible itself says nothing different), are in accord in teaching that this was originally the normal state for humanity, while the present state is merely the result of a decline, the effect of a kind of progressive materialization occurring down the ages and throughout the duration of a particular cycle. We do not believe in "evolution" in the sense the moderns have given the word; the so-called scientific hypotheses they have devised in no way correspond to reality. In any case, it is not possible here to make more than a passing mention of the theory of cosmic cycles,[1] which is particularly expounded in the Hindu doctrines; to do so would be to go beyond our subject, for cosmology is not metaphysics, although it depends closely upon it. Cosmology is no more than an application of metaphysics to the physical order, while the true natural laws are only the consequences, in a relative and contingent domain, of universal and necessary principles.

But let us return to metaphysical realization. Its second phase corresponds to supra-individual states which are still conditioned, although their conditions are completely different from those of the human state. Here the human world in which we remained in

---

[1] See *Traditional Forms and Cosmic Cycles*, chap 1. ED

the preceding stages has been entirely and definitively left behind. It must also be added that what has been left behind is the world of forms in its most general sense, comprising all possible individual states, for form is the condition common to all such states, by which individuality is defined as such. The being, which can no longer be called human, is henceforth free from the "current of forms", to use a Far-Eastern expression. There are moreover further distinctions to be made, for this stage can be subdivided: in reality it includes several stages, from the acquisition of states which, though non-formal, still belong to manifested existence, to the stage of universality which is that of pure being.

Nevertheless, as elevated as these states are when compared to the human state, and as remote as they may be from it, they are still only relative, and this is true even of the highest among them, which corresponds to the principle of all manifestation. The possession thereof is thus only a transitory result that should not be confused with the ultimate goal of metaphysical realization, which lies beyond being, and in comparison with which all the rest is but a journey and preparation. This supreme goal is the absolutely unconditioned state, set free from all limitation. For this very reason it is completely inexpressible, and anything we might say about it must be put in the form of a negation, the negation of all limits that determine and define all existence in its relativity. The attainment of this state is what the Hindu doctrine calls "Deliverance" when considering it in relation to conditioned states, and "Union" when envisaged in relation to the supreme Principle.

Moreover, all other states of the being can in principle be found in this unconditioned state, but transformed, disengaged from the particular conditions that determined them as special states. What subsists is everything that has a positive reality, since it is there that everything has its principle; the "delivered" being is truly in possession of the fullness of its own potentialities. What have disappeared are merely the limiting conditions, of which the reality is negative, since they represent no more than a "privation" in the Aristotelian sense of the word. Thus, far from being a kind of annihilation, as some Westerners believe, this final state is on the contrary absolute plenitude, the supreme reality compared to which all else is but illusion.

Let us add too that every result, even partial, obtained by the being in the course of metaphysical realization, is obtained definitively. For this being, the result is a permanent acquisition that nothing can

ever take from it; the work accomplished in this order, even if inter-
rupted before it is completed, is achieved once and for all by the very
fact that it is outside of time. This is true even of simple theoretical
knowledge, for all knowledge carries its benefit within it, in this way
quite different from action, which is but a momentary modification
of the being and is always distinct from its own effects. Furthermore,
these effects are of the same domain and the same order of existence
as that which has produced them; action cannot effectively liberate
from action, and its consequences cannot reach beyond the limits of
individuality, even when this is considered in its fullest possible extension. Action of any sort, not being opposed to the ignorance that is the
root of all limitation, cannot dispel that ignorance; only knowledge can
dispel ignorance, as sunlight disperses shadow, and it is at this point
that the "Self", the immutable and eternal principle of all manifested
and unmanifested states, appears in its supreme reality.

After this brief and very imperfect sketch, which provides only
the weakest notion of what metaphysical realization might be, it is
absolutely essential to stress one point in order to avoid grave errors of
interpretation: nothing referred to here has any connection whatsoever
with phenomena of any kind, however extraordinary they may be.
All phenomena are of the physical order; metaphysics is beyond phenomena, even taking the word in its widest sense. Among other consequences, it follows from this that the states to which we are referring
are in no way "psychological"; this must be stated plainly, since
strange confusions sometimes arise in this connection. By very definition psychology can be concerned only with human states, and even
then, as it is understood today, it reaches to only a very limited part of
the individual's potentialities, which include far more than practitio-
ners of this science could ever suspect. Indeed, the human individual
is both much more and much less than is generally supposed in the
West: much more, by reason of his possibilities of indefinite extension
beyond the corporeal modality, to which, in short, everything belongs
that is commonly studied; but he is also much less, since far from
constituting a complete and self-sufficient being, he is but an outward
manifestation, a fleeting appearance assumed by the true being, which
in no way affects the essence of the latter in its immutability.

It must be emphasized that the metaphysical domain lies entirely
outside the phenomenal world, for by dint of habit the moderns
hardly ever recognize or investigate anything but phenomena, in

which their interests lie almost exclusively, as the attention they have given to the experimental sciences bears witness; and their metaphysical inaptitude stems from the same tendency. Undoubtedly, it may happen that certain particular phenomena may occur during the labor of metaphysical realization, but in a wholly accidental manner. This is a rather unfortunate result, as occurrences of this sort can only be an impediment to those who might be tempted to attach some importance to them. Those who allow themselves to be stopped or turned aside by phenomena, and above all those who indulge in the search for extraordinary "powers", have very little chance of pressing their realization any further than the degree already achieved before this deviation occurred.

This observation leads naturally to the correction of some erroneous interpretations on the subject of the term *Yoga*; indeed, has it not been claimed that what the Hindus indicate by this word is the development of certain powers latent in the human being? What we have just said suffices to demonstrate that such a definition is to be rejected. In reality, the word *Yoga* is the same as that which we have translated as literally as possible by the word "Union". What it properly defines is thus the supreme goal of metaphysical realization; and the *yogī*, in the strictest sense of the term, is solely the person who attains this end. However, it is true that in some cases the same terms may be applied by extension to stages preparatory to "Union" or even to simple preliminary techniques, as well as to the being that has reached the states corresponding to such stages or that uses those teachings to reach them. But how can it be maintained that a word having the primary meaning of "Union" designates in its proper and original application breathing exercises or other things of that sort? Such exercises, and others generally based on what we might call the science of rhythm, do indeed figure among the means most widely practiced in promoting realization, but one must not mistake as an end that which amounts to no more than a contingent and accidental means, nor must one confuse the original meaning of a word with a secondary acceptation that is more or less distorted.

In referring to the original *Yoga*, and in saying that this word has always meant essentially the same thing, we might be prompted to pose a question regarding which we have as yet said nothing: what is the origin of these traditional metaphysical doctrines from which we have borrowed all our fundamental ideas? The answer is very simple, although it risks raising objections from those who would prefer to consider everything from an historical point of view, and the answer is that there is no origin—by which we mean no human origin—that can be determined in time. In other words, the origin of tradition, if indeed the word "origin" has any place at all in such a case, is as "non-human" as is metaphysics itself. Doctrines of this order did not appear at any particular moment in the history of humanity; the allusion we have made to the "primordial state", and also what we have said of the timeless nature of all that concerns metaphysics, should enable us to grasp this point without too much difficulty, on condition that we concede, contrary to certain prejudices, that there are some things to which the historical point of view does not apply. Metaphysical truth is eternal, and by that very fact there have always existed beings able to know it truly and completely. What changes is only external forms and contingent means, and the change has nothing to do with what people today call "evolution", it is simply an adaptation to such and such particular circumstances, to special conditions of some given race or age. From this springs the multiplicity of forms; but the foundation of the doctrine is no more modified and affected by it than the essential unity and identity of the being is altered by the multiplicity of its states of manifestation.

Thus metaphysical knowledge, as well as the realization it implies in order to truly be what it ought to be, are possible everywhere and always, at least in principle, and when this possibility is regarded in a quasi-absolute sense; but in fact, in practice so to speak, and in a relative sense, are they equally possible in just any environment and without making the least allowance for contingencies? On this score we shall be much less affirmative, at least as concerns realization, and this can be explained by the fact that in its beginning such a realization must take its support in the realm of contingencies. The conditions may be particularly unfavorable, such as those offered by the contemporary West, so much so that such a labor is almost impossible and can even be dangerous in the absence of any support offered by one's environment and in an ambiance that can only impede or even destroy the efforts of one who undertakes such a task. On the other hand, those civilizations that we call traditional are organized in a way that can actually prove an effective help, which no doubt is not strictly indispensable, any more than is anything else external, but without which it is however quite difficult to obtain effective results. Here is something that exceeds the strength of an isolated human individual, even if that individual happens to possess the requisite qualifications in other respects; hence we would not wish to encourage anyone in the present conditions to embark heedlessly upon such an undertaking, and this brings us to our conclusion.

For us, the great difference between the East and West (meaning here exclusively the modern West), the only difference that is truly essential, since all the other differences are derivative, is this: on the one hand, preservation of tradition and all that it implies, and on the other hand the neglect and loss of that same tradition; on the one side, the safeguarding of metaphysical knowledge, on the other, utter ignorance of all that relates to that realm. Between civilizations that open to their elite such possibilities as we have tried to intimate, which give the most appropriate means to realize these possibilities effectively, and in the case of at least a few, to realize them fully—between those traditional civilizations and a civilization that has developed along purely material lines, how could a common measure be found? And who, unless he were blinded by I know not what prejudice, would dare claim that material superiority compensates for intellectual inferiority? When we say intellectual, we mean true intellectuality, that which is limited neither to the human nor to the natural order, that which makes pure metaphysical knowledge possible in its absolute transcendence. A moment's reflection on these questions seems to me sufficient to leave no doubt or hesitation as to the appropriate answer in response.

The material superiority of the West is beyond dispute; nobody denies it, but it is hardly grounds for envy. But one must go further: sooner or later this excessive material development threatens to destroy the West if it does not recover itself in time and if it does not seriously consider a "return to the source", as goes a saying current in certain schools of Islamic esoterism. Today one hears from many quarters of the "defense of the West", but unfortunately it does not seem to be understood that it is chiefly against itself that the West needs to be defended, that the greatest and most formidable of the dangers that threaten it stem from its own present tendencies. It would be wise to meditate deeply on this, and one cannot urge this too strongly on all who are still capable of reflection. So it is with this that I will end my account, glad if I have succeeded in giving a sense, if not a full understanding, of that Eastern intellectuality that no longer has any equivalent in the West, and if I have been able to provide a glimpse, imperfect though it may be, of what true metaphysics is—knowledge par excellence, which alone, as the sacred texts of India say, is completely true, absolute, infinite, and supreme.

10

What is Meant by Tradition?

... We have constantly had occasion to speak of tradition, of traditional doctrines or conceptions, and even of traditional languages, and this is really unavoidable when trying to describe the essential characteristics of Eastern thought in all its modalities; but what, to be exact, is tradition? To obviate one possible misunderstanding, let it be said from the outset that we do not take the word "tradition" in the restricted sense sometimes given to it by Western religious thought, when it opposes "tradition" to the written word, using the former of these two terms exclusively for something that has been the object of oral transmission alone. On the contrary, for us tradition, taken in a much more general sense, may be written as well as oral, though it must usually, if not always, have been oral originally. In the present state of things, however, tradition, whether it be religious in form or otherwise, consists everywhere of two complementary branches, written and oral, and we have no hesitation in speaking of "traditional writings", which would obviously be contradictory if one only gave to the word "tradition" its more specialized meaning; besides, etymologically, tradition simply means "that which is transmitted" in some way or other. In addition, it is necessary to include in tradition, as secondary and derived elements that are nonetheless important for the purpose of forming a complete picture, the whole series of institutions of various kinds which find their principle in the traditional doctrine itself.

Looked at in this way, tradition may appear to be indistinguishable from civilization itself, which according to certain sociologists consists of "the whole body of techniques, institutions, and beliefs common to a group of men during a certain time";[1] but how much exactly is this definition worth? In truth, we do not think that civilization can be characterized generally by a formula of this type, which will always be either too comprehensive or too narrow in some respects, with the risk that elements common to all civilizations will be omitted or else that elements belonging to certain particular civilizations only will

---

[1] E. Doutté, *Magie et Religion dans l'Afrique du Nord*, Introduction, p. 5.

be included. Thus the preceding definition takes no account of the essentially intellectual element to be found in every civilization, for that is something that cannot be made to fit into the category known as "techniques", which, as we are told, comprises "those classes of practices specially designed to modify the physical environment"; on the other hand, when these sociologists speak of "beliefs", adding moreover that the word must be "taken in its usual sense", they are referring to something that clearly presupposes the presence of the religious viewpoint, which is really confined to certain civilizations only and is not to be found in others.[2] It was in order to avoid all difficulties of this kind that we were content at the start simply to describe a civilization as the product and expression of a certain mental outlook common to a more or less widespread group of men, thus making it possible to treat each particular case separately as regards the exact determination of its constituent elements.

However that may be, it remains nonetheless true, as far as the East is concerned, that the identification of tradition with the entire civilization is fundamentally justifiable. Every Eastern civilization, taken as a whole, may be seen to be essentially traditional. . . . As for Western civilization, we have shown that it is on the contrary devoid of any traditional character, with the exception of the religious element, which alone has retained it. Social institutions, to be considered traditional, must be effectively attached in their principle to a doctrine that is itself traditional, whether it be metaphysical or religious or of any other conceivable kind. In other words, those institutions are traditional that find their ultimate justification in their more or less direct, but always intentional and conscious, dependence upon a doctrine which, as regards its fundamental nature, is in every case of an intellectual order; but this intellectuality may be found either in a pure state, in cases where one is dealing with an entirely metaphysical doctrine, or else it may be found mingled with other heterogeneous elements, as in the case of the religious or other special modes which a traditional doctrine is capable of assuming.

---

[2] In Guénon's writings the terms "religion" and the "religious viewpoint" refer to exoterism and the exoteric viewpoint respectively. Guénon considers this outlook characteristic of the Semitic monotheistic traditions alone. ED

. . . In Islam tradition exists under two distinct aspects, one of which is religious—it is upon this aspect that the general body of social institutions is dependent—while the other aspect, which is purely Eastern, is wholly metaphysical. In a certain measure something of the same sort existed in medieval Europe in the case of the Scholastic doctrine, in which Arab influences moreover made themselves felt to an appreciable extent; but in order not to push the analogy too far it should be added that metaphysics was never sufficiently clearly distinguished from theology, that is to say from its special application to the religious mode of thought; moreover, the genuinely metaphysical portion to be found in it is incomplete and remains subject to certain limitations that seem inherent in the whole of Western intellectuality; doubtless these two imperfections should be looked upon as resulting from the double heritage of the Jewish and the Greek mentalities.

In India we are in the presence of a tradition that is purely metaphysical in its essence; to it are attached, as so many dependent extensions, the diverse applications to which it gives rise, whether in certain secondary branches of the doctrine itself, such as that relating to cosmology, or in the social order, which is moreover strictly governed by the analogical correspondence linking together cosmic existence and human existence. A fact that stands out much more clearly here than in the Islamic tradition, chiefly owing to the absence of the religious point of view and of certain extra-intellectual elements that religion necessarily implies, is the complete subordination of the various particular orders relative to metaphysics, that is to say relative to the realm of universal principles.

In China, [there is] the sharp division . . . [between] a metaphysical tradition on the one hand and a social tradition on the other, and these may at first sight appear not only distinct, as in fact they are, but even relatively independent of one another, all the more so since the metaphysical tradition always remained well-nigh exclusively the appanage of an intellectual elite, whereas the social tradition, by reason of its very nature, imposed itself upon all without distinction and claimed their effective participation in an equal degree. It is, however, important to remember that the metaphysical tradition, as constituted under the form of "Taoism", is a development from the principles of a more primordial tradition, formulated in the *I Ching*, and it is from this primordial tradition that the whole of the social institutions commonly known under the name of "Confucianism" are entirely derived, though less directly and then only as an application to a contingent sphere. Thus the essential continuity between the two principal aspects of the Far-Eastern civilization is re-established, and their true relationship made clear; but this continuity would almost inevitably be missed if it were not possible to trace them back to their common source, that is to say to the primordial tradition of which the ideographical expression, as fixed from the time of Fu Hsi onward, has been preserved intact for almost fifty centuries.

11

Essential Characteristics of Metaphysics

While the religious point of view necessarily implies the intervention of an element drawn from the sentimental order, the metaphysical point of view is exclusively intellectual; but although for our part we find such a remark sufficiently clear, to many people it might seem to describe the metaphysical point of view inadequately, unfamiliar as it is to Westerners, so that a few additional explanations will not come amiss. Science and philosophy, such as they are to be found in the Western world, also in fact have pretensions toward intellectuality; if we do not admit that these claims are well-founded and if we maintain that a gulf separates all speculations of this kind from metaphysics, this is because pure intellectuality, as we understand it, is a very different thing from the rather vague ideas that ordinarily pass under that name.

It should be explained first of all that in adopting the term "metaphysics" we are not greatly concerned with the historical origin of the word, which is open to some doubt, and which would even have to be regarded as purely accidental if one were prepared to admit the opinion, a decidedly improbable one in our view, according to which the word was first used to denote that which came "after physics" in the collected works of Aristotle. Likewise, we need not concern ourselves with various other rather far-fetched interpretations that certain authors have thought fit to attach to this word at different times; these are not reasons, however, for giving up its use, for, such as it is, it is very well suited for what it should normally be called upon to express, at least so far as any term borrowed from the Western languages ever can be. In actual fact, taken in its most natural sense, even etymologically, it denotes whatever lies "beyond physics"; the word "physics" must here be taken to denote the natural sciences viewed as a whole and considered in quite a general manner, as they always were by the ancients; it must on no account be taken to refer to one of those sciences in particular, according to the restricted meaning in vogue at the present day. It is therefore on the basis of this interpretation that we make use of the term "metaphysics", and we must make it clear once for all that if we persist in using it, this is solely for the reasons just given and because we consider that it is always undesirable to have recourse to neologisms except in cases of absolute necessity.

It may now be stated that metaphysics, understood in this way, is essentially the knowledge of the Universal, or, if preferred, the knowledge of principles belonging to the universal order, which moreover alone can validly lay claim to the name of principles; but in making this statement we are not really trying to propose a definition of metaphysics, for such a thing is a sheer impossibility by reason of that very universality which we look upon as the foremost among its characteristics, the one from which all the others are derived. In reality, only something that is limited is capable of definition, whereas metaphysics is on the contrary by its very nature absolutely unlimited, and this plainly does not allow of our enclosing it within a more or less narrow formula; and a definition in this case would be all the more inaccurate the more exact one tried to make it.

It is important to note that we have spoken of knowledge and not of science; our purpose in so doing is to emphasize the radical distinction that must be made between metaphysics, on the one hand, and the various sciences in the proper sense of the word, on the other, namely all the particular and specialized sciences which are directed to the study of this or that determinate aspect of individual things. Fundamentally, this distinction is none other than that between the universal and the individual orders, a distinction that must not however be looked upon as an opposition, since there can be no common measure nor any possible relationship of symmetry or coordination between its two terms. Indeed, no opposition or conflict of any sort between metaphysics and the sciences is conceivable, precisely because their respective domains are so widely separated; and exactly the same thing applies to the relationship between metaphysics and religion. It must however be understood that the division in question does not so much concern things themselves as the points of view from which they are considered. . . . It is easy to see that the same subject can be studied by different sciences under different aspects; similarly, anything that may be examined from an individual and particular point of view can, by a suitable transposition, equally well be considered from the universal point of view (which is not to be reckoned as a special point of view at all), and the same applies in the case of things incapable of being considered from any individual standpoint whatsoever. In this way, it may be said that the domain of metaphysics embraces all things, which is an indispensable condition of its being truly universal, as it necessarily must be; but the respective domains of the different sciences remain nonetheless distinct from the domain of metaphysics, for the latter, which does not occupy the same plane as the specialized sciences, is in no wise analogous to them, so that there can never be any occasion for making a comparison between the results arrived at by the one and by the others.

On the other hand, the metaphysical realm certainly does not consist of those things of which the various sciences have failed to take cognizance simply because their present state of development is more or less incomplete, as is supposed by certain philosophers who can hardly have realized what is in question here; the domain of metaphysics consists of that which, of its very nature, lies outside the range of those sciences and far exceeds in scope all they can legitimately claim to contain. The domain of every science is always dependent upon experimentation in one or other of its various modalities, whereas the domain of metaphysics is essentially constituted by that which cannot be investigated externally: being "beyond physics" we are also, by that very fact, beyond experiment. Consequently, the field of every separate science can, if it is capable of it, be extended indefinitely without ever finding the slightest point of contact with the metaphysical sphere.

From the preceding remarks it follows that when reference is made to the object of metaphysics it must not be regarded as something more or less comparable with the particular object of this or that science. It also follows that the object in question must always be absolutely the same and can in no wise be something that changes or that is subject to the influences of time and place; the contingent, the accidental, and the variable belong essentially to the individual domain; they are even characteristics that necessarily condition individual things as such, or, to speak still more precisely, that condition the individual aspect of things in its manifold modalities. Where metaphysics is concerned, all that can alter with time and place is, on the one hand, the manner of expression, that is to say the more or less external forms which metaphysics can assume and which may be varied indefinitely, and on the other hand, the degree of knowledge or ignorance of it to be found among men; but metaphysics in itself always remains fundamentally and unalterably the same, for its object is one in its essence, or to be more exact "without duality", as the Hindus put it, and that object, again by the very fact that it lies "beyond nature", is also beyond all change: the Arabs express this by saying that "the doctrine of Oneness is one".

Following the same line of argument, we may add that it is absolutely impossible to make any "discoveries" in metaphysics, for in a type of knowledge which calls for the use of no specialized or external means of investigation all that is capable of being known may have been known by certain persons at any and every period; and this in fact emerges clearly from a profound study of the traditional metaphysical doctrines. Moreover, even admitting that the notions of evolution and progress might have a certain relative value in biology and sociology—though this is far from having been proved—it is nonetheless certain that they cannot possibly find a place in metaphysics; besides, such ideas are completely foreign to the Easterners, just as they were foreign even to Westerners until almost the end of the eighteenth century, though people in the West now take it for granted that they are essential to human thought. This also implies, be it noted, a formal condemnation of any attempt at applying the "historical method" to the metaphysical order; in fact the metaphysical point of view is itself radically opposed to the historical point of view, or what passes for such, and this opposition will be seen to amount not only to a question of method, but also, what is far more important, to a real question of principle, since the metaphysical point of view, in its essential immutability, is the very negation of the notions of evolution and progress. One might say in fact that metaphysics can only be studied metaphysically. No notice must be taken of contingencies such as individual influences, which are strictly nonexistent from this point of view and cannot affect the doctrine in any way; the latter, being of the universal order, is thereby essentially supra-individual, and necessarily remains untouched by such influences. Even circumstances of time and space, we must repeat, can only affect the outward expression but not the essence of the doctrine; moreover there can be no question here, as there is in the relative and contingent order, of "beliefs" or "opinions" that are more or less variable and changing precisely because they are more or less open to doubt; metaphysical knowledge essentially implies permanent and changeless certitude.

Indeed, from the very fact that it in no wise shares in the relativity of the sciences, metaphysics is bound to imply absolute certainty as one of its intrinsic characteristics, not only by virtue of its object, which is certitude itself, but also by virtue of its method, if this word can still be used in the present context, for otherwise this method, or whatever else one cares to call it, would not be adequate to its object. Metaphysics therefore of necessity excludes every conception of a hypothetical character, whence it follows that metaphysical truths, in themselves, cannot in any way be contestable. Consequently, if there sometimes is occasion for discussion and controversy, this only happens as a result of a defect in exposition or of an imperfect comprehension of those truths. Moreover, every exposition possible in this case is necessarily defective, because metaphysical conceptions, by reason of their universality, can never be completely expressed, nor even imagined, since their essence is attainable by the pure and "formless" intelligence alone; they vastly exceed all possible forms, especially the formulas in which language tries to enclose them, which are always inadequate and tend to restrict their scope and therefore to distort them. These formulas, like all symbols, can only serve as a starting-point, a "support" so to speak, which acts as an aid toward understanding that which in itself remains inexpressible; it is for each man to try to conceive it according to the extent of his own intellectual powers, making good, in proportion to his success, the unavoidable deficiencies of formal and limited expression; it is also evident that these imperfections will be at their maximum when the expression has to be conveyed through the medium of certain languages, such as the European languages and especially the modern ones, which seem particularly ill-adapted to the exposition of metaphysical truths. ... Metaphysics, because it opens out a limitless vista of possibilities, must take care never to lose sight of the inexpressible, which indeed constitutes its very essence.

Knowledge belonging to the universal order of necessity lies beyond all the distinctions that condition the knowledge of individual things, of which that between subject and object is a general and basic type; this also goes to show that the object of metaphysics is in no wise comparable with the particular object of any other kind of knowledge whatsoever, and indeed it can only be referred to as an object purely by analogy, because, in order to speak of it at all, one is forced to attach to it some denomination or other. Likewise, when one speaks of the means of attaining metaphysical knowledge, it is evident that such means can only be one and the same thing as knowledge itself, in which subject and object are essentially unified; this amounts to saying that the means in question, if indeed it is permissible to describe it by that word, cannot in any way resemble the exercise of a discursive faculty such as individual human reason. As we have said before, we are dealing with the supra-individual and consequently with the supra-rational order, which does not in any way mean the irrational: metaphysics cannot contradict reason, but it stands above reason, which has no bearing here except as a secondary means for the formulation and external expression of truths that lie beyond its province and outside its scope. Metaphysical truths can only be conceived by the use of a faculty that does not belong to the individual order, and that, by reason of the immediate character of its operation, may be called "intuitive", but only on the strict condition that it is not regarded as having anything in common with the faculty which certain contemporary philosophers call intuition, a purely instinctive and vital faculty that is really beneath reason and not above it. To be more precise, it should be said that the faculty we are now referring to is intellectual intuition, the reality of which has been consistently denied by modern philosophy, which has failed to grasp its real nature whenever it has not preferred simply to ignore it; this faculty can also be called the pure intellect, following the practice of Aristotle and his Scholastic successors, for to them the intellect was in fact that faculty which possessed a direct knowledge of principles. Aristotle expressly declares[1] that "the intellect is truer than science", which amounts to saying that it is more true than the reason which constructs that science; he also says that "nothing is more true than the intellect", for it is necessarily infallible from the fact that its operation is immediate and because, not being really distinct from its object, it is identified with the truth itself.

Such is the essential basis of metaphysical certainty; it may thus be seen that error can only enter in with the use of reason, that is, with the formulation of the truths that the intellect has conceived, and this follows from the fact that reason is obviously fallible in consequence of its discursive and mediate character. Furthermore, since all expression is bound to be imperfect and limited, error is inevitable in its form, if not in its content: however exact one tries to make the expression, what is left out is always much greater than what is included; but this

---

[1] *Posterior Analytics*, Book ii.

unavoidable error in expression contains nothing positive as such and simply amounts to a lesser truth, since it resides merely in the partial and incomplete formulation of the integral truth.

It now becomes possible to grasp the profound significance of the distinction between metaphysical and scientific knowledge: the first is derived from the pure intellect, which has the Universal for its domain; the second is derived from reason, which has the general for its domain since, as Aristotle has declared, "there is no science but that of the general". One must on no account confuse the Universal with the general, as often happens among Western logicians, who more-over never really go beyond the general, even when they erroneously apply to it the name of universal. The point of view of the sciences, as we have shown, belongs to the individual order; the general is not opposed to the individual, but only to the particular, since it is really nothing else than the individual extended; moreover the individual can receive an indefinite extension without thereby altering its nature and without escaping from its restrictive and limiting conditions; that is why we say that science could be indefinitely extended without ever joining metaphysics, from which it will always remain as completely separate as ever, because metaphysics alone embraces the knowledge of the Universal.

. . . All that we have just said can be applied, without reservation, to every one of the traditional doctrines of the East, in spite of great differences in form which might conceal their fundamental identity from the eyes of a casual observer: this conception of metaphysics is equally true of Taoism, of the Hindu doctrine, and also of the inward and extra-religious aspect of Islam. Now, is there anything of the kind to be found in the Western world? If one were only to consider what actually exists at the present time, it would certainly not be possible to give any but a negative answer to this question, for that which modern philosophical thought is sometimes content to label as metaphysics bears no relation whatsoever to the conception just put forward. . . . Nevertheless, what we said about Aristotle and the Scholastic doctrine at least shows that metaphysics really existed in the West to a certain extent, if incompletely; and in spite of this neces-sary reservation, one can say that here was something that is without the slightest equivalent in the modern mentality and that seems to be utterly beyond its comprehension. On the other hand, if the above reservation is unavoidable, it is because, as we said earlier on, there are certain limitations that seem to be innate in the whole of Western intellectuality, at least from the time of classical antiquity onward; we have already noted, in this respect, that the Greeks had no notion of the Infinite. Besides, why do modern Westerners, when they imagine they are conceiving the Infinite, always represent it as a space, which can only be indefinite, and why do they persist in confusing eternity, which abides essentially in the "timeless", if one may so express it, with perpetuity, which is but an indefinite extension of time, whereas such misconceptions do not occur among Easterners? The fact is that the Western mind, being almost exclusively inclined to the study of the things of the senses, is constantly led to confuse conceiving with imagining, to the extent that whatever is not capable of sensible representation seems to it to be actually unthinkable for that very reason; even among the Greeks the imaginative faculties were preponderant. This is obviously the very opposite of pure thought; under these conditions there can be no intellectuality in the real sense of the word and consequently no metaphysics. If another common confusion be added as well, namely that of the rational with the intellectual, it becomes evident that the supposed Western intellectuality, especially among the moderns, in reality amounts to no more than the exercising of the exclusively individual and formal faculties of reason and imagination; it can then be understood what a gulf separates it from Eastern intellectuality, which regards no knowledge as real or valuable excepting that knowledge which has its deepest roots in the Universal and the formless.

12

Metaphysical Realization

When describing the essential features of metaphysics, we said that it constitutes an intuitive, or in other words, immediate knowledge, as opposed to the discursive and mediate knowledge that belongs to the rational order. Intellectual intuition is even more immediate than sensory intuition, for it is beyond the distinction between subject and object which the latter allows to subsist; it is at once the means of knowledge and the knowledge itself, and in it subject and object are identified. Indeed, no knowledge is really worthy of the name except insofar as it has the effect of bringing about such an identification, although in all cases other than that of intellectual intuition this identification always remains incomplete and imperfect; in other words, there is no true knowledge except that which participates to a greater or less extent in the nature of pure intellectual knowledge, which is the supreme knowledge. All other knowledge, being more or less indirect, has at best only a symbolic or representative value; the only genuinely effective knowledge is that which permits us to penetrate into the very nature of things, and if such a penetration may be effected up to a certain point in the inferior degrees of knowledge, it is only in metaphysical knowledge that it is fully and totally realizable.

The immediate consequence of this is that knowing and being are fundamentally but one and the same thing; they are, so to speak, two inseparable aspects of a single reality, being no longer even really distinguishable in that sphere where all is "without duality". This in itself is enough to show how purposeless are all the various "theories of knowledge" with metaphysical pretensions which occupy such a prominent place in modern Western philosophy, sometimes even going so far, as in the case of Kant for example, as to absorb, or at least to dominate, everything else. The only reason for the existence of such theories arises from an attitude of mind shared by almost all modern philosophers and originating in the Cartesian dualism; this way of thinking consists in artificially opposing knowing and being, an opposition that is the negation of all true metaphysics. Modern philosophy thus ends by wishing to substitute the theory of knowledge for knowledge itself, which amounts to an open confession of impotence on its part; nothing is more characteristic in this respect than the following declaration of Kant: "The chief and perhaps the only use of all philosophy of pure reason is, after all, exclusively negative, since it is not an instrument for extending knowledge, but a discipline for limiting it."[1] Do not such words amount purely and simply to saying that the only aim of philosophers should be to impose upon everyone else the narrow limits of their own understanding? Here we see an inevitable consequence of the systematic outlook, which, let it be repeated once more, is anti-metaphysical in the highest degree.

Metaphysics affirms the fundamental identity of knowing and being, which can only be questioned by those who are ignorant of the most elementary metaphysical principles; and since this identity is essentially implied in the very nature of intellectual intuition, it not merely affirms it but realizes it as well. This is true at least of integral metaphysics; but it must be added that such metaphysics as there has been in the West seems always to have remained incomplete in this respect. Nevertheless, Aristotle clearly laid down the principle of identification by knowledge, when he expressly declared that "the soul is all that it knows".[2] But neither he himself nor his successors ever seem to have given this affirmation its full significance, or to have extracted all the consequences implied in it, so that for them it has remained something purely theoretical. Certainly this is better than nothing, but it is nevertheless very inadequate, and thus Western metaphysics appears to have been doubly incomplete: it is already so theoretically, as previously explained, in that it does not proceed beyond Being; on the other hand it only considers things, to the extent that it does consider them, in a purely theoretical light. Theory is regarded as if it were in some way self-sufficient, an end in itself, whereas it should normally be looked upon as nothing more than a preparation, indispensable as such we admit, leading to a corresponding realization.

It is necessary to say something at this point about the way in which we use the word "theory": etymologically, its primary meaning is "contemplation", and if it is taken thus, it might be said that metaphysics in its entirety, including the realization which it implies, is

---

[1] *Kritik der reinen Vernunft*, ed. Hartenstein, p. 256.

[2] *De Anima.*

theory in the fullest sense; but usage has given the word a rather different and above all a much narrower meaning. In the first place, it has become usual to oppose theory and practice, and in its original sense, this antithesis, which meant the opposition of contemplation to action, would still be justifiable here, since metaphysics is essentially beyond the sphere of action, which is the sphere of individual contingencies; but the Western mentality, being turned almost exclusively toward action and being unable to conceive of any realization outside the sphere of action, has come to oppose theory and realization in a general sense. It is therefore this last opposition that we shall in fact accept, so as not to depart from common usage and in order to avoid any confusion that might arise owing to the difficulty of separating these terms from the meaning which rightly or wrongly is ordinarily attached to them; we will not go so far however as to qualify metaphysical realization as "practical", for in current speech this word has remained inseparable from the idea of action which it originally expressed, and which is in no wise applicable here.

In all doctrines that are metaphysically complete, as are those of the East, theory is invariably accompanied or followed by an effective realization, for which it merely provides the necessary basis; no realization can be embarked upon without a sufficient theoretical preparation, but theory is ordained entirely with a view to this realization as the means toward the end, and this point of view is presupposed, or at least is tacitly implied, even in the exterior expression of the doctrine. On the other hand, in addition to theoretical preparation and subsequent to it, other means of effective realization of a very different kind may be brought into play; but these means also are destined simply to furnish a support or a point of departure, playing the part of "aids" only, however important they may be in actual practice: this is indeed the reason for the existence of rites possessing a genuinely metaphysical character and import. . . . However, these rites, unlike theoretical preparation, are never regarded as an indispensable means, since they are only accessory and not essential, and the Hindu tradition, where they nevertheless hold an important place, is quite explicit in this respect; but they are capable nonetheless, by virtue of their own efficacy, of markedly facilitating metaphysical realization, that is to say the transformation of this virtual knowledge, which is all that theory amounts to, into effective knowledge.

13

Sanātana Dharma

The notion of *Sanātana Dharma* has no equivalent in the West, to the point that it seems impossible to find a term or an expression that could convey its meaning entirely and in all its aspects, any translation one might propose for it being, if not altogether false, at least quite inadequate. A. K. Coomaraswamy thought that the expression best approximating it would be *Philosophia Perennis*, taken in the sense in which this was understood in the Middle Ages, and this is indeed true in certain respects although there are nevertheless considerable differences, which it will be all the more useful to examine here because there are those who too easily believe in the possibility of simply assimilating these two notions.

We should note at the outset that the difficulty does not hinge on the translation of the word *sanātana*, for which the Latin *perennis* is really a true equivalent; it is properly a question here of "perenniality" or perpetuity, and not of eternity, as is sometimes claimed. Indeed, this term *sanātana* implies a notion of duration, whereas eternity on the contrary is essentially "non-duration", the duration in question being indefinite so to speak, or, more precisely, "cyclical"—as in the Greek, which likewise lacks the meaning of "eternal", which, through a regrettable confusion the moderns too often attribute to it. What is perpetual in this sense is what subsists continuously from the beginning to the end of a cycle, and according to Hindu tradition the cycle that must be considered in the case of the *Sanātana Dharma* is a *Manvantara*, that is to say the duration of manifestation of a terrestrial humanity. We must immediately add—for its full importance will become evident later—that *sanātana* also has the sense of "primordial", and it is moreover easy to understand its very direct link with what we have just noted because what is truly perpetual can only be what goes back to the very beginning of the cycle. Finally, it must be clearly understood that this perpetuity and the stability it necessarily implies, while it must not in any way be confused with eternity, with which it has no common measure, is a sort of reflection in the conditions of our world, of the eternity and the immutability belonging to those principles of which *Sanātana Dharma* is likewise the expression with respect to our world.

The word *perennis* can itself also include all we have just explained, but it would be quite difficult to say to what degree the scholastics of the Middle Ages, to whose language the term *Philosophia Perennis* more particularly belongs, were clearly aware of it, for although obviously traditional their point of view nonetheless only extended to an exterior domain and was in many respects limited. However that may be, and admitting that, independently of all historical considerations, one could restore to this word the plenitude of its meaning, what remains nonetheless a cause for more serious reservations as concerns the assimilation just discussed is the use of the term *Philosophia*, which in a certain way corresponds precisely to the very limitations of the scholastic point of view. In the first place, this word too easily gives rise to ambiguities, especially as the moderns habitually use it. One could of course resolve them by making it clear that the *Philosophia Perennis* is by no means "a" philosophy, that is to say one particular conception more or less limited and systematic and having this or that individual as its author, but is rather the common foundation from which proceeds whatever is truly valid in all philosophies; and such a way of envisaging it would certainly correspond to the thought of the Scholastics. But there is still an impropriety here, for if it is considered, as it must be, as an authentic expression of truth, it would much more likely be a question of *Sophia* than *Philosophia*: "wisdom" must not be confused with the aspiration that leads to it, or that seeks it and may lead to it, which is all the word "philosophy" properly designates according to its etymology. It can perhaps be said that the word is subject to a certain transposition, and although in our view this term does not seem indispensable (as it would be if we really had none better at our disposal), we do not intend to contest such a possibility; but even in the most favorable case it would still be very far from a legitimate equivalent of *Dharma*, for it can never designate more than one doctrine, which, whatever may be the extent of its domain, will in any event remain merely theoretical, and consequently can in no way correspond to all that the traditional point of view comprehends in its integrality. From the traditional point of view, doctrine is in fact never seen as a simple theory sufficient in itself but as knowledge that must be realized effectively, and it comprises applications moreover that extend to all modes of human life without exception.

This extension results from the very meaning of the word *dharma*, which in any case is impossible to render by a single term in Western languages; by its root *dhri*, which has the meaning of carrying, supporting, sustaining, and maintaining, it designates above all a principle of conservation of beings, and consequently of stability, at least to the extent that the latter is compatible with the conditions of manifestation. It is important to note that the root *dhri* is almost identical in form and meaning with another root *dhru*, from which is derived the word *dhruva*, which designates "pole". One must actually turn to this idea of "pole" or "axis" of the manifested world if one wishes to understand the notion of *dharma* in its most profound sense, for it is what remains invariable at the center of the revolutions of all things, ruling the course of change by the very fact that it does not participate in it. It must not be forgotten in this connection that such language, by virtue of the synthetic character of the thought it expresses, is much more closely linked to symbolism than are modern languages, where such a link no longer subsists to any extent except by virtue of a distant derivation. And if it did not lead us too far from our subject, one could even demonstrate that this notion of *dharma* is connected quite directly to the symbolic representation of the "axis" through the figure of the "World Tree".

One could say that if thus envisaged only in principle, *dharma* is necessarily *sanātana*, and is so in an even broader sense than indicated above since instead of being limited to a certain cycle and to the beings manifested therein, it applies equally to all beings and to all their states of manifestation. Indeed, here again we meet the idea of permanence and stability, but it goes without saying that this latter, outside of which there could be no question at all of *dharma*, can nevertheless be applied in a relative way to different levels and in more or less restricted domains, and this justifies all the secondary or "specialized" meanings of this term. By the very fact that it must be conceived as the principle of conservation of beings, *dharma* consists for these beings in the conformity of each to its own essential nature. In this sense one can therefore speak in this sense of the *dharma* proper to each being—designated more precisely as *svadharma*—or of each category of beings, as well as of a world or state of existence, or again of only a definite portion of the latter, that of a certain people or a certain period; and when one speaks of *Sanātana Dharma*, it is then as we have said a question of the totality of a humanity throughout the duration of its manifestation, which constitutes a *Manvantara*. It can also be said that in this case it is the "law" or the "norm" proper to that cycle, formulated from its very beginning by the *Manu* governing it, that is to say by the cosmic intelligence that reflects the divine Will and expresses universal Order therein. In principle this is the true sense of the *Mānava Dharma*, considered apart from all the particular adaptations that can be derived from it, although these latter may legitimately receive the same designation in that in the final analysis they will only be translations required by varying circumstances of time and place. We must add however that in such cases it may happen that the very idea of "law" in fact entails a certain restriction, for although it can be applied by extension to the contents of the whole body of sacred scriptures, as is true of its Hebrew equivalent *Torah*, it makes us think most immediately and naturally of the "legislative" aspect properly speaking, which is assuredly very far from constituting the entire tradition, although it is an integral part of every civilization that can be qualified as normal. This legislative aspect, although in reality only an application to the social order, necessarily presupposes (as do all other such applications) the purely metaphysical doctrine constituting the essential and fundamental part of the tradition, the principial knowledge upon which all the rest wholly depends and without which nothing really traditional, in whatever domain it may be, could in any way exist.

We have spoken of the universal order, which is the expression of the divine Will in manifestation and which in each state of existence assumes particular modalities determined by the conditions proper to that state. Now in certain respects at least, *dharma* may be defined as conformity to order, which explains the close relationship between it and *rita*, which is also order and has the etymological sense of "rectitude", as does the *Te* of the Far-Eastern traditions, with which Hindu *dharma* has much in common—and this clearly calls to mind once again the notion of "axis", of a constant and invariable direction. At the same time this term *rita* is obviously identical with the word "rite", which in its original meaning also effectively designated everything accomplished in conformity with order, all integrally traditional civilizations, especially at their inception, being characterized by a properly ritual character. Rites only began to take on a more restricted meaning in consequence of the degeneration that gave rise to "profane" activity in all domains, the distinction between "sacred" and "profane" implying of course that certain things were thenceforth envisaged as outside the traditional point of view rather than the latter applying equally to all—and these things, by the very fact that they are considered "profane", have truly become *adharma* or *anrita*. By contrast it must be understood that rites, which then correspond to the "sacred", always conserve the same "dharmic" character as it were and represent what still remains of what preceded that degeneration. In reality, it is non-ritual activity that is deviant or abnormal, in particular all mere "conventions" or "customs", which, lacking any profound reason and being of purely human invention, did not exist originally but only arose through deviation. Whatever some may think, rites envisaged from the traditional point of view (as they must be to be worthy of the name) can have absolutely no relation with such counterfeits or parodies. Furthermore—and this point is essential—when conformity to order is spoken of this must not be understood in respect of the human order alone, but also and even above all of the cosmic order. In every traditional conception there is in fact always a strict correspondence between the one and the other, and it is precisely the rite that consciously preserves the relationships, implying in a way a collaboration of man in that sphere where his activity takes place—the cosmic order itself.

From this it follows that if the *Sanātana Dharma* is considered as an integral tradition, it includes principially all branches of human activity, which moreover are "transformed" thereby, since by virtue of this integration they participate in the "nonhuman" character inherent in every tradition, or, better yet, constitute the very essence of tradition as such. It is therefore the exact opposite of "humanism", that is to say of the point of view that would like to reduce everything to the purely human level, which basically is one with the profane point of view itself. It is especially in this that the traditional conception of the sciences and of the arts and sciences differs most profoundly from their profane conception, to such a point that one could say without exaggeration that the two are separated by a veritable abyss. From the traditional point of view the sciences and arts are really only valid and legitimate insofar as they adhere to universal principles in such a way that they in fact appear as applications of the fundamental doctrine in a certain contingent order, just as social legislation and organization are such in another domain. Through this participation in the essence of the tradition, science and art, in all their modes of operation, also have that ritual character of which we have just spoken, and of which no activity is deprived so long as it remains what it must normally be. And we might add that from this point of view there is no distinction to be made between arts and crafts, which traditionally are but one and the same thing. We cannot dwell further on all these considerations, . . . but we think that we have at least said enough to show how in every respect all this goes beyond "philosophy", no matter how this latter may be understood.

It should now be easy to understand what the *Sanātana Dharma* really is: it is nothing other than the primordial tradition, which alone subsists continuously and without change across the entire *Manvantara* and thus possesses cyclical perpetuity because its very primordiality removes it from the vicissitudes of successive ages, and it is this tradition alone that can in all strictness be regarded as truly and fully integral. Moreover, owing to the descending course of the cycle and the resulting spiritual obscuration, the primordial tradition has become hidden and inaccessible to ordinary humanity. It is the primary source and the common foundation of all particular traditional forms which proceed from it by adaptation to the particular conditions of peoples and times, but none of these can be identified with the *Sanātana Dharma* itself or be considered an adequate expression of it, although they are nevertheless always more or less veiled images of it. Every orthodox tradition is a reflection of and, one could say, a "substitute" for the primordial tradition in the measure permitted by contingent circumstances, so that if it is not the *Sanātana Dharma* it nevertheless truly represents it for those who effectively adhere to it and participate in it, since they can only reach it in this way and since it expresses, if not the fullness thereof, at least everything that concerns them directly, and under the form most suited to their individual nature. In a certain sense, all these diverse traditional forms are contained principially in the *Sanātana Dharma*, for they are just so many regular and legitimate adaptations of it, and not one of the developments to which they are subject in the course of time could ultimately ever be anything else. And in another inverse and complementary sense they all contain the *Sanātana Dharma* as that in them which is most inner and "central". In their different degrees of exteriority they are like so many veils concealing the *Sanātana Dharma*, permitting it to show through only in an attenuated and more or less partial fashion.

This being true for all traditional forms, it would be an error to wish to assimilate the *Sanātana Dharma* purely and simply to one among them, whichever one that might be, even the Hindu tradition such as we find it at present. And if this error is in fact sometimes made, it can only be by those whose horizon, by reason of the circumstances in which they find themselves, is limited to that tradition alone. If however that assimilation is in a certain measure legitimate according to what we have just explained, the adherents of other traditions could in the same sense and by the same right also say that their own tradition is the *Sanātana Dharma*, such an affirmation always remaining true in a relative sense although obviously false in the absolute sense. There is however a reason why the notion of the *Sanātana Dharma* appears to be linked more particularly with the Hindu tradition, for of all the traditional forms existing today, the latter derives most directly from the primordial tradition. It prolongs it outwardly, as it were, although always of course conforming to the conditions in which the human cycle unfolds (of which moreover it gives a more complete description than is to be found elsewhere), and hence participating in its perpetuity to a higher degree than all the others. It is also interesting to note that the Hindu and the Islamic traditions explicitly affirm the validity of all the other orthodox traditions, and if this is so it is because as the temporally first and the last in the course of the *Manvantara* they must to the same extent integrate—although in different modes—all the diverse forms that have arisen in the interval, so as to render possible the "return to origins" by which the end of the cycle will rejoin its beginning, whence, at the starting-point of another *Manvantara*, the true *Sanātana Dharma* will again be outwardly manifest.

We must still point out two erroneous conceptions only too prevalent in our time, bearing witness to a lack of understanding that is far more serious and more complete than is the assimilation of the *Sanātana Dharma* to a particular traditional form. One of these misconceptions is that of the so-called "reformers"—met with today even in India—who think themselves capable of recovering the *Sanātana Dharma* by proceeding with a sort of simplification of the tradition that is more or less arbitrary, something that in reality merely corresponds to their own individual tendencies and most often betrays prejudices stemming from the influence of the modern Western spirit. What these "reformers" generally have in mind in the first instance is the elimination of precisely what has the most profound significance, either because it eludes them entirely or because it runs counter to their preconceived ideas, and this attitude is quite comparable to that of the "critics" who reject as "interpolations" everything in a text that does not agree with the idea they have of it or with the meaning they wish to discover there. When we speak of a "return to origins", as we did a moment ago, it is assuredly a matter of something else entirely, something that in no way depends on the initiative of individuals as such; besides, we do not at all see why the primordial tradition should be as simple as these people claim, if it is not that an intellectual infirmity or weakness wishes it were so. And why should truth be obliged to accommodate itself to the mediocrity of the faculties of comprehension of the average individual today? To realize that this is not at all the case it suffices to understand on the one hand that the *Sanātana Dharma* contains everything without exception, and more besides, that has been expressed through all traditional forms, and on the other that it necessarily involves truths of the highest and most profound order, such as have become most inaccessible through the spiritual and intellectual obscuration inherent in the cyclical descent. Under these conditions the simplicity dear to modernists of every ilk is obviously as far as may be from constituting a mark of the antiquity of a traditional doctrine, and with even greater reason of its primordiality.

The other erroneous conception to which we want to draw attention belongs above all to the various contemporary schools that are connected to what is fitly designated "occultism". As a rule these schools proceed "syncretically", that is, by bringing together various traditions, to the extent that they are acquainted with them, in a wholly exterior and superficial manner without even trying to draw out what they have in common, but only to juxtapose as well as they can elements borrowed from one or another of them. The results, as incongruous as they are fanciful, are nonetheless presented as the expression of an "ancient wisdom" or of an "archaic doctrine" from which all traditions would have issued, and which they identify with the primordial tradition, or with the *Sanātana Dharma*, although these terms themselves seem not to be understood by the schools concerned. It goes without saying that all of this, whatever be the pretensions, cannot have the least value and only corresponds to a purely profane point of view, the more so as these conceptions are almost invariably accompanied by a total failure to grasp the necessity of adhering above all to a given tradition for whomever wishes to penetrate the spiritual domain to any degree whatever. And in this connection it should be understood that we speak of an affective adherence with all the consequences that this implies, including the practice of the rites of that tradition, and not of a vague "ideal" feeling of connectedness such as leads some Westerners to declare themselves Hindus or Buddhists without much knowledge of what these are, and at all events without ever thinking of establishing a real and regular attachment to these traditions, although such an attachment is the indispensable point of departure from which each according to his capacity may seek to go further. In effect, what is required are not speculations in the void, but knowledge which must be essentially ordained with a view to spiritual realization. It is only in this way that from within the traditions—and one can speak with more exactitude of their very center, should it be successfully reached—one can truly realize that which constitutes their essential and fundamental unity, and thereby truly attain full knowledge of the *Sanātana Dharma.*

14

Some Remarks on the Doctrine of Cosmic Cycles

We have often been asked, regarding allusions we have been led to make here and there to the Hindu doctrine of cosmic cycles and its equivalents in other traditions, whether we might give, if not a complete explanation, at least an overview sufficient to reveal its broad outlines. In truth, this seems an almost impossible task, not only because the question is very complex in itself, but especially owing to the extreme difficulty of expressing these things in a European language and in a way that is intelligible to the present-day Western mentality, which has had no practice whatsoever with this kind of thinking. All that is really possible, in our opinion, is to try to clarify a few points with remarks such as those that follow, which can only raise suggestions about the meaning of the doctrine in question rather than to really explain it.

In the most general sense of the term, a cycle must be considered as representing the process of development of some state of manifestation, or, in the case of minor cycles, of one of the more or less restricted and specialized modalities of that state. Moreover, in virtue of the law of correspondence which links all things in universal Existence, there is necessarily and always a certain analogy, either among different cycles of the same order or among the principal cycles and their secondary divisions. This is what allows us to use one and the same mode of expression when speaking about them, although this must often be understood only symbolically, for the very essence of all symbolism is precisely founded on the analogies and correspondences which really exist in the nature of things. We allude here especially to the "chronological" form under which the doctrine of cycles is presented: since a *Kalpa* represents the total development of a world, that is to say of a state or degree of universal Existence, it is obvious that one cannot speak literally about its duration, computed according to some temporal measure, unless this duration relates to a state of which time is one of the determining conditions, as in our world. Everywhere else, this duration and the succession that it implies can have only a purely symbolic value and must be transposed analogically, for temporal succession is then only an image, both logical and ontological, of an "extra-temporal" series of causes and effects. On the other hand, since human language cannot directly express any condition other than those of our own state, such a symbolism is by that very fact sufficiently justified and must be regarded as perfectly natural and normal.

We do not intend to deal just now with the most extensive cycles, such as the *Kalpas*; we will limit ourselves to those which develop within our *Kalpa*, that is, the *Manvantaras* and their subdivisions. At this level, the cycles have a character that is at once cosmic and historical, for they particularly concern terrestrial humanity, while at the same time being closely linked to events occurring in our world but outside of the history of humanity. There is nothing to surprise us here, for the idea of seeing human history as somehow isolated from all the rest is exclusively modern and sharply opposed to what is taught by all traditions, which on the contrary unanimously affirm a necessary and constant correlation between the cosmic and the human orders.

The *Manvantaras*, or eras of successive *Manus*, are fourteen in number, forming two septenary series of which the first includes both past *Manvantaras* and our present one, and the second future *Manvantaras*. These two series, of which one relates to the past as well as to the present that is its immediate result, and the other to the future, can be linked with those of the seven *Svargas* and the seven *Pātālas*, which, from the point of view of the hierarchy of the degrees of existence or of universal manifestation, represent the states respectively higher and lower than the human state, or anterior and posterior with respect to that state if one places oneself at the viewpoint of the causal connection of the cycles symbolically described, as always, under the analogy of a temporal succession. This last point of view is obviously the most important here, for it enables us to see within our *Kalpa* a kind of reduced image of the totality of the cycles of universal manifestation according to the analogical relation we mentioned earlier; and in this sense one could say that the succession of *Manvantaras* in a way marks a reflection of other worlds in ours. To confirm this relationship, one could also note that the words *Manu* and *Loka* are both used as symbolic designations for the number 14; to say that this is simply a "coincidence" would be to give proof of a complete ignorance of the profound reasons inherent in all traditional symbolism.

Yet another correspondence with the *Manvantaras* concerns the seven *Dvīpas* or "regions" into which our world is divided. Although according to the proper meaning of the word that designates them these are represented as islands or continents distributed in a certain way in space, one must be careful not to take this literally and to regard them simply as different parts of present-day earth; in fact, they "emerge" in turns and not simultaneously, which is to say that only one of them is manifested in the sensible domain over the course of a certain period. If that period is a *Manvantara*, one will have to conclude that each *Dvīpa* will have to appear twice in the *Kalpa* or once in each of the just mentioned septenary series; and from the relationship of these two series, which correspond to one another inversely as do all similar cases, particularly the *Svargas* and the *Pātālas*, one can deduce that the order of appearance for the *Dvīpas* will likewise have to be, in the second series, the inverse of what it was in the first. In sum, this is a matter of different "states" of the terrestrial world rather than "regions" properly speaking; the *Jambu-Dvīpa* really represents the entire earth in its present state, and if it is said to extend to the south of *Meru*, the "axial" mountain around which our world revolves, this is because *Meru* is identified symbolically with the North Pole, so that the whole earth is really situated to the south with respect to it. To explain this more completely it would be necessary to develop the symbolism of the directions of space according to which the *Dvīpas* are distributed, as well as correspondences existing between this spatial symbolism and the temporal symbolism on which the whole doctrine of cycles rests; but since we cannot here go into these considerations, which alone would require a whole volume, we must be content with these summary indications, which can be easily completed by all who already have some knowledge of what is involved.

This way of envisaging the *Dvīpas* is also confirmed by concordant data from other traditions which also speak of "seven lands", particularly Islamic esoterism and the Hebrew Kabbalah. Thus in the latter, even while these "seven lands" are outwardly represented by as many divisions of the land of Canaan, they are related to the reigns of the "seven kings of Edom" which clearly correspond to the seven *Manus* of the first series; and all are included in the "Land of the Living" which represents the complete development of our world considered as realized permanently in its principal state. We can note here the coexistence of two points of view, one of succession, which refers to manifestation in itself, and the other of simultaneity, which refers to its principle or to what one could call its "archetype"; and at root the correspondence between these two points of view is in a certain way equivalent to that between temporal symbolism and spatial symbolism, to which we just alluded in connection with the *Dvīpa*s of the Hindu tradition.

In Islamic esoterism, the "seven lands" appear, perhaps even more explicitly, as so many *tabaqāt* or "categories" of terrestrial existence, which coexist and in a way interpenetrate, but only one of which is presently accessible to the senses while the others are in a latent state and can only be perceived exceptionally and under certain special conditions; these too are manifested outwardly in turn, during the different periods that succeed one another in the course of the total duration of this world. On the other hand, each of the "seven lands" is governed by a *Quṭb* or "Pole", which thus corresponds very clearly to the *Manu* of the period during which his land is manifested; and these seven *Aqtāb* are subordinate to the supreme "Pole" just as the different *Manu*s are subordinate to the *Adi-Manu* or primordial *Manu*; but because these "seven lands" coexist, they also in a certain respect exercise their functions in a permanent and simultaneous way. It is hardly necessary to point out that the designation of "Pole" is closely related to the "polar" symbolism of *Meru* which we just mentioned, for *Meru* itself has in any case its exact equivalent in the mountain of *Qāf* in Islamic tradition. Let us also add that the seven terrestrial "Poles" are considered to be reflections of the seven celestial "Poles" which preside respectively over the seven planetary heavens; and this naturally evokes the correspondence with the *Svarga*s in Hindu doctrine, which shows in sum the perfect concordance in this regard between the two traditions.

We shall now consider the divisions of a *Manvantara*, that is to say the *Yuga*s, which are four in number. First of all, and without dwelling on it at length, let us point out that this quaternary division of a cycle is susceptible of multiple applications and that it is in fact found in many cycles of a more particular order. One can cite as examples the four seasons of the year, the four weeks of the lunar month, and the four ages of human life; here too there is correspondence with a spatial symbolism, in this case principally related to the four cardinal points. On the other hand, we have often called attention to the obvious equivalence of the four *Yuga*s with the four ages of gold, silver, bronze, and iron as they were known to Greco-Latin antiquity, in both cases, each period is marked by a degeneration in regard to the age that preceded it; and this, which is directly opposed to the idea of "progress" as understood by the modern world, is very simply explained by the fact that every cyclical development, that is in sum every process of manifestation, quite truly constitutes a "descent" since it necessarily implies a gradual distancing from the principle, and this is moreover the real meaning of the "fall" in the Judeo-Christian tradition.

From one *Yuga* to the next the degeneration is accompanied by a decrease in duration, and this is thought to influence the length of human life; and what is most important in this respect are the ratios that exist between the respective durations of these different periods. If the total duration of the *Manvantara* is represented by 10, that of the *Krita-Yuga* or *Satya-Yuga* is 4, that of the *Treta-Yuga* is 3, that of the *Dvapara-Yuga* is 2, and that of the *Kali-Yuga* is 1. These numbers are also those belonging to the feet of the symbolic bull of *Dharma* which are represented as resting on the earth during the same periods. The division of the *Manvantara* is therefore carried out according to the formula $10 = 4+3+2+1$, which is, in reverse, that of the Pythagorean *Tetraktys*: $1+2+3+4 = 10$. This last formula corresponds to what the language of Western Hermeticism calls the "circling of the square", and the other to the opposite problem of the "squaring of the circle", which expresses precisely the relation of the end of a cycle to its beginning, that is, the integration of its total development. Here there is an entire symbolism both arithmetic and geometric which we can only indicate in passing so as not to digress too far from our principal subject.

As for the numbers given in different texts for the duration of the *Manvantara* and consequently for that of the *Yuga*s, it must be understood that they are not to be regarded as a "chronology" in the ordinary sense of the word, we mean as expressing a literal number of years; and this is also why certain apparent differences in these numbers do not really imply any contradiction. Generally speaking, it is only the number 4,320 that is to be considered in these figures, for a reason that we shall explain later, and not the many zeros that follow it, which may well be meant to lead astray those who wish to devote themselves to certain calculations. At first glance, such a precaution might seem strange, and yet it is easily explained: if the real duration of the *Manvantara* were known, and if in addition its starting-point were exactly determined, anyone could without difficulty draw there from deductions allowing him to foresee certain future events. But no orthodox tradition has ever encouraged inquiries by means of which someone might see more or less into the future, since in practice such a knowledge has more drawbacks than real advantages. This is why the starting-point and the duration of the *Manvantara* have always been more or less carefully concealed, either by adding or subtracting a given number of years from the real dates, or by multiplying or dividing the durations of the cyclical periods so as to conserve only their exact proportions; and we will add that certain correspondences have also sometimes been reversed for similar reasons.

If the duration of the *Manvantara* is 4,320, those of the four *Yuga*s will respectively be 1,728, 1,296, 864, and 432; but by what number must we multiply them to obtain an expression of these durations in years? It is easy to see that all the cyclical numbers are directly related to the geometric division of the circle; thus 4,320 = 360 x 12. Besides, there is nothing arbitrary or purely conventional in this division because, for reasons relating to the correspondence between arithmetic and geometry, it is normal for it to be carried out according to multiples of 3, 9, and 12, whereas decimal division is that best suited for the straight line. And yet this observation, although truly fundamental, would not enable us to go very far in determining cyclical periods if we did not also know that in the cosmic order their principal basis is the astronomical period of the precession of the equinoxes, of which the duration is 25,920 years, so that the displacement of the equinoctial points is one degree in 72 years. This number 72 is precisely a sub-multiple of 4,320 = 72 x 60 and 4,320 is in turn a sub-multiple of 25,920 = 4,320 x 6. The fact that we find in the precession of the equinoxes numbers linked to the division of the circle is yet another proof of its truly natural character; but the question that now arises is this: what multiple or sub-multiple of the astronomical period in question really corresponds to the duration of the *Manvantara*?

The period that appears most frequently in different traditions is in truth not so much the precession of equinoxes as its half; actually, it is this that corresponds in particular to the "great year" of the Persians and the Greeks which is often expressed by approximation as either 12,000 or 13,000 years, its exact duration being 12,960 years. Given the very particular importance which is thus attributed to that period, it is to be presumed that the *Manvantara* will have to comprise a whole number of these "great years"; but what will that number be? Here we find, elsewhere than in Hindu tradition, at least a precise indication which this time seems plausible enough to be accepted literally: among the Chaldeans, the duration of the reign of *Xisuthros*, which is manifestly identical to *Vaivasvata*, the *Manu* of the present era, is fixed at 64,800 years, or exactly five "great years". Let us note incidentally that the number 5, being that of the *bhūtas* or elements of the sensory world, must necessarily have a special importance from the cosmological point of view, something that tends to confirm the reality of such an evaluation; perhaps there is reason to consider a correlation between the five *bhūtas* and the successive five "great years" in question, all the more so in fact since in the ancient traditions of Central America one encounters an explicit association of the elements with certain cyclical periods; but this question would require closer examination. However that may be, if such is indeed the real duration of the *Manvantara*, and if we continue to take as a base the number 4,320, which is equal to the third part of the "great year", it is then by 15 that this number will have to be multiplied. On the other hand, the five "great years" will naturally be distributed unequally but according to simple relationships among the four *Yugas*: the *Krita-Yuga* will contain 2 of them, the *Treta-Yuga* 1½, the *Dvapara-Yuga* 1, and the *Kali-Yuga* ½; these numbers are of course half of those we previously used when representing the duration of the *Manvantara* by 10. Expressed in ordinary years, these same durations of the four *Yugas* will be respectively 25,920, 19,440, 12,960, and 6,480 years, forming the total of 64,800 years; and it will be recognized that these numbers are at least within perfectly plausible limits and may very well correspond to the true chronology of present terrestrial humanity. We will end these considerations here, for as concerns the starting-point of our *Manvantara* and consequently the exact point in its course where we are presently situated, we do not intend to risk an attempt to determine them. By all traditional data we know that we have been in the *Kali-Yuga* for a long time already; and we can say without fear of error that we are in an advanced phase, a phase whose description in the *Purānas* corresponds in the most striking fashion to the characteristics of our present epoch. But would it not be imprudent to wish to be more exact, and would this not inevitably end in the kinds of predictions to which traditional doctrine has, not without good reasons, posed so many obstacles?

15

Foundation of the Theory of the Multiple States

The preceding exposition[1] contains the basis for the theory of the multiple states in all its universality: if one envisages any being whatsoever in its totality, it must include, at least virtually, states of manifestation and states of non-manifestation, for it is only in this sense that one can truly speak of "totality", as otherwise one is only dealing with something incomplete and fragmentary that cannot truly constitute the total being;[2] and since, as we have said above, non-manifestation alone possesses the character of absolute permanence, manifestation in its transitory condition draws all its reality from it; and by this it is evident that Non-Being, far from being "nothingness", is exactly the opposite, if indeed "nothingness" could have an opposite, for this would imply granting it a certain degree of "positivity" incompatible with its absolute "negativity", which is pure impossibility.[3]

This being so, it follows that it is essentially the states of non-manifestation that assure the being permanence and identity, for aside from these states, that is, taking the being only in its manifested aspect, without reference to its non-manifested principle, this permanence and this identity can only be illusory, since the domain of manifestation is properly the domain of the transitory and multiple, involving continual and indefinite modifications. This being so, one will readily understand what, from the metaphysical point of view, one should think of the supposed unity of the "self", that is, the individual being so indispensable to Western and profane psychology: on

---

[1] See chap. 3, "Being and Non-Being", in *The Multiple States of Being*. ED

[2] As we indicated at the outset, if one wishes to speak of the total being, one must still speak analogically of "a being" for lack of another more adequate term at our disposal, but this expression is not strictly applicable.

[3] "Nothingness" is then not opposed to Being, despite what is commonly said; it is to Possibility that it would be opposed, if it could really enter as a term into any opposition—but this is not the case, since nothing can oppose itself to Possibility, something that should be understood without any difficulty in view of the fact that Possibility is in reality identical with the Infinite.

the one hand it is a fragmentary unity, since it refers to a part of the being only, to one of its states taken in isolation and arbitrarily from among an indefinite number of others (and this state, too, is far from being envisaged in its integrality), while on the other hand this unity, even if only considered in reference to this special state, is as relative as possible, since this state is itself composed of an indefinite number of diverse modifications and so has even less reality when abstracted from its transcendent principle (the "Self" or personality), which alone could truly give it reality by maintaining the identity of a being in permanent mode throughout all these modifications.

The states of non-manifestation are of the domain of Non-Being, and the states of manifestation are of the domain of Being envisaged in its integrality; it could also be said that these latter correspond to the different degrees of Existence, which are nothing other than the different modes of universal manifestation, indefinite in their mul-tiplicity. In order to establish a clear distinction between Being and Existence, we must, as we have already said, consider Being strictly as the very principle of manifestation; universal Existence will then be the integral manifestation of the ensemble of possibilities that Being comprises, and which moreover are all the possibilities of manifesta-tion, implying the effective development of those possibilities in a conditioned mode. Being thus envelops Existence, and is metaphysi-cally more than the latter since it is its principle; Existence is thus not identical with Being, for the latter corresponds to a lesser degree of determination, and consequently to a higher degree of universality.[4]

Although Existence is essentially unique because Being in itself is one, it nonetheless comprises the indefinite multiplicity of the modes of manifestation, for it contains them all equally by the very fact that they are all equally possible, this possibility implying that each one of them must be realized according to the conditions proper to it. As we have said elsewhere, in connection with this "unicity of Existence" (in Arabic, *al-waḥdat al-wujūd*) as found in the teachings of Islamic

---

[4] Let us recall again that to "exist", in the etymological sense of the word (from Latin *ex-stare*), is properly speaking to be dependent or conditioned; it is then, finally, not to possess in oneself one's own principle or sufficient reason, which is indeed true of manifestation, as we shall explain further on when we define contingency with more precision.

esoterism,[5] it follows that Existence comprises in its very "unicity" an indefinitude of degrees corresponding to all the modes of universal manifestation (which is basically the same thing as Existence itself); and for any being whatsoever envisaged in the entire domain of that Existence, this indefinite multiplicity of degrees of existence implies correlatively a like indefinite multiplicity of possible states of manifestation, each of which must be realized in a determined degree of universal Existence. A state of a being is then the development of a particular possibility contained in such a degree, that degree being defined by the conditions to which the possibility is subject insofar as it is envisaged as realizing itself in the domain of manifestation.[6]

Thus, each state of manifestation of a being corresponds to a degree of Existence, and in addition includes diverse modalities in accordance with the different combinations of conditions to which one and the same general mode of manifestation is susceptible; and finally, each modality comprises in itself an indefinite series of secondary and elementary modifications. If, for example, we consider the being in the particular state of human individuality, the corporeal part of this individuality is only one of its modalities, and this modality is not precisely determined by a single condition but by an ensemble of conditions that delimit its possibilities, these conditions taken in combination defining the perceptible or corporeal world.[7] As we have already noted,[8] each of these conditions considered in isolation from the others can extend beyond the domain of that modality, and, whether through its own extension or through its combination with different conditions, can then constitute the domain of other

---

[5] *The Symbolism of the Cross*, chap. 1.

[6] This restriction is necessary because, in its non-manifested essence, the same possibility obviously cannot be subject to such conditions.

[7] It is this that Hindu doctrine designates as the domain of "gross" manifestation. It is sometimes called the "physical world", but this expression is equivocal, and even if it can be justified by the modern sense of the word "physical", which actually applies only to what concerns sensible qualities, we think it better to preserve the ancient etymological meaning (from the Greek word meaning "nature") for this word, because when understood thus, "subtle" manifestation is no less "physical" than gross manifestation, for "nature", which is properly speaking the domain of "becoming", is in reality identical to the whole of universal manifestation.

[8] *The Symbolism of the Cross*, chap. 11.

modalities that are part of the same integral individuality. Moreover, each modality must be regarded as susceptible of development in the course of a certain cycle of manifestation, and, for the corporeal modality in particular, the secondary modifications that this development includes will be all the moments of its existence (envisaged under the aspect of temporal succession), or, what comes to the same thing, all the actions and gestures, whatever they may be, that it will carry out in the course of its existence.[9]

It is almost superfluous to stress how little place the individual "self" occupies in the totality of the being,[10] since even given its entire extension when envisaged in its integrality, and not merely in one particular modality such as the corporeal, it constitutes only one state like the others, among an indefinitude of others. This is so even when one limits one's consideration to the states of manifestation; and beyond this, the latter are themselves the least important elements in the total being from the metaphysical point of view, for the reasons given above.[11] Among the states of manifestation are those, apart from human individuality, that can likewise be individual (that is, formal) states, whereas others are non-individual (that is, non-formal), the nature of each being determined, together with its place in the hierarchically organized totality of the being, by the conditions proper to it, for it is always a matter of conditioned states, by the very fact that they are manifested. As for the states of non-manifestation, it is evident that, not being more subject to form than to any other condition of any mode whatsoever of manifested existence, they are essentially extra-individual; we can say that they constitute whatever is truly universal in each being, and therefore that by which each being, in all that it is, is linked to its metaphysical and transcendent principle, a link without which it would have only an altogether contingent and in fact purely illusory existence.

[9] Ibid., chap. 12.

[10] Ibid., chap. 27.

[11] One might say that the "self", with all the prolongations of which it is susceptible, has incomparably less importance than modern Western psychologists and philosophers attribute to it, although at the same time it contains possibilities of an indefinitely greater extension than they can even suspect (see *Man and His Becoming*, chap. 2. . .).

16

The Realization of the Being through Knowledge

We have just said that the being assimilates more or less completely everything of which it is conscious; indeed, there is no true knowledge in any domain whatsoever, other than that which enables us to penetrate into the intimate nature of things, and the degrees of knowledge consist precisely in the measure to which this penetration is more or less profound and results in a more or less complete assimilation. In other words, the only genuine knowledge is that which implies an identification of the subject with the object, or, if one prefers to consider the relationship inversely, an assimilation of the object by the subject,[1] and consequently the measure to which such an identification or such an assimilation is actually implied constitutes precisely the degrees of knowledge themselves.[2] We must therefore maintain, despite all the more or less idle philosophical discussions that this point has given rise to,[3] that all true and effective knowledge is immediate, and that mediate knowledge can have only a purely symbolic and representative value.[4] As for the actual possibility of immediate knowledge, the whole theory of multiple states makes it sufficiently comprehensible. Besides, to wish to cast doubt upon it is merely to

---

[1] It should be clearly understood that here we take the terms "subject" and "object" in their usual sense, as designating respectively "the one who knows" and "that which is known" (see *Man and His Becoming*, chap. 15).

[2] We have already mentioned on various occasions that in principle Aristotle posited identification by knowledge, but also that this affirmation, in his works as in those of his Scholastic followers, seems to have remained purely theoretical, for they seem never to have drawn any conclusions from it as concerns metaphysical realization (see especially *Introduction to the Study of the Hindu Doctrines*, pt. 2, chap. 10; and *Man and His Becoming*, chap. 24).

[3] We allude here to the modern "theories of knowledge", whose futility we have already explained elsewhere (*Introduction to the Study of the Hindu Doctrines*, pt. 2, chap. 10), a point to which we shall shortly return.

[4] This difference is that between intuitive and discursive knowledge, about which we have already spoken so often that we need not linger over it here.

give proof of complete ignorance of the most elementary metaphysical principles, since without this immediate knowledge, metaphysics itself would be impossible.[5]

We have spoken of identification or assimilation, and we can employ these two terms almost indifferently here, although they do not arise from exactly the same point of view; in the same way, one can regard knowledge as proceeding simultaneously from the subject to the object of which it becomes conscious (or, more generally, and in order not to limit ourselves to the conditions of certain states, from which it makes a secondary modality of itself), and from the object to the subject that assimilates it to itself; and in this context it is worth recalling the Aristotelian definition of knowledge in the sensible domain as "the common act of perceiver and perceived", which in effect implies such a reciprocity of relationship.[6] Where the sensible and corporeal domain is concerned, the sense organs are thus the "entryways" of knowledge for the individual being;[7] but from another point of view they are also precisely the "outlets" in that all knowledge implies an act of identification starting from the knowing subject and proceeding toward the known (or to be known) object, like the emission of a sort of exterior prolongation of itself. And it is important to note that such a prolongation is only exterior in relation to the individuality envisaged in its most restricted sense, for it is an integral part of the extended individuality; in extending itself thus by a development of its own possibilities, the being has no need at all to go outside of itself, which, in reality, would make no sense since under no conditions can a being become other than itself. This is also a direct response to the principal objection of modern Western philosophers against the possibility of immediate knowledge, from which it is evident that this objection could only arise from a pure and simple metaphysical incomprehension, in consequence of which these

---

[5] See *Introduction to the Study of the Hindu Doctrines*, pt. 2, chap. 5.

[6] One might note also that the act common to two beings, following the sense which Aristotle gives to the word "act", is that by which their natures coincide, and are thus identified, at least partially.

[7] See *Man and His Becoming*, chap. 12. The symbolism of the "mouths" of *Vaishvānara* is related to the analogy of cognitive with nutritive assimilation.

philosophers have failed to recognize the possibilities of being, even individual being, in its indefinite extension.

All this is true *a fortiori* if, leaving behind the limits of the individuality, we apply it to superior states; true knowledge of these states implies their effective possession, and, inversely, it is by this very knowledge that the being takes possession of them, for the two acts are inseparable one from another, and we could even say that fundamentally they are but one. Naturally, this must be understood only of immediate knowledge, which, when it extends to the totality of states, includes in itself their realization, and which, consequently, is "the only means of obtaining complete and final Deliverance".[8] As for knowledge that has remained purely theoretical, it is obvious that it could in no way be equivalent to such a realization, and that, not being an immediate seizure of its object, it can only have an altogether symbolic value, as we have already said; but it nonetheless constitutes an indispensable preparation for the acquisition of that effective knowledge whereby, and whereby alone, the realization of the total being takes place.

Whenever occasion arises, we must insist particularly upon the realization of the being through knowledge, because it is altogether foreign to modern Western conceptions, which do not go beyond theoretical knowledge, or, more exactly, beyond a slender portion of it, and which artificially oppose "knowledge" to "being" as if they were not the two inseparable faces of one and the same reality.[9] There can be no true metaphysics for anyone who does not truly understand that the being realizes itself through knowledge, and that it can only realize itself in this way. Pure metaphysical doctrine does not need to trouble itself in the least with all the "theories of knowledge" that modern philosophy so laboriously elaborates; in these efforts to substitute a "theory of knowledge" for knowledge itself one can even see a veritable admission of impotence, albeit certainly unconscious, on the part of this philosophy, so completely ignorant is it of any possibility of effective realization. What is more, true knowledge being immediate as we have said, can be more or less complete, more or less

---

[8] Shankaracharya, *Ātma-Bodha* (ibid., chap. 22).

[9] See also *Introduction to the Study of the Hindu Doctrines*, pt. 2, chap. 10.

profound, more or less adequate, but it cannot be essentially "relative", as this same philosophy would have it, or at least it could be so only insofar as its objects are themselves relative. In other words, relative knowledge, metaphysically speaking, is nothing but knowledge of the relative or of the contingent, that is to say of what applies only to the realm of manifestation; but the validity of this knowledge within its own domain is only as great as the nature of the domain allows,[10] which is not what is meant by those who speak of the "relativity of knowledge". Apart from consideration of the degrees of a more or less complete and profound knowledge—degrees that change nothing of its essential nature—the only legitimate distinction to be made as to the validity of knowledge is the distinction we have already noted between immediate and mediate knowledge, that is, between effective and symbolic knowledge.

[10] This applies even to simple sensible knowledge, which in its own inferior and limited order is also immediate, and thus necessarily true.

PART THREE

THE HINDU WORLD

The entire Hindu tradition is founded upon the *Veda*, a scripture which portrays traditional knowledge in its most essential form. Since its origin is considered to be "non-human", the Vedic scriptures exude a timeless and immutable quality and convey metaphysical knowledge that possesses the character of absolute certainty. In the Hindu world, knowing and being are two aspects of the same reality; theory has its place, so long as it is accompanied by a corresponding realization.

17

On the Exact Meaning of the Word "Hindu"

Everything that has been said up to now might serve as a general introduction to the study of all Eastern doctrines; what follows will relate more closely to the Hindu doctrines in particular, adapted as they are to modes of thought which, while retaining those characteristics common to Eastern thought as a whole, also exhibit certain distinctive features of their own, with corresponding differences in the forms of expression. These differences arise even when strict identity exists with other traditions as regards the basis of the doctrine, which in fact must always remain the same when it is a question of pure metaphysics, for reasons we have already explained. At this point in our treatise it is important, before passing on to anything else, to indicate the exact meaning of the word "Hindu", for the more or less haphazard manner in which it has been used has given rise to frequent misunderstandings in the West.

In order to define clearly what is Hindu and what is not Hindu, we cannot avoid recalling briefly certain points that we have touched on already. In the first place, this word cannot denote a race, since it is applied without distinction to persons belonging to various races; still less can it denote a nationality, since nothing of the kind exists in the East. India considered as a whole is more comparable to the whole continent of Europe than to any single European state, not only because of its size or the numerical strength of its population, but also because of the variety of ethnic types to be found there; from the north to the south of India the differences are at least as great in this respect as from one extremity of Europe to another. Moreover, no governmental or administrative bond exists between the various regions, other than that recently established in an entirely artificial way by the Europeans. This administrative unity, it is true, had already been achieved before them by the Mogul emperors, and perhaps even before that by others, but it never had a more than transitory existence in relation to the permanence of Hindu civilization, and it is noteworthy that it was nearly always the result of a foreign domination, or in any case the work of non-Hindu influences; furthermore, it never went so far as completely to suppress the autonomy of the separate states, the intention being rather to include them in a federal organization. On the other hand, there exists nothing in India comparable to the kind of unity that is achieved elsewhere by the recognition of a common religious authority, which may either be represented by a single individual, as in Catholicism, or by a plurality of distinct functions, as in Islam. Though the Hindu tradition in no wise partakes of a religious character, there is yet no reason why it should not possess a more or less analogous organization, but such is not actually the case despite the gratuitous assumptions certain people make in this respect because they are unable to understand how unity can be effectively achieved simply by the inherent power of the traditional doctrine itself. That is certainly very different from anything obtaining in the West, but nevertheless it is a fact: Hindu unity, as we have already emphasized, is a unity of a traditional order purely and exclusively and has no need to depend upon any more or less exterior form of organization, or upon the support of any authority other than that of the doctrine itself.

From these facts the following conclusions may be drawn: Hindus are those who adhere to the Hindu tradition, on the understanding that they are duly qualified to do so really effectively, and not simply in an exterior and illusory way; non-Hindus, on the contrary, are those who, for any reason whatsoever, do not participate in the tradition in question. This is, for example, the case of the Jains and the Buddhists; it is also, in more modern times, the case of the Sikhs, who moreover were subject to Muslim influences, the mark of which is clearly to be seen in their particular doctrine. Such is the true distinction, and there can be no other, although it is admittedly a rather difficult one for Western people to grasp, accustomed as they are to judging by quite different standards, which are entirely absent here. Under these circumstances it is absurd to speak, for example, of "Hindu Buddhism", as has actually been known to occur; if one wishes to refer to Buddhism as it formerly existed in India, the only appropriate expression is "Indian Buddhism", just as one speaks of "Indian Muslims", that is to say the Muslims of India, who are in no sense Hindus. The true gravity of an error of the kind indicated above, and the reason why we look upon it as something more than a mere fault of detail, lies in the fact that it implies a profound misunderstanding of the essential nature of Hindu civilization; but the remarkable thing is not that such ignorance should be widespread in the West, but that it should even have been known to occur among professional orientalists.

Certain evidences that we have already mentioned go to show that the tradition in question was brought to the country now known as India, at a comparatively remote date which it would be very difficult to determine exactly, by men who came from the North; nevertheless, it has never been proved that these men, who must have settled successively in various regions, ever formed what could properly be called a people, in the beginning at least, or that they belonged originally to a single race. At all events, the Hindu tradition, or at least the tradition now bearing this name—since it may at that time have had a different name or even have had no name at all—when it became established in India, was adopted sooner or later by the majority of the descendants of the indigenous populations; the latter, the Dravidians for example, consequently became Hindus as it were by adoption, but once they had been admitted into the unity of the traditional civilization, they were just as genuinely Hindus as those who had always been so, even though some traces of their origin may still have persisted in the form of particular modes of thought and action, always provided that these were compatible with the spirit of the tradition.

Prior to its establishment in India, this particular tradition belonged to a civilization . . . for which, in the absence of a better term, the name Indo-Iranian may be accepted, not because the place of development of the tradition is any more likely to have been in Iran than in India, but simply to indicate that it subsequently gave birth to two civilizations, distinct and even opposed in certain respects, namely the Hindu and the Persian civilizations. At some period or other therefore a rupture must have occurred not unlike that brought about by Buddhism at a later date, and the separated branch, constituting a deviation from the primordial tradition, then became what is known as "Iranism", eventually destined to form the basis of the Persian tradition, known also as Mazdaism. We have already drawn attention to the tendency, often met with in the East, for such doctrines as were at first opposed to the regular tradition to become established in their turn as independent traditions; and there is no doubt that this happened in the case under consideration long before the tradition was codified in the *Avesta* under the name of Zarathustra or Zoroaster, which moreover should not be taken for the name of a man but rather as denoting a collectivity, as is often the way in such cases: the examples of Fu Hsi in China, Vyāsa in India, and Thoth or Hermes in Egypt show this very clearly. On the other hand, a very distinct mark of the deviation has survived in the Persian language itself, where certain words have taken on an exactly contrary meaning to the one they bore originally and which is the meaning they still preserve in Sanskrit; the word *deva* is the best known example, but it would be possible to cite others (such as the name *Indra*) that cannot be due to pure accident. The dualistic character usually attributed to the Persian tradition, if it were a fact, would also be a manifest proof of an alteration in the doctrine, though it must be stated that this character appears to have become attached to it only as the result of a false or incomplete interpretation; another more serious proof consists in the presence of certain sentimental elements, but there is no need to insist upon this point here.

Starting from the moment when the separation of which we have just been speaking occurred, the regular tradition may properly be called Hindu, wherever the region may have lain in which it was first established and whether or not this name was actually given to it at that time. The use of this name, however, should on no account give rise to the idea that the tradition had undergone some profound and essential change; any modifications that may from time to time have taken place are attributable merely to a natural and normal development of the primordial tradition. This leads us to point out another error committed by orientalists, who, understanding nothing of the essential immutability of the doctrine, have imagined the existence, subsequent to the Indo-Iranian period, of three successive and supposedly distinct doctrines, to which they give the names of Vedism, Brāhmanism, and Hinduism respectively. If this classification were only intended to refer to three periods in the history of Hindu civilization, it would no doubt be admissible, notwithstanding the fact that the names are very inappropriate and that it is extremely difficult to fix the limits of these periods and to relate them chronologically. Even if it were only intended to state that the traditional doctrine, while always remaining fundamentally the same, received successively several more or less different forms of expression in order to adapt itself to the particular mental and social conditions of such and such a period, this again, with similar reservations, would be admissible. But this is not the sole contention of the orientalists: in using a plurality of denominations, they expressly assume a series of deviations or alterations, which are not only incompatible with traditional regularity, but have never existed save in their own imaginations.

In reality, the entire Hindu tradition is founded upon the *Veda*; it always was so and has never ceased to be so; it might therefore quite legitimately be called Vedism, and the name Brāhmanism also would be equally applicable to it at all periods. The name actually preferred is really a matter of little importance, provided one clearly understands that, under one or several names, it is always the same thing that is being referred to; and this can only be the development of the doctrine contained in principle in the *Veda*, a word which literally means traditional knowledge without further qualification. There is therefore no such thing as Hinduism in the sense of a deviation from traditional thought, since that which is correctly and purely Hindu is just that which, by definition, admits of no such deviation; and if nonetheless certain more or less grave irregularities have sometimes occurred, the power of the tradition has always kept them within certain limits, or else has rejected them entirely from the unity of Hindu civilization, and in any case has prevented them from acquiring any real authority; but to be properly understood, this calls for further explanation.

18

Perpetuity of the *Veda*

The name *Veda*, the proper meaning of which has just been explained,
is applied in a general way to all the basic scriptures of the Hindu tradition; these are divided into four collections known respectively as
the *Rig-Veda*, the *Yajur-Veda*, the *Sāma-Veda*, and the *Atharva-Veda*.
The question of the date when these collections were composed is one
of those that worry orientalists the most, and they have never managed to agree on its solution, even when confining themselves to a very
approximate computation of their antiquity. Here as everywhere else
may be observed the usual tendency to refer everything to a period as
little remote in time as possible, and likewise to contest the authenticity of such and such parts of the traditional writings, the whole
argument being based on a minute analysis of texts, accompanied by
dissertations that are as endless as they are superfluous on the use of a
word or of a certain grammatical form. These are in fact the habitual
preoccupations of orientalists, and the general purpose, in the minds
of those who occupy themselves with such things, is to show that
the text under discussion is not as old as was believed, that it cannot
be the work of the author to whom it had hitherto been ascribed (if
indeed it ever had an author), or at least that it has been "interpolated"
or has suffered some alteration or other at a comparatively recent date;
anyone acquainted with the products of "biblical criticism" can form
a clear enough idea of the nature of these proceedings. It is hardly
surprising that researches undertaken in such a spirit only lead to the
piling up of volumes of tedious discussions, and that the pitiful results
of this undermining "criticism", when they come to the knowledge of
Easterners, contribute substantially to inspiring them with a contempt
for the West. In fact, it is always questions of principle that escape
the orientalists, and as it is precisely this knowledge which is essential to a proper understanding (seeing that everything else is derived
from it and should logically be deduced from it), these scholars are
led to neglect the one essential thing through their inability to grasp
its primary importance; the consequence is that they lose their way
hopelessly in a maze of the most insignificant details or in a tangle of
quite arbitrary theorizing.

The question of the date when the different portions of the *Veda* may have been composed appears to be truly insoluble; it is not however a matter of any real importance because, prior to the more or less distant epoch when the text was written down for the first time, it is necessary to consider a period of oral transmission of indeterminate length, as we have already pointed out. It is probable that the origin of writing in India in fact dates from considerably earlier than is usually admitted; furthermore, it is most unlikely that the Sanskrit characters have been derived from a Phoenician alphabet, which they resemble neither in shape nor arrangement. However that may be, one thing is certain, namely that nothing more than an ordering and final codifying of pre-existing traditional texts is to be seen in the work attributed to Vyāsa, a name which in reality does not refer to an historical person, still less to a "myth", but denotes an intellectual collectivity, as we mentioned before. This being the case, the determining of the epoch of Vyāsa, even admitting that such a thing were possible, is only of interest as a simple historical fact, devoid of any doctrinal implication; moreover, it is obvious that this epoch may comprise a period of several centuries, or may even never have been completed, so that the question of its starting-point alone is open to discussion; this however does not mean that it can of necessity be answered, least of all by resorting to the methods favored by Western scholarship.

The preceding oral transmission is often indicated in a text, though without the addition of any chronological data, by what is called the *vansha* or traditional filiation; this is the case, for example, in most of the Upanishads. As regards the origin, however, it is always necessary to refer back to a direct inspiration, likewise implied in the *vansha,* for here there is no question of an individual work; it makes little difference that the tradition has been expressed or formulated by such and such an individual, for this does not make him its author, given that the tradition belongs essentially to the supra-individual order. That is why the origin of the *Veda* is said to be *apaurusheya* or "non-human": historical circumstances exert no more influence on the essence of the doctrine than any other contingent factor, since it is endowed with an immutable and entirely timeless character, and it is moreover clear that the inspiration just referred to can manifest itself at any period. Perhaps the only difficulty here is to get Westerners to accept the theory of inspiration and especially to make them understand that this theory is neither mystical nor psychological, but can only be purely metaphysical; to pursue this question would however necessitate developments which do not fit in with our present scheme. These few explanations should suffice to give at least some idea of what the Hindus mean when they speak of the perpetuity of the *Veda*. From another point of view this doctrine is also correlated with the cosmological theory of the primordial place of sound among the sensory qualities, though we cannot undertake to expound this theory here; this last point may provide a clue to the fact that even after the adoption of writing, the oral transmission of the doctrine has always continued to play a preponderant part in India.

Since the *Veda* represents traditional knowledge unqualified, it therefore constitutes the principle and common basis of all the more or less secondary and derived branches of the doctrine; and even in their case the question of chronological development is of small importance. The tradition has to be considered in its entirety, and there is no point in asking which part of it is or is not primitive, since we are dealing with a perfectly coherent whole (which does not mean a systematic whole), and since all the points of view included in it can be considered simultaneously just as well as successively; consequently it is of no great interest to ascertain the historical order in which they were actually unfolded. Indeed, such a proceeding is all the less interesting because one can do no more than trace the actual development of the points of view in question as formulated in those works that are available to us; once one has learned to look beyond texts and has begun to penetrate further into the nature of things, one is bound to recognize that the various points of view have always been conceived as co-existing simultaneously in the unity of their principle; that is why a traditional text is capable of manifold interpretations or applications corresponding to these different points of view. It is not possible to assign a definite author to this or that portion of the doctrine any more than to the Vedic texts themselves, in which the doctrine in its entirety is contained synthetically, at least insofar as it is capable of expression; and if such and such a known author or commentator has expounded a certain more or less special point, that certainly does not imply that no one else had done so before him, and still less that no one had previously thought about it, even if until then it had not been formulated in a definite text.

Undoubtedly the exposition can be modified in its external form in order to be adapted to circumstances; but—and we can never repeat it too often—the foundation always remains absolutely identical and its outward modifications in no wise touch or affect the essence of the doctrine. These considerations, by raising the question to the plane of principles, serve to show the chief reasons for the embarrassment of the chronologists, as well as the pointlessness of their researches; and since these reasons, which they are unfortunately unaware of, are inherent in the very nature of things, it would assuredly be better if they resigned themselves to the inevitable and stopped debating insoluble questions; indeed, they would have no hesitation in following this course once they realized that these inquiries were without serious import: this is the point we were more particularly concerned to clear up in the present chapter, since it was not possible to treat the main theme fully and in its more profound aspects.

19

The Law of *Manu*

As an example of the kind of idea that is apt to cause confusion in the minds of Western people, through the absence of any equivalent term in their own vocabulary, one might cite the conception denoted by the Sanskrit word *dharma*;[1] orientalists have certainly proposed any number of translations for the word, but most of these are only rough approximations or even completely erroneous, owing as usual to the confusion of points of view we have alluded to before. Thus, attempts are sometimes made to translate *dharma* by "religion", though the religious point of view is here quite inapplicable; furthermore, it should at the same time be realized that it is not the conception of a doctrine, wrongly supposed to be religious, that this word properly designates. On the other hand, if it be a question of the accomplishment of rites, which likewise are not religious in character, these are described in their entirety by the word *karma*, the general meaning of which is "action", but which is here taken in a special and, as it were, technical sense. For those who wish at all costs to see a religion in the Hindu tradition, there would still remain what they believe to be a moral aspect, and it is this more especially that they would call *dharma*; hence, according to circumstances, several more or less secondary interpretations have arisen, such as "virtue", "justice", "merit", and "duty", all of which are in fact exclusively moral ideas and for this very reason do not in any way express the idea in question. The moral point of view, apart from which these ideas have no meaning, does not belong to India; we have already sufficiently insisted on this point, and we have even observed that Buddhism, which alone might perhaps have been thought likely to introduce it, never made any such advance along the path of sentimentality. Furthermore, we may note in passing that these same ideas are not all equally essential to the moral point of view itself; that is to say, there are some of them which are not common to all moral conceptions: for example, the idea of duty or obligation is absent from most ancient codes of morality,

---

[1] See *Studies in Hinduism*, chap. 5. ED

among others from that of the Stoics, and it is only recently, and especially since Kant, that it has come to play such a preponderant part. An important thing to notice in this connection, since it is one of the most frequent sources of error, is that ideas or points of view which have become habitual tend for that very reason to appear essential; that is why attempts are made to introduce them into the interpretation of every kind of conception, even those most remote in time or space, although there would often be no need to go back very far to discover their real source.

Having said this much by way of dealing with the false interpretations most commonly met with, we will try to show as clearly as possible what should really be understood by *dharma*. As the meaning of the verbal root *dhri*, from which it is derived, indicates, this word, in its most general sense, simply denotes "manner of being"; it is, so to speak, the essential nature of a being, comprising the sum of its particular qualities or characteristics, and determining, by virtue of the tendencies or dispositions it implies, the manner in which this being will conduct itself, either in a general way or in relation to each particular circumstance. The same idea may be applied, not only to a single being, but also to an organized collectivity, to a species, to all the beings included in a cosmic cycle or state of existence, or even to the whole order of the Universe; at one level or another, then, it signifies conformity with the essential nature of beings, which is realized in the ordered hierarchy where all beings have their place, and it is also, in consequence, the fundamental equilibrium or integral harmony resulting from this hierarchical disposition, which is moreover precisely what the idea of "justice" amounts to when stripped of its specifically moral character.

Considered in this way, as a principle of order and therefore as an inherent organization and disposition either of a being or group of beings, *dharma* may in one sense be regarded as opposed to *karma*, which is simply the action by which this disposition will be manifested outwardly, always provided the action is normal, or in other words provided it conforms to the nature of beings and the states of existence to which they belong, and to the relationships arising in consequence. Under these circumstances, that which is *adharma*, or contrary to *dharma*, is not "sin" in the theological sense of the word, neither is it "evil" in the moral sense, since both these ideas are equally foreign to the Hindu mind; it is simply "non-conformity" with the nature of beings, disequilibrium, a rupture of harmony, a destruction or upsetting of hierarchical relations. Without doubt, in the universal order, the sum total of all particular disequilibriums always goes to make up the total equilibrium, which nothing can destroy; but at each point regarded separately and by itself, disequilibrium is both possible and conceivable, and whether it occurs in the social sphere or elsewhere, there is absolutely no need to attribute to it anything of a moral character when defining it as something that is contrary, within its own sphere, to the "law of harmony" that governs at the same time both the cosmic and the human orders. The meaning of "law" being thus defined, and, care being taken to distinguish it from all the particular and derivative applications to which it can give rise, we may accept the word "law" as a translation of *dharma*, no doubt an imperfect one, but less inexact than other terms borrowed from Western languages; it must be emphasized once more, however, that it is not a moral law that is here in question; while the notions of scientific law and social or juridical law, even by definition, only refer to special cases.

The "law" may by an analogical transposition be regarded in principle as a "universal will", which however does not allow anything personal to subsist in the conception, nor, for still stronger reasons, anything anthropomorphic. The expression of this will in each state of manifested existence is called *Prajāpati* or the "Lord of produced beings"; and in each particular cosmic cycle this same will manifests itself as the *Manu* who gives the cycle its proper law. *Manu* should not therefore be taken for the name of a mythical, legendary, or historical personage; it is properly speaking the name of a principle, which can be defined, in accordance with the meaning of the verbal root *manas*, as "cosmic intelligence" or "thought reflecting the universal order". On the other hand, this principle is also regarded as the prototype of man, who is called *manava* insofar as he is considered essentially as a "thinking being", characterized by the possession of *manas*, the mental or rational faculty; the concept of *Manu* is therefore equivalent, at least in certain respects, to what other traditions, notably the Hebrew Kabbalah and Islamic esoterism, refer to as Universal Man, or what Taoism calls "the King". We have seen previously that the name Vyāsa does not denote a man but a function; in that case, however, the function is in a general way an historical one, while *Manu* represents a cosmic function which can only become historical when specially applied to the social order, but without this in itself presupposing any kind of "personification". In fact, the law of *Manu*, for any cycle or collectivity whatsoever, is nothing else but the observance of the natural hierarchical relations existing between the beings subject to the special conditions of that cycle or collectivity, together with the whole body of precepts normally pertaining thereunto. We do not propose to dwell here on the subject of cosmic cycles,[2] especially as rather lengthy explanations would be necessary to make the theory plainly intelligible; we will simply point out that the connection between them is not chronological but logical and causal, each cycle being determined in its entirety by the preceding cycle and determining in its turn the following one, through a continuous production governed by the "law of harmony" which establishes the fundamental analogy between all the modes of universal manifestation.

When it comes to applying it to the social sphere, the "law", which then takes on its specifically juridical sense, may be formulated in a *shāstra* or code, which, insofar as it expresses the "cosmic will" at that particular level, is referred to *Manu*, or, more precisely, to the *Manu* of the actual cycle; but it is evident that this attribution does not make *Manu* the author of the *shāstra*, at least not in the ordinary sense in which something purely human is said to be the work of such or such an author. Here again, as in the case of the Vedic texts, there is no definitely assignable historical origin, and indeed, as we have already explained, the question of such an origin is of no consequence from the doctrinal point of view. However, an important distinction is to be noted between the two cases: while the Vedic texts are described by the term *shruti*, as being the fruit of direct inspiration, the *dharma-shāstra* only belongs to the class of traditional writings called *smriti*, the authority of which is of a less fundamental character; among the writings of this class are also included the *Purānas* and the *Itihāsas*, which Western scholars take to be mythological or epic poems only, having failed to grasp the profound symbolism that makes of them something quite other than "literature" in the ordinary sense of the word. Fundamentally, the distinction between *shruti* and *smriti* is equivalent to that between pure and direct intellectual intuition on the one hand, and reflected consciousness of the rational order

---

[2] See *Traditional Forms and Cosmic Cycles*, pt. 1, chap. 1. ED

on the other hand, the former applying exclusively to the domain of metaphysical principles, the latter exercising itself upon objects of knowledge in the individual sphere, as must necessarily be the case where social or other applications are in question. Despite this, the traditional authority of the *dharma-shāstra* does not in any way derive from the human authors whose task it has been to formulate it, doubtless orally at first and later on in writing, and that is why these writers have remained unknown and unidentified; its authority derives exclusively from the fact that it represents a true expression of the law of *Manu,* that is to say from its conformity with the natural order of the existences it is destined to govern.

20

Principles Governing the Institution of Caste

In order to complete what has just been said, we may usefully add a few explanations on the subject of caste, which is of primary importance in the law of *Manu* and which has been persistently misunderstood by Europeans in general. First of all we will give the following definition: caste, which the Hindus describe indifferently by one or other of the two words *jāti* and *varna*, is a social function determined by the particular nature of each human being. The word *varna* in its original sense means "color", and some people have attempted to see in this a proof, or at least an indication, of the supposed fact that the distinction between the castes was originally founded upon racial differences; but this is not a tenable view, for the same word bears by extension the meaning of "quality" in general, whence its analogical use to denote the particular nature of a being, or what might be called its "individual essence"; and it is in fact the latter that determines caste, racial considerations intervening merely as one of the elements capable of exercising an influence upon the constitution of the individual nature. As for the word *jāti*, its proper meaning is "birth", and some have therefore concluded from this that caste is essentially hereditary, but this again is an error. If it is most often hereditary in actual practice, it is not strictly so in principle, for although the part played by heredity in the formation of the individual nature may be preponderant in the majority of cases, it is by no means exclusive; this however calls for some supplementary explanations.

The individual being is regarded in its totality as a compound of two elements, called respectively *nāma*, "name", and *rūpa*, "form", which in effect represent the "essence" and the "substance" of the individuality, or what the Aristotelian school calls "form" and "matter"; these last two terms however have a technical meaning very different from their ordinary ones, and it should be observed in particular that the word "form", instead of denoting the element we have so named to translate the Sanskrit *rūpa*, denotes on the contrary the other element, which is properly speaking the "individual essence". It should be added that the distinction we have just pointed out, although analogous to that made in the West between soul and body, is far from being its exact equivalent: the form referred to is not an exclusively corporeal form, although we cannot at present insist on this point; as for the name, it represents the sum of all the being's characteristic qualities or attributes. A further distinction is to be made within the individual essence itself: *nāmika*, that which refers to the name in a more restricted sense, or "that which the particular name of each individual should express", is the sum of the qualities properly belonging to the individual, without his deriving them from anything other than himself; *gotrika*, "that which belongs to the race or family", is the sum of the qualities which the being derives from his heredity. An analogical representation of this second distinction may be observed in the attribution to an individual, on the one hand, of a prenomen belonging exclusively to himself and, on the other hand, of a family name. Much might be said about the original significance of names and what they should normally be intended to express; but since questions of this kind do not fall within the scope of the present work, we will only point out that the determination of the true name is bound up in principle with the determination of the individual nature itself. Birth, within the meaning of the Sanskrit word *jāti*, is properly speaking the resultant of the two elements *nāmika* and *gotrika*: allowance must therefore be made for the part played by heredity, and this may be considerable, but account has also to be taken of those qualities by which the individual is distinguished from his parents and other members of his family. It is clear, in fact, that no two beings possess exactly the same qualities, either physical or psychic: apart from what they have in common, there are also certain distinguishing characteristics, and those people who try to ascribe everything in the individual to the influence of heredity would undoubtedly have considerable difficulty in applying their theory to any particular case; this influence is undeniable, but there are other elements that must be taken into account, and allowance is in fact made for them in the theory we are explaining.

The particular nature of each individual necessarily comprises from the beginning all the tendencies and aptitudes which will be developed and manifested in the course of his existence, and which, for instance, will determine his qualification for this or that social function, this being the point that more especially concerns us here. Knowledge of the individual nature should therefore make it possible to assign to each human being the function for which his nature fits him, or in other words to assign him the place that he should normally occupy in the social organization. It will be easily understood that we have here the basis of an organization that is truly hierarchical, that is to say in conformity with the nature of beings, following the interpretation we have given of the notion of *dharma*. Errors of application are no doubt always possible, especially in periods when the light of tradition has grown dim, but they do not in any way affect the validity of the principle, and it can be said that to deny it implies theoretically, if not always in practice, the overturning of every legitimate hierarchy. At the same time it can be seen how absurd is the attitude of those Europeans who feel indignant because a man cannot pass from his own caste into a higher one: in effect this would imply nothing more nor less than a change of individual nature, or in other words a man would have to cease being himself in order to become another man, which is obviously absurd; a being will remain throughout the whole of his individual existence what he is potentially at the time of his birth. The question why a being is himself and not another is a pointless one; the truth is that every being, each according to his own nature, is a necessary element in the total and universal harmony. It is only too clear, however, that considerations of this kind are completely foreign to people living in societies such as are to be found in the West today, the constitution of which is without principle and does not rest upon any hierarchy; in these societies any man may exercise almost indifferently the most diverse functions, including those for which he is not in the least fitted, while material riches are generally accepted as the only real mark of superiority.

From what has been said about the meaning of *dharma*, it follows that the social hierarchy ought to reproduce analogically, in accordance with its own conditions, the constitution of "Universal Man"; by this we mean that there is a correspondence between the cosmic and the human orders, and that this correspondence, which finds natural expression in the organization of the individual, whether the latter is regarded integrally or even simply corporeally, should also be realized in an appropriate manner in the organization of society. The conception of a "social organism", with organs and functions comparable to those of a living being, is already familiar to modern sociologists; but the latter have gone much too far in this direction, forgetting that correspondence and analogy do not mean assimilation and identity, and that in any legitimate comparison between the two cases allowance would necessarily have to be made for differences in the respective modes of application; furthermore, being ignorant of the profound reasons for the analogy, they have never been able to draw any valid conclusions concerning the establishment of a true hierarchy. It is clear from these reservations that expressions which may appear to indicate an assimilation must only be understood in a purely symbolical sense, in the same way that designations borrowed from different parts of the human individual are applied analogically to "Universal Man".

These indications will suffice to explain the meaning of the symbolical description of the origin of castes, as it is to be found in numerous texts, notably in the *Purusha-sukta* of the *Rig-Veda*, from which the following quotation is taken: "of Purusha, the Brahmin was the mouth, the Kshatriya the arms, the Vaishya the thighs; the Shudra was born under his feet."[1] Here we find the enumeration of the four castes the differentiation of which constitutes the basis of the social order, and which are susceptible of more or less numerous secondary subdivisions: the Brahmins represent essentially the spiritual and intellectual authority; the Kshatriyas, the administrative prerogative comprising both the judicial and the military offices, of which the royal function is simply the highest degree; to the Vaishyas belongs the whole varied range of economic functions in the widest sense of the word, including the agricultural, industrial, commercial, and financial functions; as for the Shudras, they carry out the tasks necessary to assure the purely material subsistence of the community.[2] It should be added that the Brahmins are not "priests" in the Western and religious sense of the word: no doubt their functions include the accomplishment of various kinds of rites, because they must possess the knowledge necessary to make them fully effective; but they also include, above everything else, the conservation and regular transmission of the traditional doctrine. Indeed, the function of teaching, represented by the mouth in the symbolism we have just mentioned, was regarded by nearly all ancient peoples as the highest priestly function, because their civilizations were based in their entirety upon a doctrinal principle. For the same reason deviations from the doctrine were generally bound up with a subversion of the social hierarchy, as can be seen for example in the repeated attempts made by the Kshatriyas to throw

---

[1] *Rig-Veda* x. 90.

[2] See *Spiritual Authority and Temporal Power*, especially chap. 3. ED

off the overlordship of the Brahmins, an overlordship the justification of which will be apparent from all that has been said concerning the real nature of Hindu civilization.

These summary remarks would not be complete without some reference to the traces which these traditional and primordial conceptions have left in the ancient institutions of Europe, notably in connection with the conferring of the divine right upon kings, whose function was originally regarded as being essentially that of regulators of the social order, as the root of the word *rex* indicates; but we can only note these things in passing, without dwelling upon them as much as would be necessary to bring out their full significance.

Participation in the tradition is only fully effective for the members of the first three castes; this finds expression in the various designations exclusively reserved for them, such as *ārya* ["noble"] . . . and *dvija* or "twice born"; the idea of a "second birth", understood in a purely spiritual sense, is indeed common to all traditional doctrines, and Christianity itself provides an equivalent in religious mode in the rite of Baptism. For the Shudras, participation is primarily indirect and as it were virtual, for in a general way it only results from their relations with the superior castes; moreover, to revert to the analogy of the "social organism", the part they play does not properly speaking constitute a vital function, but an activity that is in some sense mechanical, and this is why they are represented as springing, not from a part of the body of *Purusha* or "Universal Man", but from the earth beneath his feet, which is the element in which the substances of bodily nourishment are compounded. In connection with this same representation, it may also be noted that the distinction between the castes is sometimes applied by analogical transposition not merely to the whole human collectivity, but to the totality of beings, both animate and inanimate, as comprised within nature in its entirety, since all these beings are likewise said to be sprung from *Purusha*: it is thus that the Brahmin is regarded as the type of immutable beings, that is to say of those which are above change, and the Kshatriya as the type of beings subject to change, because their functions refer respectively to the sphere of contemplation and the sphere of action. That is clear enough evidence of the questions of principle involved in all this, for they are of a kind that contain implications going far beyond the limits of the social sphere, in relation to which they have more particularly been considered here.

21

Yoga

The word *Yoga* properly means "union";[1] it should be mentioned in passing, though it is really a matter of small importance, that we do not know why numerous European authors make this a feminine word, whereas in Sanskrit it is masculine. The principal meaning of the term is the effective union of the human being with the Universal; applied to a *darshana*, of which the formulation in *sūtra*s is attributed to Patañjali, it signifies that the *darshana* in question has as its goal the realization of this union and provides the means of attaining it. While the *Sāṇkhya* viewpoint remains a theoretical one, we are here essentially concerned with realization in the metaphysical sense that we have already explained, notwithstanding the opinions of the professional orientalists, who imagine that they are concerned with a "philosophy", or of the would-be "esoterists" who, attempting to make up for their own lack of doctrine by fanciful inventions, look upon *Yoga* as a "method for developing the latent powers of the human organism". The point of view in question refers to a totally different order of things, incomparably superior to anything that is implied in such interpretations, and it escapes the comprehension of both orientalists and occultists alike; this is natural enough, however, since nothing of the kind is to be met with in the West.

On the theoretical side, *Yoga* completes *Sāṇkhya* by introducing the conception of *Īshvara* or Universal Being; and this conception permits of the unification, first of *Purusha*, a multiple principle only so long as it is considered in relation to separate existences, and next of *Purusha* and *Prakriti*, since Universal Being, as their common principle, is beyond the distinction between them. *Yoga* again admits the development of nature or manifestation as described in *Sāṇkhya*, but since it is here taken as the basis of a realization that is destined to lead beyond its own contingent sphere, it is considered, so to speak, in an order inverse to that of its development, namely, from the standpoint of return to its final end, which is identical with its initial principle.

---

[1] The same root, in almost identical form, appears in the English word "yoke". ED

In relation to manifestation, the first principle is *Īshvara* or Universal Being; that is not to say that this principle is absolutely first in the universal order, since we have explained the fundamental distinction to be made between *Īshvara*, who is Being, and *Brahma*, which is beyond Being; but for the manifested being, union with Universal Being may be looked upon as constituting a necessary stage on the way toward ultimate union with the supreme *Brahma*. Besides, the possibility of going beyond Being, either theoretically or from the point of view of realization, implies a complete metaphysical doctrine, which the *Yoga-Shāstra* of Patañjali does not claim to represent by itself alone.

Since metaphysical realization essentially consists in identification through knowledge, whatever is not itself knowledge has value only as an accessory means; accordingly, *Yoga* takes as its starting-point and fundamental means what is called *ekāgrya*, that is to say "concentration". This concentration, as Max Müller admitted,[2] is something quite foreign to the Western mind, accustomed as it is to direct all its attention upon externals and to disperse itself amid their indefinitely changing multiplicity; it has indeed become almost an impossibility for this type of mind, and yet it is the first and most important of all the conditions of effective realization. Concentration, especially at the outset, can take for its support either a thought or else a symbol such as a word or an image; subsequently, however, these auxiliary means become needless, along with the rites and other "aids" that may be employed concurrently in view of the same end. It is evident, moreover, that this end could not be attained solely by use of the accessory means we have just mentioned, which are extraneous to knowledge; but it is nonetheless true that these means, though in no wise essential, are not to be despised, for they can possess a large measure of efficacy in assisting realization, and in leading, if not to its final goal, at least to its earlier stages. Such is the real utility of everything that is covered by the term *hatha-yoga*, which is designed, on the one hand, to destroy or, rather, to "transform" those elements in the human being which pose an obstacle to union with the Universal, and, on the other hand, to prepare for that union by the assimilation of certain rhythms, connected chiefly with the control of the breath; but for reasons previously given, we do not intend to dwell here on questions affecting

---

[2] *Preface to the Sacred Books of the East*, pp. xxiii–xxiv.

realization. In any case, it must always be borne in mind that, of all preliminary means, theoretical knowledge alone is really indispensable, and that later, when one passes to actual realization, it is concentration that matters most and that leads to it in the most immediate way, for it is directly bound up with knowledge. An action is always separated from its results, but meditation or intellectual contemplation, called in Sanskrit *dhyāna*, bears its fruit within itself; moreover, action cannot bring about deliverance from the realm of action, a result that is implicit in the final aim of metaphysical realization. However, this realization may not always be complete, and it is possible for it to stop short at the attainment of states that are of a higher order but not final; it is to these lesser degrees of realization that the special observances prescribed by the *Yoga-Shāstra* refer; but instead of traversing them in succession, it is also possible, though doubtless more difficult, to pass them over in one leap in order to arrive directly at the final goal, and it is this last way which is often referred to by the term *raja-yoga*. Actually, this last expression should be taken to refer also, in a stricter sense, to the goal of realization itself, whatever may be the means or particular modes employed, which should naturally be those best adapted to the mental and even to the physiological conditions of each person; in this case the chief purpose of *hatha-yoga*, at all its stages, will be to lead up to *rāja-yoga*.

The *yogī*, in the strict sense of the word, is he who has realized perfect and final union. The name cannot therefore be applied without abuse to the man who simply gives himself up to the study of *Yoga* as a *darshana*, nor even to one who in fact follows the path of realization indicated in it but without having yet reached the supreme goal toward which it leads. The state of a true *yogī* is that of a being who has attained and possesses the highest possibilities in their fullest development; all the secondary states we have mentioned belong to him as well, automatically so, but as it were by superaddition, and without being given greater importance than is their due, each according to its rank, in the complete hierarchy of existence of which they form so many constituent elements. The same can be said of the possession of certain special and more or less extraordinary powers, such as those called *siddhis* or *vibhūtis*: far from being worth pursuing for their own sake, these powers amount to no more than simple accidents, derived from the realm of the "great illusion", as does all that belongs to the phenomenal order, and the *yogī* only exercises them in quite exceptional circumstances; regarded otherwise, they can only form obstacles to complete realization. It can be seen how unfounded is the popular opinion that would make of the *yogī* a sort of magician, not to say a sorcerer. In truth, those who make a display of certain peculiar faculties, corresponding to the development of possibilities that do not however belong exclusively to the "organic" or physiological order, are not *yogīs* at all, but they are men who, for one reason or another, and most often through intellectual insufficiency, have stopped short at a partial and inferior realization that does not extend beyond the limits of human individuality, and one can rest assured that they will never travel any further. On the other hand, through true metaphysical realization, detached from all contingencies and therefore essentially of a supra-individual order, the *yogī* has become identical with "Universal Man", to use an expression borrowed from Islamic esoterism to which we have already referred; but in order to draw the conclusions that this implies, we should have to go beyond the limits we wish to set ourselves in the present work. Furthermore, it is especially to *hatha-yoga*, that is to say to the preparatory tasks, that the present *darshana* refers, and our remarks were chiefly intended to strike at the root of the commonest errors on the subject; what remains to be said, namely whatever concerns the final goal of realization, should be reserved rather for the purely metaphysical side of the doctrine, which is represented by the *Vedānta*.

22

General Remarks on the *Vedānta*

The *Vedānta*, contrary to an opinion widely held among orientalists, is neither a philosophy nor a religion, nor does it partake to a greater or lesser extent of the character of either. To deliberately consider this doctrine under these aspects is one of the gravest of errors, calculated to result in failure to understand anything about it from the outset; in fact one reveals oneself thereby as a complete stranger to the true character of Eastern thought, the modes of which are quite different from those of the West and cannot be included within the same categories. We have already explained in a previous work[1] that religion, if one is not to extend the scope of this word beyond its just limits, is something wholly Western; the same term cannot be applied to Eastern doctrines without stretching its meaning to such a degree that it becomes quite impossible to give it any definition, even of the vaguest kind. As for philosophy, it also represents an exclusively Western point of view, one, moreover, much more external than the religious point of view and therefore still further removed from that of the subject we are about to study. As we said above, it is an essentially "profane"[2] kind of knowledge even when it is not purely illusory, and we cannot help thinking, particularly when we consider what philosophy has become in modern times, that its absence from a civilization is hardly a matter for regret. In a recent book a certain orientalist has asserted that "philosophy is philosophy everywhere", a statement which opens the door to undesirable assimilations of every kind, including those against which he himself quite justly protested on other occasions. That philosophy is to be found everywhere is just what we are at present contesting; and we decline to accept as "universal thought" (to adopt a phrase of the same author) what is in

---

[1] *Introduction to the Study of the Hindu Doctrines.* ED

[2] A single exception can be made for the very special sense in which the word is used in reference to the "Hermetic philosophy"; but it goes without saying that it is not this unusual sense that we at present have in mind, a sense which is moreover almost unknown to the moderns.

reality but an extremely special mode of thought. Another historian of the Eastern doctrines, while in principle admitting the inadequacy and inexactitude of those Western terms which have been persistently imposed upon them, nevertheless declared that he could see no way of dispensing with such terms, and he made as free a use of them as any of his predecessors. This appears all the more surprising inasmuch as for our part we have never experienced the slightest need to resort to this philosophical terminology, which would still suffer from the disadvantage of being somewhat repellent and needlessly complicated, even if it were not wrongly applied, as is always the case under such circumstances. But we do not wish to embark at present upon the kind of discussions to which these questions might give rise; we were merely concerned with showing, by these examples, how difficult it is for some people to step outside the "classical" framework within which their Western education has confined their thought from the outset.

To return to the *Vedānta*, it must be regarded in reality as a purely metaphysical doctrine, opening up truly unlimited possibilities of conception, and, as such, it can in no wise be contained within the more or less narrow framework of any system whatsoever. In this respect and without looking any further, one can observe a profound and irreducible difference, a difference of principle, distinguishing it from anything that Europeans include under the name of philosophy. Indeed, the avowed aim of all philosophical conceptions, especially among the moderns, who carry to extremes the individualist tendency and the resultant quest for originality at any price, is precisely to establish systems that are complete and definite, or in other words essentially relative and limited on all sides. Fundamentally, a system is nothing but a closed conception, the more or less narrow limits of which are naturally determined by the "mental horizon" of its author. But all systematization is absolutely impossible in pure metaphysics, where everything belonging to the individual order is truly non-existent, metaphysics being entirely detached from all relativities and contingencies, philosophical or otherwise. This is necessarily so, because metaphysics is essentially knowledge of the Universal, and such knowledge does not permit of being enclosed within any formula, however comprehensive.

The diverse metaphysical and cosmological conceptions of India are not, strictly speaking, different doctrines, but only developments of a single doctrine according to different points of view and in various, but by no means incompatible, directions. Besides, the Sanskrit word *darshana*, which is attached to each of these conceptions, properly signifies "view" or "point of view", for the verbal root *drish*, whence it is derived, has as its primary meaning that of "seeing": it cannot in any way denote "system", and if orientalists translate it thus, that is merely the result of Western habits of thought which lead them into false assimilations at every step. Seeing nothing but philosophy everywhere, it is only natural that they should also see systems wherever they go.

The single doctrine to which we have just alluded is represented essentially by the *Veda*, that is to say, the sacred and traditional Science in its integrality, for this precisely is the proper meaning of that term.[3] It furnishes the principle and the common basis of all the more or less secondary and derivative branches which go to make up those diverse conceptions in which certain people have seen so many rival and opposed systems. In reality, these conceptions, insofar as they are in accord with their principle, obviously cannot contradict one another; on the contrary, they are bound mutually to complete and elucidate each other. Moreover, there is no need to read into this statement the suggestion of a more or less artificial and belated "syncretism", for the entire doctrine must be considered as being synthetically comprised within the *Veda*, and that from its origin. Tradition, in its integrality, forms a perfectly coherent whole, which however does not mean to say a systematic whole; and since all the points of view which it comprises can as well be considered simultaneously as in succession, there cannot be any real object in enquiring into the historical order in which they may actually have been developed and rendered explicit, even apart from the fact that the existence of oral transmission, probably lasting over a period of indefinite duration, would render any proposed solution quite misleading. Though the exposition may be modified to a certain degree externally in order to

---

[3] The root *vid*, from which *Veda* and *vidya* are derived, bears the twofold meaning of "seeing" (*videre* in Latin) and "knowing" (as in the Greek οἶδα): sight is taken as a symbol of knowledge because it is its chief instrument within the sensible order; and this symbolism is carried even into the purely intellectual realm, where knowledge is likened to "inward vision", as is implied by the use of such words as "intuition" for example.

adapt itself to the circumstances of this or that period, it is nonetheless true that the basis of tradition always remains exactly the same, and that these external modifications in no wise reach or affect the essence of the doctrine.

The concordance of a conception with the fundamental principle of the tradition is the necessary and sufficient condition of its orthodoxy, which term must however on no account be taken in this instance merely according to its religious mode; it is necessary to stress this point in order to avoid any error in interpretation, because in the West there is generally no question of orthodoxy except as viewed from the purely religious standpoint. In everything that concerns metaphysics or that proceeds more or less directly from it, the heterodoxy of a conception is fundamentally not different from its falsity, resulting from its disagreement with the essential principles. Since these are contained in the *Veda*, it follows that it is agreement with the *Veda* that constitutes the criterion of orthodoxy. Heterodoxy is found, therefore, at that point where contradiction with the *Veda* arises; whether voluntary or involuntary, it indicates a more or less far-reaching deviation or alteration of the doctrine, which moreover generally occurs only within somewhat restricted schools and can only affect special points, sometimes of very secondary importance, the more so since the power inherent in the tradition has the effect of limiting the scope and bearing of individual errors, of eliminating those which exceed certain bounds, and, in any case, of preventing them from becoming widespread and acquiring real authority. Even where a partially heterodox school has become to a certain extent representative of a *darshana*, such as the Atomist school in the case of the *Vaisheshika*, no slur is cast on the legitimacy of that *darshana* in itself; for it to remain within the bounds of orthodoxy it is only necessary to reduce it again to its truly essential content. On this point we cannot do better than quote by way of general indication this passage from the *Sāṇkhya-Pravachana-Bhashya* of Vijñāna-Bhikshu:

> In the doctrine of Kaṇāda [the *Vaisheshika*] and in the *Sāṇkhya* [of Kapila], the portion which is contrary to the *Veda* must be rejected by those who adhere strictly to the orthodox tradition; in the doctrine of Jaimini and that of Vyāsa [the two *Mīmānsās*], there is nothing which is not in accordance with the Scriptures [considered as the basis of that tradition].

The name *Mīmānsā*, derived from the verbal root *man*, "to think", in its iterative form, denotes the reflective study of the "Sacred Science": it is the intellectual fruit of meditation on the *Veda*. The first *Mīmānsā* (*Pūrva-Mīmānsā*) is attributed to Jaimini; but we must recall in this connection that the names which are thus attached to the formulation of the different *darshana*s cannot be related in any way to particular individuals: they are used symbolically to describe what are really "intellectual groupings", composed of all those who have devoted themselves to one and the same study over the course of a period the duration of which is no less indeterminable than the date of its beginning. The first *Mīmānsā* is also called *Karma-Mīmānsā* or practical *Mīmānsā* because it is concerned with actions, and, more particularly, with the accomplishment of rites. The word *karma* indeed possesses a double meaning: in a general sense, it means action in all its forms; in a special and technical sense, it means ritual action, such as is prescribed by the *Veda*. This practical *Mīmānsā* has for its aim, as the commentator Somanātha says, "to determine in an exact and precise manner the sense of the Scriptures", but chiefly insofar as they include precepts, and not in respect of pure knowledge or *jñāna*, which is often placed in opposition to *karma*, an opposition corresponding precisely to the distinction between the two *Mīmānsā*s.

The second *Mīmānsā* (*Uttara-Mīmānsā*) is attributed to Vyāsa, that is to say to the "collective entity" which arranged and finally codified the traditional texts constituting the *Veda* itself. This attribution is particularly significant, for it is easy to see that it is, not a historical or legendary person with whom we are dealing in this instance, but a genuine "intellectual function", amounting, one may say, to a permanent function, since Vyāsa is described as one of the seven *Chiranjīvī*s, literally "beings endowed with longevity", whose existence is not confined to any particular epoch.[4] To describe the second *Mīmānsā* in relation to the first, one may regard it as belonging to the purely intellectual and contemplative order. We cannot say theoretical *Mīmānsā* by way of symmetry with practical *Mīmānsā*, because this description

---

[4] Something similar is to be found in other traditions: thus in Taoism they speak of eight "immortals"; elsewhere we have Melchizedek, who is "without father, without mother, without descent, having neither beginning of days, nor end of life" (Heb. 7:3); and it would probably be easy to discover yet other parallelisms of a similar kind.

would give rise to ambiguity. Although the word "theory" is indeed etymologically synonymous with contemplation, it is nonetheless true that in current speech it has come to convey a far more restricted meaning; in a doctrine which is complete from the metaphysical point of view, theory, understood in this ordinary sense, is not self-sufficient, but is always accompanied or followed by a corresponding "realization", of which it is, in short, but the indispensable basis, and in view of which it is ordained, as the means in view of the end.

The second *Mīmānsā* is further entitled *Brahma-Mīmānsā* as being essentially and directly concerned with "Divine Knowledge" (*Brahma-Vidya*). It is this which constitutes the *Vedānta* strictly speaking, that is to say, according to the etymological significance of that term, the "end of the *Veda*", based principally upon the teaching contained in the *Upanishads*. This expression "end of the *Veda*" should be understood in the double sense of conclusion and of aim. On the one hand, the *Upanishads* do in fact form the last portion of the Vedic texts, and, on the other hand, that which is taught therein, insofar at least as it can be taught, is the final and supreme aim of traditional knowledge in its entirety, detached from all the more or less particular and contingent applications derivable from it. In other words, with the *Vedānta*, we find ourselves in the domain of pure metaphysics.

The *Upanishads*, forming an integral part of the *Veda*, are one of the very foundations of the orthodox tradition, a fact which has not prevented certain orientalists, such as Max Müller, from professing to detect in them the germs of a Buddhism interpreted after the modern fashion, that is to say of heterodoxy; such a statement obviously amounts to a contradiction in terms, and it would assuredly be difficult to carry misunderstanding further. One cannot insist too strongly on the fact that it is the *Upanishads* which here represent the primordial and fundamental tradition and consequently constitute the *Vedānta* in its essence; it follows from this that in a case of doubt as to the interpretation of the doctrine, it is always to the authority of the *Upanishads* that it is necessary to appeal in the last resort.

The principal teachings of the *Vedānta*, as extracted expressly from the *Upanishads*, have been coordinated and synthetically formulated in a collection of aphorisms known either as the *Brahma-*

*Sūtra*s or the *Shārīraka-Mīmānsā*;[5] the author of these aphorisms, who is called Bādarāyana and Krishna-Dwaipāyana, is identified with Vyāsa. It is important to note that the *Brahma-Sūtras* belong to the class of traditional writings called *smriti*, while the *Upanishads*, like all the other Vedic texts, form part of *shruti*; but the authority of *smriti* is derived from that of *shruti*, on which it is based. *Shruti* is not "revelation" in the religious and Western sense of the word, as most orientalists would have it, who, here again, confuse two very different points of view; it is the fruit of direct inspiration, so that it is in its own right that it holds its authority. *Shruti*, says Shankarāchārya,

> is a means of direct perception [in the sphere of transcendent knowledge], since, in order to be an authority it is necessarily independent of all other authority; while *smriti* plays a part that is analogous to induction, in that it derives its authority from an authority other than itself.[6]

But to avoid any misunderstanding as to the force of the analogy thus indicated between transcendent and sensory knowledge, it is necessary to add that, like every true analogy, it must be applied inversely;[7] thus, while induction rises above sensible perception and permits one to pass on to a higher level, it is on the contrary direct perception or inspiration alone which, in the transcendent order, attains the Principle itself, to what is highest, after which nothing remains but to draw the consequences and to determine the manifold applications. It may further be said that the distinction between *shruti* and *smriti* is, fundamentally, equivalent to that between immediate intellectual

---

[5] The term *Shārīraka* has been interpreted by Rāmānuja in his commentary (*Shrī-Bhāshya*) on the *Brahma-Sūtras* I.1.13 as referring to the "Supreme Self" (*Paramātmā*) which is in a sense, "incorporated" (*sharīra*) in all things.

[6] In Hindu logic, perception (*pratyaksha*) and induction or inference (*anumāna*) are the two "means of proof" (*pramāna*s) that can be legitimately employed in the realm of sensible knowledge.

[7] In the Hermetic tradition, the principle of analogy is expressed by the following sentence from the *Emerald Table*: "That which is below is like that which is above, and that which is above is like that which is below"; but in order to understand this formula and apply it correctly it is necessary to refer it to the symbol of "Solomon's Seal", made up of two superposed triangles pointing opposite ways.

intuition and reflective consciousness; if the first is described by a word bearing the primitive meaning of "hearing", this is precisely in order to indicate its intuitive character, and because according to the Hindu cosmological doctrine sound holds the primordial rank among sensible qualities. As for *smriti*, its primitive meaning is "memory": in fact, memory, being but a reflex of perception, can be taken as denoting, by extension, everything which possesses the character of reflective or discursive, that is to say, of indirect knowledge. Moreover, if knowledge is symbolized by light, as is most often the case, pure intelligence and recollection, otherwise the intuitive faculty and the discursive faculty, can be respectively represented by the sun and the moon. This symbolism, which we cannot enlarge upon here, is capable of numerous applications.[8]

The *Brahma-Sūtras*, the text of which is extremely concise, have given rise to numerous commentaries, the most important of which are those by Shankarāchārya and Rāmānuja; they are, both of them, strictly orthodox, so that we must not exaggerate the importance of their apparent divergences, which are in reality more in the nature of differences of adaptation. It is true that each school is naturally enough inclined to think and to maintain that its own point of view is the most worthy of attention and ought, while not excluding other views, nevertheless to take precedence over them. But in order to settle the question in all impartiality one has but to examine these points of view in themselves and to ascertain how far the horizon extends which they embrace respectively; it is, moreover, self-evident that no school can claim to represent the doctrine in a total and exclusive manner. It is nevertheless quite certain that Shankarāchārya's point of view goes deeper and further than that of Rāmānuja; one can, moreover, infer this from the fact that the first is of Shaivite tendency while the second is clearly Vaishnavite. A curious argument has been raised by Thibaut, who translated the two commentaries into English: he suggests that that of Rāmānuja is more faithful to the teaching

---

[8] Traces of this symbolism are to be detected even in speech: for example, it is not without reason that the same root *man* or *men* has served, in various languages, to form numerous words denoting at one and the same time the moon, memory, the "mental faculty" or discursive thought, and man himself insofar as he is specifically a "rational being".

of the *Brahma-Sūtras* but at the same time recognizes that that of
Shankarāchārya is more in conformity with the spirit of the *Upanishads*. In order to be able to entertain such an opinion it is obviously
necessary to maintain that there exist doctrinal differences between
the *Upanishads* and the *Brahma-Sūtras*; but even were this actually
the case, it is the authority of the *Upanishads* which must prevail,
as we have explained above, and Shankarāchārya's superiority would
thereby be established, although this was probably not the intention
of Thibaut, for whom the question of the intrinsic truth of the ideas
concerned hardly seems to arise. As a matter of fact, the *Brahma-
Sūtras*, being based directly and exclusively on the *Upanishads*, can
in no way be divergent from them; only their brevity, rendering them
a trifle obscure when they are isolated from any commentary, might
provide some excuse for those who maintain that they find in them
something besides an authoritative and competent interpretation of
the traditional doctrine. Thus the argument is really pointless, and
all that we need retain is the observation that Shankarāchārya has
deduced and developed more completely the essential contents of the
Upanishads: his authority can only be questioned by those who are
ignorant of the true spirit of the orthodox Hindu tradition, and whose
opinion is consequently valueless.

To complete these preliminary observations we must again make
it clear, although we have already explained this elsewhere, that it is
incorrect to apply the label "Esoteric Brāhmanism" to the teachings
of the *Upanishads*, as some have done. The inadmissibility of this
expression arises especially from the fact that the word "esoterism"
is a comparative, and that its use necessarily implies the correlative
existence of an "exoterism"; but such a division cannot be applied
to the doctrine in question. Exoterism and esoterism, regarded not
as two distinct and more or less opposed doctrines, which would be
quite an erroneous view, but as the two aspects of one and the same
doctrine, existed in certain schools of Greek antiquity; there is also
a clear example of this relationship to be met with in the Islamic
tradition, but the same does not apply in the case of the more purely
Eastern doctrines. In their case one can only speak of a kind of "natural
esoterism" such as inevitably pertains to every doctrine, especially in
the metaphysical sphere, where it is important always to take into
account the inexpressible, which is indeed what matters most of all,
since words and symbols, all told, serve no purpose beyond acting as

aids to conceiving it, by providing "supports" for a task which must necessarily remain a strictly personal one. From this point of view, the distinction between exoterism and esoterism would amount to no more than the distinction between the "letter" and the "spirit"; and one could also apply it to the plurality of meanings of greater or lesser depth contained in the traditional texts or, if preferred, the sacred scriptures of all races. On the other hand, it goes without saying that the same teaching is not understood in an equal degree by all who receive it: among such persons there are therefore those who in a certain sense discern the esoterism, while others, whose intellectual horizon is narrower, are limited to the exoterism; but this is not how people who talk about "Esoteric Brāhmanism" understand that expression. As a matter of fact, in Brāhmanism, the teaching is accessible in its entirety to all those who are intellectually "qualified" (*adhikārī*), that is, capable of deriving a real advantage from it; and if there are doctrines reserved for a chosen few, it is because it cannot be otherwise where instruction is allotted with discretion and in accordance with the real capacities of men. Although the traditional teaching is not esoteric in the strict sense of the word, it is indeed "initiatic", and it differs profoundly in all its methods from that "profane" education which the credulity of modern Westerners so strangely overrates: this we have already pointed out when speaking of "sacred science" and of the impossibility or "popularizing" it.

This last observation prompts us to a further remark. In the East the traditional doctrines always employ oral teaching as their normal method of transmission, even in cases where they have been formulated in written texts; there are profound reasons for this, because it is not merely words that have to be conveyed, but above all it is a genuine participation in the tradition which has to be assured. In these circumstances, it is meaningless to say, with Max Müller and other orientalists, that the word "Upanishad" denotes knowledge acquired "by sitting at the feet of a teacher"; this title, if such were the meaning, would then apply without distinction to all parts of the *Veda*; moreover, it is an interpretation which has never been suggested or admitted by any competent Hindu. In reality, the name of the *Upanishads* denotes that they are ordained to destroy ignorance by providing the means of approach to supreme Knowledge; and if it is solely a question of approaching, then that is because the supreme

Knowledge is in its essence strictly incommunicable, so that none can attain to it save by himself alone.

Another expression which seems to us even more unhappy than "Esoteric Brāhmanism" is "Brāhmanic Theosophy", which has been used by Oltramare; and he indeed admits that he did not adopt it without hesitation, since it seems to "justify the claims of Western Theosophists" to have derived their sanction from India, claims which he perceives to be ill-founded. It is true that we must certainly avoid anything which might lend countenance to certain most undesirable confusions; but there are still graver and more decisive reasons against admitting the proposed designation. Although the self-styled Theosophists of whom Oltramare speaks are almost completely ignorant of the Hindu doctrines, and have derived nothing from them but a terminology which they use entirely at random, they have no connection with genuine theosophy either, not even with that of the West; and this is why we insist on distinguishing carefully between "theosophy" and "Theosophism".[9] But leaving Theosophism aside, it can still be said that no Hindu doctrine, or more generally still, no Eastern doctrine, has enough points in common with theosophy to justify describing it by that name; this follows directly from the fact that the word denotes exclusively conceptions of mystical inspiration, therefore religious and even specifically Christian ones. Theosophy is something peculiarly Western; why seek to apply this same word to doctrines for which it was never intended, and to which it is not much better suited than are the labels of the philosophical systems of the West? Once again, it is not with religion that we are dealing here, and consequently there cannot be any question of theosophy any more than of theology; these two terms, moreover, began by being almost

---

[9] Guénon is at pains here to distinguish between "theosophy", or the "wisdom of God" strictly speaking, and "Theosophy", understood as designating the movement of the same name founded by H. S. Olcott and Mme Blavatsky. The matter is somewhat complicated by the fact that Guénon also introduces the term "Theosophism" (with very little precedent in English) to designate not only Blavatsky's Theosophy, but other similar movements. We will use the capitalized "Theosophy", and, where necessary, "Theosophism" when reference is being made to these latter movements, and the uncapitalized "theosophy" when the word is used in its strictly etymological sense. ED

synonymous although, for purely historical reasons, they have come to assume widely differing acceptations.[10]

It will perhaps be objected that we have ourselves just made use of the phrase "Divine Knowledge", which is equivalent, after all, to the original meaning of the words "theosophy" and "theology". This is true, but, in the first place, we cannot regard the last-named terms exclusively from an etymological standpoint, for they are among those with reference to which it has by now become quite impossible to ignore the changes of meaning which long usage has brought about. Moreover, we readily admit that this term "Divine Knowledge" is not itself entirely adequate; but owing to the unsuitability of European languages for the purpose of expressing purely metaphysical ideas, there was no better expression available. Besides, we do not think that there are any serious objections to its use, since we have already been careful to warn the reader not to apply a religious shade of meaning to it, such as it must almost inevitably bear when related to Western conceptions. All the same, a certain ambiguity might still remain, for the Sanskrit term which can be least inaccurately rendered by "God" is not *Brahma*, but *Īshvara*. However, the adjective "divine", even in current speech, is used less strictly, more vaguely perhaps, and therefore lends itself better to such a transposition as we make here than the substantive whence it was derived. The point to note is that such terms as "theology" and "theosophy", even when regarded etymologically and apart from all intervention of the religious point of view, can only be translated into Sanskrit as *Īshvara-Vidyā;* on the other hand, what we render approximately as "Divine Knowledge", when dealing with the *Vedānta* is *Brahma-Vidyā*, for the purely metaphysical point of view essentially implies the consideration of *Brahma* or the Supreme Principle, of which *Īshvara*, or the "Divine Personality", is merely a determination, as Principle of, and in relation to, universal Manifestation. The consideration of *Īshvara* therefore already implies a relative point of view; it is the highest of the relativities, the first of all determinations, but it is nonetheless true that it is "qualified" (*saguna*) and "conceived distinctively" (*savishesha*), whereas *Brahma*

---

[10] A similar remark could be made with regard to the terms "astrology" and "astronomy", which were originally synonyms; among the Greeks either term denoted both the meanings which these terms have later come to convey separately.

is "unqualified" (*nirguṇa*), "beyond all distinctions" (*nirvishesha*), absolutely unconditioned, universal manifestation in its entirety being strictly nil beside Its Infinity. Metaphysically, manifestation can only be considered from the point of view of its dependence upon the Supreme Principle and in the quality of a mere "support" for raising oneself to transcendent Knowledge; or again, taking things in inverse order, as an application of the principial Truth. In any case, nothing more should be looked for in everything pertaining thereto than a kind of "illustration" ordained to facilitate the understanding of the Unmanifested, the essential object of metaphysics, thus permitting, as we explained when interpreting the title of the *Upanishads*, of an approach being made to Knowledge unqualified.[11]

---

[11] For a fuller account of all these preliminary questions, which have had to be treated in rather summary fashion in the present chapter, we would refer the reader to our *Introduction to the Study of the Hindu Doctrines*, where these matters form the main subject of study and have been discussed in greater detail.

23

The Vital Center of the Human Being:
Seat of *Brahma*

The "Self" . . . must not be regarded as distinct from *Ātmā*, and, moreover, *Ātmā* is identical with *Brahma* itself. This is what may be called the "Supreme Identity", according to an expression borrowed from Islamic esoterism, where the doctrine on this and on many other points is fundamentally the same as in the Hindu tradition, in spite of great differences of form. The realization of this identity is brought about through *Yoga*, that is to say, through the intimate and essential union of the being with the Divine Principle, or, if it is preferred, with the Universal. The exact meaning of this word *Yoga* is in fact "union", neither more nor less,[1] despite the numerous interpretations, each more fanciful than the last, which orientalists and Theosophists have suggested. It should be noted that this realization ought not strictly speaking to be considered as an "achievement", or as "the production of a non-pre-existing result", according to Shankarāchārya's expression, for the union in question, even though not actually realized in the sense here intended, exists nonetheless potentially, or rather virtually: it is simply a matter of the individual (for it is only in respect of the individual that one can speak of realization) becoming effectively conscious of what really is from all eternity.

That is why it is said that it is *Brahma* which dwells in the vital center of the human being; this is true of every human being, not only of one who is actually "united" or "delivered"—these two words denoting the same thing viewed under two different aspects, the first in relation to the Principle, the second in relation to manifested or conditioned existence. This vital center is considered as corresponding analogically with the smaller ventricle (*guhā*) of the heart (*hridaya*); but it must not be confused with the heart in the ordinary sense of the word, that is to say with the physiological organ bearing that name,

---

[1] The root of this word is to be found, scarcely altered, in the Latin *jungere* and its derivatives: and the English word "yoke" shows this root in a form almost identical with the Sanskrit.

since it is in reality the center not only of the corporeal individuality, but of the integral individuality, capable of indefinite extension in its own sphere (which occupies, moreover, but one degree of existence), and of which the corporeal modality constitutes only a portion, and indeed, as we have already stated, only a very limited portion. The heart is regarded as the center of life, and in fact, from the physiological point of view, it is so by reason of its connection with the circulation of the blood, with which vitality itself is essentially linked in a very special way, as all traditions are unanimous in recognizing; but it is further considered as a center on a higher plane and in a more symbolical sense, through its connection with the universal Intelligence (in the sense of the Arabic term *al-Aqlu*) as related to the individual. It should be noted in this connection that the Greeks themselves, and Aristotle among others, assigned the same part to the heart, also making it the seat of intelligence, if one may so express it, and not of feeling as the moderns commonly do; the brain, in actual fact, is only the instrument of the mental faculty, that is, of thought in its reflective and discursive mode: and thus, in accordance with a symbolism which we have previously mentioned, the heart corresponds to the sun and the brain to the moon. It goes without saying, moreover, that in describing the center of the integral individuality as the heart, the greatest care should be taken not to regard what is merely an analogy as an identification; between the two there is strictly speaking a correspondence only, in which, it may be added, there is nothing arbitrary, but which is perfectly valid, although our contemporaries no doubt may be led by their habits of thought to disregard the profound reasons for such a thing. "In this seat of *Brahma* [*Brahma-pura*]", that is to say, in the vital center of which we have just been speaking, "there is a small lotus, a place in which is a small cavity [*dahara*] occupied by Ether [*Ākāsha*]; we must seek That which is in this place, and we shall know It."[2]

That which, in fact, dwells at the center of the individuality is not merely the etheric element, the principle of the four other sensible elements, as might be supposed by those who confine themselves to its most external meaning, that relating to the corporeal world only. In the latter world, this element does in fact play the part of a principle,

---

[2] *Chhāndogya Upanishad* VIII.1.1.

but in a wholly relative sense, inasmuch as this world is eminently relative, and it is precisely this acceptation which has to be analogically transposed. It is indeed only in the capacity of a "support" for this transposition that Ether is mentioned here; the conclusion of the text expressly denotes this, since, if nothing more were really being referred to, there would obviously be nothing to seek. And it may further be added that the lotus and the cavity in question must also be regarded symbolically, for such a "localization" is in no wise to be conceived literally once the point of view of corporeal individuality has been transcended, the other modalities being no longer subject to the spatial condition.

Nor is what we are at present considering merely the "living soul" (*jīvātmā*), that is, the particularized manifestation of the "Self" in life (*jīva*) and consequently in the human individual, viewed here more especially under the vital aspect which is one of the conditions of existence specifically determining the human individual state, and which applies moreover to the sum-total of modalities comprised in that state. Metaphysically, in fact, this manifestation should not be regarded separately from its Principle, which is the "Self"; and although this appears as *jīva* in the sphere of individual existence, in illusory mode therefore, it is *Ātmā* in its supreme Reality.

> This *Ātmā*, which dwells in the heart, is smaller than a grain of rice, smaller than a grain of barley, smaller than a grain of mustard, smaller than a grain of millet, smaller than the germ which is in the grain of millet; this *Ātmā*, which dwells in the heart, is also greater than the earth [the sphere of gross manifestation], greater than the atmosphere [the sphere of subtle manifestation], greater than the sky [the sphere of formless manifestation], greater than all the worlds together [that is, beyond all manifestation, being the unconditioned].[3]

---

[3] *Chhandogya Upanishad* III.14.3. In this context one cannot help recalling the Gospel parable: "The Kingdom of heaven is like a grain of mustard seed which a man took and sowed in his field; it is the smallest of all seeds, but when it has grown it is the greatest of shrubs and becomes a tree, so that the birds of the air come and make nests in its branches" (Matt. 13:31-32). Though the point of view is certainly a different one, it is easy to understand how the conception of the "Kingdom of Heaven" can be transposed metaphysically; the growing of the tree stands for the development of possibilities; and there is no single feature of the parable, even to the "birds of the

This is so, in fact, because analogy is necessarily applied in an inverse sense, as we have already pointed out, and just as the image of an object is inverted relative to that object, that which is first or greatest in the principial order is, apparently at any rate, last and smallest in the order of manifestation.[4] To make a comparison with mathematics by way of clarification, it is thus that the geometrical point is quantitatively nil and does not occupy any space, though it is the principle by which space in its entirety is produced, since space is but the development of its intrinsic virtualities.[5] Similarly, though arithmetical unity is the smallest of numbers if one regards it as situated in the midst of their multiplicity, yet in principle it is the greatest, since it virtually contains them all and produces the whole series simply by the indefinite repetition of itself. The "Self" is only potentially in the individual so long as "Union" is not achieved,[6] and this is why it is comparable to a grain or a germ; but the individual, and manifestation in its entirety, exist through it alone and have no

---

air", representing in this case the higher states of the being, which does not recall a similar symbolism occurring in another text of the *Upanishads*: "Two birds, insepa-rably united companions, dwell in the same tree; the one eats of the fruit of the tree, while the other looks on without eating" (*Muṇḍaka Upanishad* III.1.1; *Shvetāshvatara Upanishad* IV.6). The first of the two birds is *jīvātmā*, who is involved in the realm of action and its consequences; the second is the unconditioned *Ātmā*, which is pure Knowledge; and if they are inseparably associated, this is because the former is only distinguishable from the latter in an illusory manner.

[4] The same idea is very clearly expressed in the Gospel text, "So the last will be first, and the first last" (Matt. 20:16).

[5] Even from a more external point of view, that of ordinary elementary geometry, the following observation can be made: by continuous displacement the point engenders the line, the line engenders the surface, and the surface engenders the solid; but in the contrary sense, a surface is the intersection of two solids, a line is the intersection of two surfaces, a point is the intersection of two lines.

[6] In reality, however, it is the individual who dwells in the "Self", and the being becomes effectively conscious of this when "Union" is realized; but this conscious realization implies a freeing from the limitations that constitute individuality as such, and which, in a more general way, condition all manifestation. When it is said of the "Self" that it is in a certain sense indwelling in the individual, this means that one has taken up the viewpoint of manifestation, and this is yet another example of applica-tion in an inverse sense.

reality except through participation in its essence; while it immensely transcends all existence, being the sole Principle of all things.

When we say that the "Self" is potentially in the individual, and that "Union" exists only virtually before its realization, it goes without saying that this must be understood only from the point of view of the individual himself. In point of fact, the "Self" is not affected by any contingency, since it is essentially unconditioned; it is immutable in its "permanent actuality", and therefore there cannot be anything potential about it. Moreover, it is important to distinguish very carefully between "potentiality" and "possibility". The first of these two words implies aptitude for a certain development; it presupposes a possible "actualization" and can only be applied therefore in respect of "becoming" or of manifestation; possibilities, on the contrary, viewed in the principial and unmanifested state, which excludes all "becoming", can in no way be regarded as potential. To the individual, however, all possibilities which transcend him appear as potential, since so long as he regards himself in separative mode, deriving his own being seemingly from himself, whatever he attains is strictly speaking but a reflection and not those possibilities themselves; and although this is only an illusion, we may say that for the individual they always remain potential, since it is not as an individual that he can attain them, for, once they are realized, no individuality really exists any longer, as we shall explain more fully when we come to speak of "Deliverance". Here, however, we need to place ourselves outside the individual point of view, although, even while declaring it illusory, we nonetheless recognize in it that degree of reality which belongs to it within its own order; even when we do come to consider the individual, it can only be in virtue of his essential dependence upon the Principle, sole basis of that reality, and insofar as, virtually and effectively, he is integrated with the whole being; metaphysically, all must ultimately be related to the Principle, which is the "Self".

Thus, the dweller in the vital center is, from the physical point of view, ether; from the psychic point of view, it is the "living soul", and thus far we have not transcended the realm of individual possibilities; but also, and from the metaphysical point of view, above all, it is the principial and unconditioned "Self". It is therefore, in the truest sense, the "Universal Spirit" (*Ātmā*), which is in reality *Brahma* Itself, the "Supreme Ruler"; and thus the description of this center as *Brahma-pura* is found to be fully justified. But *Brahma*, considered in this manner as within man (and one might consider It in like manner in relation to every other state of the being) is called *Purusha*, because It rests or dwells in the individuality (we are dealing, let us repeat once more, with the integral individuality, and not merely with individuality restricted to its corporeal modality) as in a city (*puri-shaya*), for *pura*, in its proper and literal sense, signifies "city".[7]

In the vital center, dwelling of *Purusha*,

> the sun shines not, nor the moon, nor the stars; still less this visible fire [the igneous sensible element, or *Tejas*, of which visibility is the peculiar quality]. All shines by the radiance of *Purusha* [by reflecting its brightness]; it is by its splendor that this whole [the integral individuality regarded as "microcosm"] is illuminated.[8]

So, too, we read in the *Bhagavad-Gītā*:[9]

> One must seek the place [symbolizing a state] whence there is no return [to manifestation] and take refuge in the primordial *Purusha* from whom hath issued the original impulse [of universal manifestation]. . . . This place neither sun, nor moon, nor fire illumines; it is there I have my supreme abode.[10]

---

[7] This explanation of the word *Purusha* should of course not be regarded as an etymological derivation; it belongs to *Nirukta*, that is to say to the science of interpretation chiefly based on the symbolical value of the elements out of which words are built up. This method is generally not understood by orientalists; it is however quite comparable to the method found in the Jewish Kabbalah, and it was not even entirely unknown to the Greeks, examples being found in the *Cratylus* of Plato. As for the meaning of *Purusha*, it may be pointed out that *puru* expresses the idea of "plenitude".

[8] *Katha Upanishad* II.5.15: *Muṇḍaka Upanishad* II.2.10; *Shvetāshvatara Upanishad* VI.14.

[9] It is well known that the *Bhagavad-Gītā* is an episode in the *Mahābhārata*, and in this connection it should also be remembered that the *Itihāsas*, namely, the *Rāmāyana* and the *Mahābhārata* being included in the *Smriti*, are therefore something quite different from mere "epic poems" in the profane sense of the expression as understood by Westerners.

[10] *Bhagavad-Gītā* XV.4 and 6. In these texts one can observe an interesting similarity with the following passage from the description of the "Heavenly Jerusalem" in Rev. 21:23: "And the city has no need of sun or moon to shine upon it, for the glory of God is its light, and its lamp is the Lamb." From this it can be seen that the "Heavenly

Purusha is represented as light (*jyotis*), because light symbolizes Knowledge: and it is the source of all other light, which is but its reflection, no relative knowledge being able to exist save by participation, however indirect or remote, in the essence of supreme Knowledge. In the light of this Knowledge all things are in perfect simultaneity, for, principially, there cannot be anything but an "eternal present", since immutability excludes all succession; and it is only in the sphere of the manifested that the relations of possibilities which, in themselves, are eternally contained in the Principle, are transposed in terms of succession.

> This *Purusha*, of the size of a thumb [*angushtha-mātra*, an expression which must not be taken literally as denoting a spatial dimension, but which refers to the same idea as the comparison with a grain],[11] is of a clear luminosity like a smokeless fire [without any admixture of obscurity or ignorance]; it is the Lord of the past and of the future [being eternal, therefore omnipresent, in such wise that it contains in its permanent actuality all that appears as past or future relatively to any given moment of manifestation, a relationship that is, moreover, capable of transference beyond that particular mode of succession which is time proper]; it is today [in the actual state which constitutes the human individuality] and it will be tomorrow [and in all cycles or states of existence] such as it is [in itself, principially, to all eternity].[12]

Jerusalem" is not unrelated to the "city of *Brahma*"; and for those who are aware of the relationship between "the Lamb" of Christian symbolism and the Vedic *Agni*, this comparison is still more significant. In order to preclude any false interpretations, it can be said, without unduly stressing the last point, that we are in no wise trying to suggest that *Agnus* and *Ignis* (the Latin equivalent of *Agni*) are related etymologically; but resemblances such as the one that connects these two words often play an important part in symbolism; and moreover, in our view, there is nothing fortuitous in this, since everything, including forms of language, has a reason for its existence. It is also worth noting, in the same context, that the vehicle of *Agni* is a ram.

[11] A comparison could also be made here with the "endogeny of the Immortal", as it is taught by the Taoist tradition.

[12] *Katha Upanishad* II.4.12-13. In the Islamic esoteric doctrine the same idea is expressed, in almost identical terms, by Muḥyi 'd-Dīn ibn al-'Arabī in his *Treatise on Unity* (*Risālat al-Aḥadiyah*): "He [*Allāh*] is now such as He was [from all eternity] every day in the state of Sublime Creator." The only difference concerns the idea of

creation, which is only to be found in those traditional doctrines that are in some way or other attached to Judaism: fundamentally it is nothing but a particular way of expressing the idea of universal manifestation and its relation with the Principle.

24

The Degrees of Individual Manifestation

We must now pass on to consider the different degrees of the manifestation of *Ātmā*, regarded as the personality, insofar as this manifestation constitutes human individuality; and it may indeed literally be said to constitute it, since this individuality would enjoy no existence at all if it were separated from its principle, that is to say from the personality. The expression just used calls, however, for one reservation; by the manifestation of *Ātmā* must be understood manifestation referred to *Ātmā* as its essential principle, but it must not be inferred from this that *Ātmā* manifests itself in some way, since it never enters into manifestation, as we have previously stated, and that is why it is not in any way affected thereby. In other words, *Ātmā* is "that by which all things are manifested, and which is not itself manifested by anything";[1] and it is this point which must never be lost sight of throughout all that follows. We will repeat once more that *Ātmā* and *Purusha* are one and the same principle, and that it is from *Prakriti* and not from *Purusha* that all manifestation is produced; but if the *Sāṇkhya*, because its point of view is chiefly "cosmological" and not strictly speaking metaphysical, sees this manifestation as the development or "actualization" of the potentialities of *Prakriti*, the *Vedānta* necessarily sees it quite differently, because it regards *Ātmā*, which is outside any change or "becoming", as the true principle to which everything must ultimately be referred. It might be said that, viewed in this manner, the *Sāṇkhya* and the *Vedānta* represent respectively the points of view of "substance" and of "essence", and that the first can be called a "cosmological" point of view, because it is that of Nature and of "becoming"; but, on the other hand, metaphysics does not limit itself to "essence" regarded as the correlative of "substance", nor even to Being, in which these two terms are unified; it extends much further, since it attains to *Paramātmā* or *Purushottama*, which is the Supreme *Brahma*, and therefore its point of view (assuming that such an expression is still applicable here) is truly unlimited.

---

[1] *Kena Upanishad* I.5-9.

Furthermore, when we speak of the different degrees of individual manifestation, it should be readily understood that they correspond with the degrees of universal manifestation, by reason of the basic analogy between the "macrocosm" and the "microcosm" to which we have already alluded. This will be still better understood if one remembers that all manifested beings alike are subject to the general conditions which limit the states of existence in which they are placed; if we cannot, when considering any given being, really isolate one state of that being from the whole composed of all the other states among which it is situated hierarchically at a given level, no more can we, from another point of view, isolate that state from all that belongs, not to the same being, but to the same degree of universal Existence; and thus all appears linked together in various different ways, both within manifestation itself, and also insofar as the latter, forming a single whole in its indefinite multiplicity, is attached to its principle, that is, to Being, and through Being to the Supreme Principle. Multiplicity, once it is a possibility, exists according to its own mode, but this mode is illusory, in the sense we have already ascribed to that word (that of a lesser reality), because the very existence of this multiplicity is based upon unity, from which it is derived and within which it is principially contained. When viewing the whole of universal manifestation in this manner, we may say that in the very multiplicity of its degrees and of its modes "Existence is one", according to a formula borrowed from Islamic esoterism; furthermore, there is a fine distinction which it is important to note here as between "unicity" and "unity": the first embraces multiplicity as such while the second is its principle (not its "root", in the sense in which this word is applied to *Prakriti* only, but as containing within itself, "essentially" as well as "substantially", all the possibilities of manifestation). It can therefore correctly be said that Being is one, and that it is Unity itself[2] in the metaphysical sense, however, and not in the mathematical sense, for at this stage we have passed quite outside the domain of quantity. Between metaphysical Unity and mathematical unity there is analogy but not identity; and similarly, when we speak of the multiplicity of universal manifestation, it is again not with a quantitative multiplicity that we are concerned, for quantity is merely a special condition of certain manifested states.

---

[2] The same idea is expressed by the Scholastic adage: *Esse et unum convertuntur.*

Finally, if Being is one, the Supreme Principle is "without duality", as we shall see in what follows: Unity is indeed the first of all determinations, but it is already a determination, and, as such, it cannot properly be applied to the Supreme Principle.

Having given these few indispensable explanations, let us return to the consideration of the degrees of manifestation. It is necessary, as we have seen, to draw a distinction first of all between formless and formal manifestation; but when we confine our attention to the individuality, it is always exclusively with the latter that we are concerned. The human state properly so called, like every other individual state, belongs wholly to formal manifestation, since it is precisely the presence of form among the conditions contributing to make up a particular mode of existence which characterizes that mode as individual. If, therefore, we have to consider a formless element, it will also necessarily be a supra-individual element, and, as regards its relationship with human individuality, it must never be considered as constitutive of it, nor for any reason at all as forming a part of it, but as linking the individuality to the personality. The personality, indeed, is unmanifested, even insofar as it is regarded more especially as the principle of the manifested states, just as Being, although it is properly the principle of universal manifestation, remains outside of and beyond that manifestation (and we may recall Aristotle's "unmoved mover" at this point); on the other hand, formless manifestation is also, in a relative sense, principial in relation to formal manifestation, and thus it establishes a link between the latter and its higher unmanifested principle, which is, moreover, the common principle of these two orders of manifestation. Similarly, if we distinguish, in formal or individual manifestation, between the subtle and the gross state, the first is, more relatively still, principial in relation to the second, and hence placed hierarchically between it and formless manifestation. We have, therefore, through a series of principles becoming progressively more relative and determined, a chain at once logical and ontological (the two points of view, moreover, corresponding in such a way that they can only be separated artificially) extending from the unmanifested downward to gross manifestation, passing through the intermediary of formless manifestation and then of subtle manifestation; and, whether we are dealing with the "macrocosm" or with the "microcosm", such is the general order which must be followed in the development of the possibilities of manifestation. . . .

One last observation is called for; in speaking of the order of development of the possibilities of manifestation, or of the order in which the elements corresponding to the different phases of this development should be enumerated, great care must be taken to explain that such an order implies a purely logical succession, signifying, however, a real ontological connection, and that there cannot be any question at all here of a temporal succession. Development in time, indeed, only corresponds with a special condition of existence, which is one of those conditions defining the domain in which the human state is contained; and there is an indefinite number of other modes of development equally possible, and included also within universal manifestation. Human individuality cannot therefore be related in the order of time to other states of the being, since these, in a general way, are extra-temporal: and that is also true even when it is only a question of states which likewise belong to formal manifestation. It might further be added that certain extensions of the human individuality, outside its corporeal modality, are already freed from time, without on that account being exempt from the general conditions of the state to which this individuality belongs; these extensions are really situated in mere prolongations of that state, and we shall doubtless have occasion in other studies to explain just how such prolongations may be reached through the suppression of one or other of the conditions which together contribute to make up the corporeal world. Such being the case, it is all the more apparent that there cannot be any question of the temporal condition applying outside this same state, nor, consequently, of its governing the relation of the integral human state with other states; and this is even less admissible when it is a question of a principle common to all the states of manifestation, or of an element which, though indeed manifested, is nevertheless superior to all formal manifestation, as is the element to be considered next.

25

Buddhi or the Higher Intellect

The first degree of the manifestation of *Ātmā*, taking this expression in the sense explained in the last chapter, is the higher intellect (*Buddhi*), which . . . is also called *Mahat* or the "great principle"; it is the second of the twenty-five principles of the *Sāṅkhya* and the first therefore of all the productions of *Prakriti*. This principle still pertains to the universal order, since it is formless; we must not, however, forget that it already belongs to manifestation, and therefore proceeds from *Prakriti*, for all manifestation, at whatever degree we take it, necessarily implies the two correlative and complementary terms, *Purusha* and *Prakriti*, "essence" and "substance". It is nonetheless true that *Buddhi* transcends the domain not only of human individuality but of every individual state whatsoever, and it is this which justifies its other name of *Mahat*: it is never really individualized, therefore, and it is not until the next stage, that of the particular (or rather "particularist") consciousness of the "ego", that we shall find individuality realized.

Buddhi, considered in relation to the human individuality or to any other individual state, is, then, its immediate but transcendent principle, just as, from the point of view of universal Existence, form-less manifestation is the principle of formal manifestation; and it is at the same time what may be called the expression of the personality in manifestation, therefore that which unifies the being throughout the indefinite multiplicity of its individual states (the human state, in its utmost extension, being but one state among all the rest). In other words, if we view the "Self" (*Ātmā*) or personality, as the Spiritual Sun[1] which shines at the center of the entire being, *Buddhi* will be the ray directly emanating from this Sun and illuminating in its entirety the particular individual state that more especially concerns us, while at the same time linking it to the other individual states of the same being, or rather, more generally still, to all the manifested states (individual or non-individual) of that being, and, beyond these, to the

---

[1] As to the sense in which this expression should be taken, we would refer the reader to the remark previously made concerning the "Universal Spirit".

center itself. Further, it should be remarked, without however going into the question so far as to interrupt the course of our exposition, that, owing to the fundamental unity of the being in all its states, the center of each state, where this spiritual ray is projected, should be regarded as virtually, if not effectively, identified with the center of the entire being; and it is for this reason that any state whatsoever, the human state as well as any other, can be taken as a basis for the realization of the Supreme Identity. It is precisely in this sense, and in virtue of this identification, that one may say, as we did in the first place, that *Purusha* itself dwells at the center of the human individuality, that is to say at the point where the intersection of the spiritual ray with the realm of the vital possibilities determines the "living soul" (*jīvātmā*).[2]

Furthermore, *Buddhi*, like everything that proceeds from the potentialities of *Prakriti*, participates in the three *guṇas*; that explains why, when viewed from the standpoint of distinctive knowledge (*vijñāna*), it is regarded as ternary, and, in the sphere of universal Existence, it is then identified with the divine *Trimūrti*:

> *Mahat* is conceived distinctively as three Gods [in the sense of three aspects of the intelligible Light, for this is the real meaning of the Sanskrit word *Deva*, of which the Latin word *Deus* is, moreover, etymologically the exact equivalent],[3] through the influence of the three *guṇas*, being one single manifestation [*mūrti*] in three Gods. In the universal order, it is the Divinity [*Īshvara*, not in himself, but under his three principal aspects as *Brahmā*, *Vishnu*, and *Shiva*,

---

[2] Clearly, we are not referring in this instance to a mathematical point, but to what might by analogy be called a metaphysical point, always with the proviso however that such an expression must not be allowed to evoke the notion of the "monad" of Leibnitz, since *jīvātmā* is nothing more than a particular and contingent manifestation of *Ātmā*, so that its separate existence is really illusory. The geometrical symbolism referred to will however be set forth in a separate work, together with all the developments to which it lends itself. [See *The Symbolism of the Cross*, in which this geometrical symbolism is treated in detail. ED]

[3] Were one to give to the word "God" the meaning that it has subsequently assumed in Western languages, its use in the plural would make nonsense from the Hindu just as much as from the Christian or Islamic point of view, since as we pointed out before, it could then only apply to *Īshvara* exclusively, in his indivisible unity which is that of Universal Being, whatever multiplicity of aspects can be considered as pertaining to it in a secondary way.

constituting the *Trimūrti*, or "triple manifestation"]; but regarded distributively [under the aspect of "separativity", which is, moreover, purely contingent] it belongs [without however being itself individualized] to individual beings [to whom it communicates the possibility of participating in the divine attributes, that is to say in the very nature of Universal Being, the Principle of all existence].[4]

It is easy to see that *Buddhi* is here considered in its respective relations with the first two of the three *Purusha*s which are spoken of in the *Bhagavad-Gītā*: in the "macrocosmic" order the "immutable" *Purusha* is *Īshvara* himself, of whom the *Trimūrti* is the expression in manifested mode (we are speaking, of course, of formless manifestation, for there is nothing individual about it); and it is stated that the other *Purusha* is "disseminated among all beings". Similarly, in the "microcosmic" order, *Buddhi* may be viewed relatively to the personality (*Ātmā*) and relatively the "living soul" (*jīvātmā*), the latter moreover only being the reflection of the personality in the individual human state, a reflection which could not exist without the mediation of *Buddhi*. To recall here the symbol of the sun and its reflected image in the water, *Buddhi* is, as we have stated, the ray which determines the formation of the image and at the same time unites it with its luminous source.

It is in virtue of the twofold relationship which has just been indicated, and of this function of intermediary between the personality and the individuality, that we may regard the intellect, in spite of the inevitable inadequacy of such a way of speaking, as passing in some sort from the state of universal potentiality to the individualized state, but without really ceasing to be such as it was, since this apparent passage only comes about through its intersection with the particular domain constituted by certain conditions of existence defining the individuality in question; it then produces as a resultant of this intersection the individual consciousness (*ahankāra*), implied in the "living soul" (*jīvātmā*) in which it is inherent. As we have already pointed out, this consciousness, which is the third principle of the *Sānkhya*, gives rise to the notion of the "ego" (*aham*, whence the name *ahankāra*, literally

---

[4] *Matsya-Purāna*. It will be noticed that *Buddhi* is not unrelated to the Logos of the Alexandrians.

"that which makes the me"), since its proper function is to establish the individual conviction (*abhimāna*), that is to say precisely the notion that the "I am" is concerned with external (*bāhya*) and internal (*abhyantara*) objects, which are respectively the objects of perception (*pratyaksha*) and contemplation (*dhyāna*); and the sum total of these objects is described by the term *idam*, "this", when conceived as in opposition to *aham* or "me", a purely relative opposition, however, and for that reason quite different from that which modern philosophers claim to establish between "subject" and "object" or between "mind" and "things". Thus the individual consciousness proceeds directly, but simply as a conditioned modality, from the intellectual principle, and, in its turn, produces all the other principles or elements specially attaching to the human individuality. . . .

26

Final Deliverance

"Deliverance" (*Moksha* or *Mukti*), that is to say that final liberation of the being . . . which is the ultimate goal toward which the being tends, differs absolutely from all states which that being may have passed through in order to reach it, since it is the attainment of the supreme and unconditioned state, whereas all the other states, no matter how exalted, are still conditioned, that is to say subject to certain limitations which define them, making them to be what they are and characterizing them as determinate states. These remarks apply to the supra-individual states as well as to the individual states, in spite of the differences in their respective conditions; and even the degree of pure Being itself, although it is beyond all existence in the strict sense of the word, namely beyond all manifestation both formless and formal, still implies a determination, which, though primordial and principial, is nonetheless already a limitation. It is through Being that all things in every mode of universal existence subsist, and Being subsists through itself; it determines all the states of which it is the principle and is only determined by itself; but to determine oneself is nonetheless to be determined and therefore limited in some respect, so that Infinity cannot be attributed to Being, which must under no circumstances be regarded as the Supreme Principle. It is here that one may observe the metaphysical incompleteness of the Western doctrines, even of those, it must be admitted, in which some degree of true metaphysics is nevertheless present:[1] stopping short at Being, they remain incom-

---

[1] We are alluding here to the philosophical doctrines of antiquity and of the Middle Ages, since the points of view of modern philosophy are the very negation of metaphysics; and the above statement is as true of conceptions of a pseudo-metaphysical stamp as of those in which the negation is frankly expressed. Naturally, our present remarks only apply to doctrines that are known to the "profane" world, and do not refer to the esoteric traditions of the West, which, so long at least as they possessed a character that was genuinely and fully "initiatic", could not be limited in this way, but must on the contrary have been metaphysically complete under the twofold heading of theory and realization; these traditions however have never been known to any but an elite far more restricted in numbers than in the Eastern countries.

plete even theoretically (without referring to realization, which they leave out of account altogether), and, as usually happens in such cases, they exhibit an undesirable tendency to deny that which lies outside their sphere and which, from the viewpoint of pure metaphysics, is precisely the most important part of all.

The acquisition or, to speak more accurately, the taking possession of higher states, whatever their nature, is thus only a partial, secondary, and contingent result; and although this result may appear immense by comparison with the individual human state (and above all by comparison with the corporeal state, the only one effectively possessed by ordinary people during their earthly existence), it is nonetheless true that, in itself, it amounts strictly to nothing in relation to the supreme state, since the finite, while becoming indefinite through the extensions of which it is capable, that is to say through the development of its own possibilities, always remains nothing in comparison with the Infinite. Ultimately, therefore, a result of this kind is only of value by way of preparation for "Union", that is to say it is still only a means and not an end; to mistake it for the end is to continue in illusion, since all the states in question, up to and including Being, are themselves illusory in the sense we have attributed to that word from the beginning. Besides, in any state where some form of distinction remains, that is to say in all the degrees of Existence, including those not belonging to the individual order, it is impossible for the universalization of the being to become effective; and even union with Universal Being, according to the mode in which it is accomplished in the condition of *Prājña* (or in the posthumous state corresponding to that condition), is not "Union" in the full sense of the word; were it so, the return to a cycle of manifestation, even in the formless order, would no longer be possible. It is true that Being is beyond all distinction, since the first distinction is that of "essence" and "substance" or of *Purusha* and *Prakriti*; nevertheless, *Brahma*, as *Īshvara* or Universal Being, is described as *savishesha*, that is to say as "implying distinction", since He is the immediate determining principle of distinction: only the unconditioned state of *Ātmā*, which is beyond Being, is *prapancha-upashama*, "without any trace of the development of manifestation". Being is one, or rather it is metaphysical Unity itself; but Unity embraces multiplicity within itself, since it produces it by the mere extension of its possibilities; it is for this reason that even in Being itself a multiplicity of aspects may be conceived, which constitute so many attributes or qualifications of it, although these aspects are not effectually distinguished in it, except insofar as we conceive them as such: yet at the same time they must be in some way distinguishable for us to be able so to conceive them. It might be said that every aspect is distinguishable from the others in a certain respect, although none of them is really distinguishable from Being, and that all are Being Itself;[2] we therefore find here a kind of principial distinction, which is not a distinction in the sense in which the word applies in the sphere of manifestation, but which is its analogical transposition. In manifestation, distinction implies separation; but that separation has nothing really positive about it, since it is only a mode of limitation;[3] pure Being, on the contrary, is beyond "separateness". That which exists at the level of pure Being is therefore "non-distinguished", if distinction (*vishesha*) be taken in the sense applicable within the manifested states; and yet, in another sense there is still present an element that is "distinguished" (*vishishta*): in Being all beings (meaning thereby their personalities) are "one" without being confused and distinct without being separated.[4] Beyond Being one cannot speak of distinction of any kind, even principial, although at the same time it cannot be said that there is confusion either; one is beyond multiplicity and beyond Unity as well; in the absolute transcendence of this supreme state none of these expressions can any longer be applied even by analogical transposition, and that is why recourse must be had to a term of negative form, namely to "non-duality" (*advaita*), as we have already explained; even the word "Union" is undoubtedly imperfect, because it evokes the idea of Unity, but we are obliged nevertheless to make

---

[2] This can be applied, in Christian theology, to the conception of the Trinity: each Divine Person is God, but is not the other Persons. In Scholastic philosophy the same might also be said of the "transcendentals", each one of which is coextensive with Being.

[3] In the individual states, separation is determined by the presence of form; in the non-individual states, it must be determined by some other condition, since these states are formless.

[4] In this is to be found the chief difference separating the point of view of Rāmānuja, who maintains the principial distinction, from that of Shankarāchārya, who transcends it.

use of it for the translation of the term *Yoga*, since the Western languages have no alternative to offer.

Deliverance, together with the faculties and powers which it implies, so to speak, "by superaddition" (because all states with all their possibilities are necessarily comprised in the absolute totalization of the being), but which, we repeat, must only be considered as accessory and even "accidental" results and in no wise as constituting a final goal in themselves—Deliverance, we say, can be obtained by the *yogī* (or rather by him who becomes such in virtue of obtaining it), with the help of the observances indicated in the *Yoga-Shāstra* of Patañjali. It can also be favored by the practice of certain rites,[5] as well as of various particular styles of meditation (*hārda-vidyā* or *dahara-vidyā*);[6] but it must be understood that all such means are only preparatory and have nothing essential about them, for

> man can acquire true Divine Knowledge even without observing the rites prescribed [for each of the different human categories, in conformity with their respective natures, and especially for the different *āshrama*s or regular stages of life];[7] and indeed many examples are to be met with in the *Veda* of persons who have neglected to carry out such rites [the function of which is compared in the *Veda* to that of a saddle-horse, which helps a man to reach his destination more easily and more rapidly, but without which he is able to reach it all the same], or who have been prevented from doing so, and yet, by maintaining their attention perpetually concentrated and fixed on the Supreme *Brahma* [in which consists the one and only

[5] These rites are in every respect comparable to those classed by the Muslims under the general denomination of *dhikr*, they are mostly based, as we have already mentioned, on the science of rhythm and its correspondences in all the various orders. Such are also the rites called *vrata* ("vow") and *dvāra* ("gate") in the otherwise partially heterodox doctrine of the Pāshupatas; under different forms all this is fundamentally the same as *Hatha-Yoga*, or at least equivalent to it.

[6] *Chhāndogya Upanishad* I.

[7] Furthermore, the man who has reached a certain degree of realization is called *ativarnāshrami*, that is to say beyond caste (*varna*) and beyond the stages of earthly existence (*āshramas*); none of the usual distinctions any longer apply to such a being from the moment that he has effectively transcended the limits of individuality, even though he has not yet arrived at the final goal.

really indispensable preparation], have acquired true Knowledge concerning It [Knowledge which, for that reason, is, likewise called "supreme"].[8]

Deliverance, then, is only effective insofar as it essentially implies perfect Knowledge of *Brahma*; and, inversely, that Knowledge, to be perfect, presupposes of necessity the realization of what we have already termed the "Supreme Identity". Thus, Deliverance and total and absolute Knowledge are truly but one and the same thing; if it be said that Knowledge is the means of Deliverance, it must be added that in this case means and end are inseparable, for Knowledge, unlike action, carries its own fruit within itself;[9] and moreover, within this sphere a distinction such as that of means and end can amount to no more than a mere figure of speech, unavoidable no doubt when one wishes to express these things, insofar as they are expressible, in human language. If therefore Deliverance is looked upon as a consequence of Knowledge, it must be specified that it is a strict and immediate consequence. This is most clearly affirmed by Shankarāchārya in the following terms:

> There is no other means of obtaining complete and final Deliverance excepting Knowledge; it alone loosens the bonds of passion [and of all other contingencies to which the individual being is subjected]; without Knowledge, Beatitude [*Ānanda*] cannot be obtained. Action [*karma*, whether understood in its general sense or as applied specially to the performance of rites], not being opposed to ignorance [*avidyā*],[10] cannot remove it; but Knowledge disperses ignorance as light disperses darkness. As soon as the ignorance born of earthly affections [and other analogous bonds] is banished [and every illusion with it], the "Self" [*Ātmā*], by its own splendor, shines afar [through every degree of existence] in an undivided state

---

[8] *Brahma-Sūtras* III.4.36-38.

[9] Besides, both action and its fruits are equally transient and "momentary"; whereas on the contrary Knowledge is permanent and final, and the same applies to its fruit, which is not distinct from Knowledge itself.

[10] Some would like to translate *avidyā* or *ajñāna* as "nescience" rather than "ignorance"; we confess that we cannot clearly see the need for this subtlety.

[penetrating all and illuminating the totality of the being], as the sun spreads its brightness abroad when the clouds have scattered.[11]

A most important point to note is the following: action, no matter of what sort, cannot under any circumstances liberate from action; in other words, it can only bear fruit within its own domain, which is that of human individuality. Thus it is not through action that it is possible to transcend individuality, taking individuality here, more-over, in its integral extension, for we do not for a moment pretend that the consequences of action are limited to the corporeal modality only. . . . Hence it follows immediately that "Salvation" in the religious sense given to the word by Western people, being the fruit of certain actions,[12] cannot be identified with "Deliverance"; and it is all the more urgent to state this explicitly since orientalists constantly confuse the two together.[13] "Salvation" is properly speaking the attainment of the *Brahma-Loka*; and we will further specify that by *Brahma-Loka* must here be understood exclusively the abode of *Hiranyagarbha*,[14] since any more exalted aspect of the "Non-Supreme" lies outside individual possibilities. This accords perfectly with the Western con-ception of "immortality", which is simply an indefinite prolongation of individual life transposed into the subtle order and extending to the *pralaya*. All this . . . represents but one stage in the process of *krama-mukti*;[15] moreover, the possibility of a return into a state of manifestation (supra-individual, however) is not definitely excluded for the being that has not passed beyond this stage. To go further and to free oneself entirely from the conditions of life and duration which

---

[11] *Ātmā-Bodha* ("Knowledge of the Self").

[12] The common expression "to work out one's salvation" is therefore perfectly ac-curate.

[13] Thus Oltramare, for example, translates *Moksha* by the word "salvation" from be-ginning to end in his works, without seeming to suspect, we will not say the real dif-ference which has been explained here, but even the mere possibility of inaccuracy in this identification.

[14] Literally, the "Golden Embryo"; the God *Brahmā* (of the *Trimūrti*) enveloped with-in the "World Egg", the principle or origin of formal manifestation. ED

[15] Deferred or gradual liberation. ED

are inherent to individuality, there is no other path but that of Knowledge, either "non-supreme" and leading to *Īshvara*,[16] or "supreme"
and conferring immediate Deliverance. In the latter case there is no
longer even occasion to consider a passage at death through various
higher, though still transitory and conditioned states:

> The Self [*Ātmā*, since there can be no further question of *jīvātmā*,
> all distinction and all "separateness" having disappeared] of him who
> has attained the perfection of Divine Knowledge [*Brahma-Vidyā*]
> and who has consequently obtained final Deliverance, ascends, on
> quitting its bodily form [and without passing through any interme-
> diate stages], to the Supreme [spiritual] Light which is *Brahma*, and
> identifies itself with It, in an undivided and conformable manner,
> just as pure water, mingling itself with the clear lake [without how-
> ever losing itself in it in any way] conforms itself in every respect
> therewith.[17]

[16] It is hardly necessary to point out that theology, even if it comprised a realization
rendering it truly effective, instead of remaining simply theoretical as is in practice the
case (unless the "mystical states" can be said to represent such a realization, which is
only partially and in certain respects true), would always be included in its entirety in
this "non-supreme" Knowledge.

[17] *Brahma-Sūtras* IV.4.1-4.

PART FOUR

THE TRADITIONAL WORLD

The traditional world comprises many religious forms and disciplines that are based upon a primordial tradition as the primary source of all traditional forms. These authentic traditions provide an effective means to arrive at an unexpected destination, namely knowledge of universal principles that lead to spiritual realization. Guénon's erudite insights into a broad range of traditional forms give clear, yet profound exposure to many different paths that always lead to one and the same truth at the heart of the perennial philosophy.

27

Kabbalah

The term *Kabbalah*[1] in Hebrew means nothing else than "tradition" in the most general sense, and although it generally designates the esoteric or initiatic tradition when used with no further precision, it also sometimes happens that it may be applied to the exoteric tradition itself.[2] This term can therefore designate any tradition; but since it belongs to the Hebraic language, it is normal to reserve it to the Hebrew tradition alone, as we have noted on other occasions, or, if one prefers perhaps a more exact way of speaking, to the specifically Hebrew form of the tradition. If we insist on this point, it is because we have noted that some people have a tendency to attach another meaning to this word, to make it the name of a special type of traditional knowledge, wherever this may be found, and this because they believe they have discovered in the word all sorts of more or less extraordinary things that really are not there at all. We do not intend to waste our time bringing up all these fanciful interpretations; it is more useful to clarify the original meaning of the word, which will suffice to reduce them to nothing, and this is all we propose to do here.

The root QBL in Hebrew and Arabic[3] signifies essentially the relationship of two things placed face to face with one another, and from this come all the varied meanings of the words derived from it, as for example those of encounter and even opposition. From this relationship also comes the idea of a passage from the one to the other of the two terms, whence ideas like those of receiving, welcoming, and accepting expressed in the two languages through the verb *qabal;*

---

[1] Although the initial "K" has been retained in spelling *Kabbalah*, since this represents current practice, when other terms and roots are introduced, the letter "Q" has been used, as in the original French and in common philological practice. ED

[2] This has not failed to cause certain errors: thus, we have seen some claim to link the *Talmud* to the "Kabbalah", understood in the esoteric sense; indeed, the *Talmud* is certainly from the "tradition", but is purely exoteric, religious, and legal.

[3] We call attention to the fact, which perhaps is not sufficiently noticed, that these two languages, which share most of their roots, can very often shed light on one another.

and *Kabbalah* derives directly from this, that is to say "that which is received" or transmitted (in Latin *traditum*) from one to the other. Here there appears, along with the idea of transmission, that of a succession; but it must be noted that the primary meaning of the root indicates a relationship that can be simultaneous as well as successive, spatial as well as temporal. And this explains the double meaning of the preposition *qabal* in Hebrew and *qabl* in Arabic, which signify both "in front of" (that is, "facing" in space) and "before" (in time); and the close relationship of these two words, "in front of" and "before", even in French, clearly shows that there is always a certain analogy between these two different modalities, one in simultaneity and the other in succession. This also allows the resolution of an apparent contradiction: although the usual idea when it comes to a temporal relationship is that of anteriority, which relates therefore to the past, it also happens that derivatives from the same root designate the future (in Arabic *mustaqbal*, that is to say literally that toward which one goes, from *istaqbal*, "to go toward"). But do we not also say in French that the past is "before" [*avant*] us, and the future is "in front of" [*devant*] us, which is quite comparable? In sum, it suffices in every case that one of the two terms considered be "in front of" or "before" the other, whether it be a question of a spatial relationship or a temporal one.

All these remarks can be further confirmed by the examination of another root, equally common to Hebrew and Arabic, and which has meanings very close to these, one could even say identical in great part, for even though their starting-point is clearly different the derived meanings converge. This is the root QDM, which in the first place expresses the idea of "to precede" (*qadam*), whence all that refers not only to a temporal anteriority but to a priority of any order. Thus for words derived from this root one finds, besides the original and ancient meanings (*qedem* in Hebrew, *qidm* or *qidam* in Arabic) that of primacy or precedence and even that of walking, advancing, or progression (in Arabic *taqaddum*);[4] and here again, the preposition *qadam* in Hebrew and *quddam* in Arabic has the double meaning of "in front of" and "before". But the principal meaning designates what

---

[4] From which comes the word *qadam*, meaning "foot", that is, what serves for walking.

is first, whether hierarchically or chronologically; thus the idea most frequently expressed is that of origin or primordiality, and by extension, that of antiquity when the temporal order is involved. Thus, *qadmon* in Hebrew and *qadim* in Arabic signify "ancient" in current usage, but when they are related to the domain of principles, they must be translated by "primordial".[5]

Concerning these same words, there are other reasons that are not without interest. In Hebrew, derivatives of the root QDM also serve to designate the East,[6] that is, the direction of the "origin" in the sense that it is there that the rising sun appears (*oriens*, from *oriri*, from which comes also *origo* in Latin), the starting-point of the diurnal course of the sun; and at the same time it is also the point used when "orienting" oneself by turning toward the rising sun.[7] Thus *qedem* also means "East", and *qadmon* "eastern"; but one should not see in these designations the affirmation of a primordiality of the East from the point of view of the history of terrestrial humanity, since, as we have often said, the original tradition is Nordic, "polar" even, and neither Eastern nor Western; moreover, the explanation we just indicated seems to us fully sufficient. We will add in this connection that these questions of "orientation" are generally quite important in traditional symbolism and in rites based on that symbolism; they are, besides, more complex than one might think and can give rise to certain errors, for in the different traditional forms there are many different modes of orientation. When one turns toward the rising sun, as we have just said, the South is designated as the "right side" (*yamīn* or *yaman*; cf. the Sanskrit *dakshina*, which has the same meaning) and

---

[5] *Al-insān al-qadim*, that is, "primordial Man" is, in Arabic, one of the designations of "Universal Man" (synonym of *al-insān al-kāmil*, which is literally "perfect or complete Man"); it is precisely the Hebraic *Adam Qadmon*.

[6] In French, *Orient*, whence oriental, "eastern". As pointed out below, the Latin *oriri* means "to rise". ED

[7] It is curious to note that Christ is sometimes called *Oriens*, a designation that can doubtless be related to the symbolism of the rising sun; but by reason of the double meaning we are indicating here it is possible that we should also, and even above all, relate it to the Hebrew *Elohi Qedem* or the expression designating the Word as the "Ancient of Days", that is, He who is before the days, or the Principle of the cycles of manifestation represented symbolically as "days" by various traditions (the "days of *Brahmā*" in the Hindu tradition, the "days of the creation" in the Hebrew *Genesis*).

the North as the "left side" (*shemōl* in Hebrew, *shimāl* in Arabic); but it also happens that orientation is established by turning toward the sun at the meridian, and the point before one is then no longer the East but the South. Thus in Arabic the South has among other names that of *qiblah*, and the adjective *qibli* means "southern" [*meridional*]. These last terms bring us to the root QBL; the same word *qiblah* is also known in Islam to designate the ritual orientation; in all cases it is the direction one has in front of one; and what is also rather curious is that the spelling of the word *qiblah* is exactly identical to that of the Hebrew *qabbalah*.

Now, one can ask why it is that in Hebrew "tradition" is designated by a word coming from the root QBL, and not from the root QDM. It is tempting to answer that since the Hebrew tradition constitutes only a secondary and derived form, a name evoking the idea of origin or primordiality would not be fitting; but this argument does not seem to us to be essential, for directly or not, every tradition is linked to its origins and proceeds from the primordial tradition, and we have even seen elsewhere that every sacred language, including Hebrew itself and Arabic, is thought to represent the primordial language in some way. The real reason, it seems, is that the idea that must especially be highlighted here is that of a regular and uninterrupted transmission, which is therefore properly expressed by the word "tradition", as we noted at the beginning. This transmission constitutes the "chain" (*shelsheleth* in Hebrew, *silsilah* in Arabic) that unites the present to the past and that must continue from the present into the future; it is the "chain of tradition" (*shelsheleth haqabbalah*) or the "initiatic chain". . . ; and it is also the determination of a "direction" (we find here the meaning of the Arabic *qiblah*) which, through the course of time, orients the cycle toward its end and joins it again with its origin, and which, extending even beyond these two extreme points by the fact that its principial source is timeless and "non-human", links it harmoniously to the other cycles, forming with these a greater "chain", that which certain Eastern traditions call the "chain of worlds" into which by degrees is integrated the entire order of universal manifestation.

28

The Symbolism of the Grail

In connection with the Knights of the Round Table it is not irrelevant to show the meaning of the "Grail quest", which, in legends of Celtic origin, is represented as their principal function. Every tradition contains such allusions to something which, at a certain time, became lost or hidden. There is, for example, the Hindu *Soma*—the Persian *Haoma*—the "draught of immortality" which has a most direct relationship with the Grail, for the latter is said to be the sacred vessel that contained the blood of Christ, which is also the "draught of immortality". In other cases the symbolism is different: thus according to the Jews it is the pronunciation of the great divine Name which is lost; but the fundamental idea always remains the same, and it will shortly appear to what, exactly, it corresponds.

The Holy Grail is said to be the cup used at the Last Supper, wherein Joseph of Arimathea received the blood and water from the wound opened in Christ's side by the lance of Longinus the Centurion.[1] According to legend, this cup was carried to Britain by Joseph of Arimathea himself along with Nicodemus;[2] and in this can be seen the indication of a link established between the Celtic tradition and Christianity. In fact, the cup plays a most important part in the majority of ancient traditions, and this, no doubt, applied particularly in the case of the Celts. The cup is also to be observed in frequent association with the lance, the two symbols then becoming in a certain way complementary; but it would take us far from our subject to enter into this.[3]

---

[1] The name Longinus is related to the name of the lance itself, Greek *logké* (pronounced *lonké*); the Latin *lancea* has the same root.

[2] These two personages here respectively represent the royal and sacerdotal powers, as did Arthur and Merlin at the institution of the Round Table.

[3] We merely observe that the symbolism of the lance frequently relates to the World Axis; under this aspect the blood which drips from the lance has the same significance as the dew emanating from the Tree of Life; it is well known that all traditions unanimously affirm that the vital principle is intimately linked with the blood.

Perhaps the clearest expression of the Grail's essential significance is found in the account of its origin: it tells that this cup had been carved by the angels from an emerald which fell from Lucifer's forehead at his downfall.[4] That emerald strikingly recalls the *urnā*, the frontal pearl which, in Hindu (and hence in Buddhist) symbolism, frequently replaced the third eye of Shiva, representing what might be called the "sense of eternity".[5] It is then said that the Grail was given into Adam's keeping in the Earthly Paradise, but that Adam, in his turn, lost it when he fell, for he could not bear it with him when he was driven out of Eden. Clearly, man being separated from his original center, thereafter found himself enclosed in the temporal sphere; he could no longer rejoin the unique point whence all things are contemplated under the aspect of eternity. In other words the possession of the "sense of eternity" is linked to what every tradition calls the "primordial state", the restoring of which constitutes the first stage of true initiation, since it is the necessary preliminary to conquest of "supra-human" states. . . .[6]

What follows might appear more enigmatic: Seth obtained reentry into the Earthly Paradise and was thus able to recover the precious vessel; now the name *Seth* expresses the ideas of foundation and stability and, consequently, indicates, in a certain manner, the restoration of the primordial order destroyed by the fall of man.[7] It can therefore be understood that Seth and those who possessed the

---

[4] Some say it was an emerald which fell from Lucifer's crown, but there is here a confusion arising from the fact that, before his fall, Lucifer was "The Angel of the Crown", which is in Hebrew *Hakathriel* (that is *Kether* [Hebrew for "crown"], the first *Sephirah*). The name has, incidentally, the numerical value 666.

[5] On this point see *Man and His Becoming According to the Vedānta*, chap. 20.

[6] On this "primordial" or "edenic" state, see *The Esoterism of Dante*, chaps. 6 and 8 and *Man and His Becoming According to the Vedānta*, chap. 23.

[7] Seth is said to have remained in the Earthly Paradise for forty years. The number 40 also carries a meaning of "reconciliation" or "return to the principle". Periods measured with this number are very frequently encountered in the Judeo-Christian tradition: for instance, the forty days of the Flood, the forty years in which the Israelites wandered in the desert, the forty days which Moses passed on Sinai, the forty days of Christ's fasting (Lent has, naturally, the same meaning); and there are, no doubt, other examples.

Grail after him were by this very fact, able to establish a spiritual center destined to replace the lost Paradise, and to serve as an image of it; thus possession of the Grail represents integral preservation of the primordial tradition in a particular spiritual center. The legend tells neither where nor by whom the Grail was preserved until the time of Christ; but its recognizably Celtic origin leaves it to be understood that the Druids had a part therein and must be counted among the regular custodians of the primordial tradition.

The loss of the Grail, or of one of its symbolic equivalents, is, in brief, the loss of tradition with all that the latter includes; nevertheless, the tradition is, in truth, hidden rather than lost; or at least it can only be lost as regards certain secondary centers, when they cease to be in direct relation with the supreme center. So far as the latter is concerned, it always preserves the deposit of tradition intact, and is not affected by the changes which occur in the outer world; thus, according to various Fathers of the Church and in particular Saint Augustine, the flood could not touch the Earthly Paradise which is "the dwelling of Enoch and the Land of the Saints"[8] and whose summit "touches the lunar sphere", that is to say finds itself beyond the domain of change (which is identified with the "sublunary world"), at the point of communication between the Earth and the Heavens. . . .[9]

The Grail, accordingly, represents two strictly interdependent things at the same time: one who integrally possesses the "primordial tradition", who has attained the degree of effective knowledge which this possession essentially implies, is thereby reintegrated into the fullness of the "primordial state". The double meaning inherent in the very word *Grail* relates to these two things, "the primordial state" and "the primordial tradition", for, through one of those verbal assimilations which frequently play a far from negligible role in symbolism, and which further have much more profound reasons than one would imagine at first glance, the Grail is at once a vessel (Old

---

[8] "And Enoch walked with God; and he was not (in the exterior and visible world), for God took him" (Gen. 5:24). He was then carried into the Earthly Paradise, as certain theologians such as Tostat and Cajetan have also believed. . . .

[9] In conformity with the symbolism used by Dante which places the Earthly Paradise at the summit of the mountain of Purgatory, identified by him with the "polar mountain" of all the traditions.

French *grasale*) and a book (*gradale* or *graduale*); this latter aspect plainly designates the tradition while the other more directly concerns the state itself.[10]

We do not intend to enter here upon the secondary details of the legend of the Holy Grail, though each has its symbolic value, nor to pursue the history of the "Knights of the Round Table" and their exploits; we merely recall that the "Round Table", constructed by King Arthur[11] from the plans of Merlin, was designed to receive the Grail when one of the Knights had succeeded in overcoming it and had brought it from Great Britain to Brittany. This table is also a symbol, probably of great antiquity, one of those always associated with the idea of spiritual centers that preserved tradition; the presence of twelve principal personages around the circular shape of the table is, moreover, a formal link with the cycle of the zodiac. . . .[12]

One other symbol relating to a different aspect of the Grail legend, merits special attention: it is that of *Montsalvat* (literally "Mountain of Salvation"), the peak standing "on distant shores that no mortal approaches", which is represented as situated, in an inaccessible region, in the midst of sea, and behind which the sun rises. It is at once the "sacred isle" and the "polar mountain", two equivalent symbols; it is the "Land of Immortality" which is naturally to be identified with the Earthly Paradise.[13]

Returning to the Grail itself, it is easy to realize that its primary significance is fundamentally the same as that of the sacred vessel

---

[10] In certain versions of the legend of the Holy Grail these two meanings are firmly fused, for the book becomes an inscription traced by Christ or by an angel on the cup itself. There are ready comparisons to be made here with the *Book of Life* and with certain elements of the symbolism of the Apocalypse.

[11] The name Arthur has an extremely remarkable meaning which attaches it to the "polar" symbolism and which we shall perhaps explain on some other occasion.

[12] The "Knights of the Round Table" are sometimes fifty in number (fifty was, among the Hebrews, the number of the Jubilee, and also relates to the "reign of the Holy Spirit"); but, even then, there were always twelve who played a preponderant role. The twelve peers of Charlemagne in other legendary medieval accounts may also be here borne in mind.

[13] The similarity of *Montsalvat* to *Meru* was pointed out to us by Hindus, and this led us to examine more closely the significance of the Western legend of the Grail.

wherever it is encountered, and notably in the East that of the sacrificial cup which originally contained, as pointed out above, the Vedic *Soma* or the Mazdean *Haoma*, that is, "the draught of immortality" which confers or restores, for those who receive it with the requisite disposition, the "sense of eternity". . . .

29

Islamic Esoterism

Of all traditional doctrines, perhaps Islamic doctrine most clearly distinguishes the two complementary parts, which can be labeled exoterism and esoterism. In Arabic terminology, these are the *sharī'ah*, literally the "great way", common to all, and the *ḥaqīqah*, literally the "inward truth", reserved to an elite, not because of some arbitrary decision, but by the very nature of things, since not all men possess the aptitudes or "qualifications" required to reach knowledge of the truth. To express their respective "outward" and "inward" natures, exoterism and esoterism are often compared to the "shell" (*qishr*) and the "kernel" (*lubb*), or to the circumference and its center. The *sharī'ah* comprises everything that in Western languages would be called "religious", and especially the whole of the social and legislative side which, in Islam, is essentially integrated into the religion. It could be said that the *sharī'ah* is first and foremost a rule of action, whereas the *ḥaqīqah* is pure knowledge; but it must be well understood that it is this knowledge that gives even the *sharī'ah* its higher and deeper meaning and its true *raison d'être*, so that even though not all those participating in the religion are aware of it, the *ḥaqīqah* is nevertheless its true principle, just as the center is the principle of the circumference.

But this is not all, for esoterism comprises not only the *ḥaqīqah*, but also the specific means for reaching it, and taken as a whole, these means are called the *ṭarīqah*, the "way" or "path" leading from the *sharī'ah* to the *ḥaqīqah*. If we return to the symbol of the circumference and its center, we can say that the *ṭarīqah* is represented by the radius that runs from the former to the latter. And this leads us to the following: to each point on the circumference there corresponds a radius, and all the radii, which are indefinite in number, terminate in the center. It can thus be said that these radii are so many *ṭuruq* (plural of *ṭarīqah*) adapted to the beings "situated" at the different points on the circumference according to the diversity of their individual natures. This is why it is said that "the ways to God are as numerous as the souls of men" (*at-ṭuruqu ila 'Llāhi ka-nufūsi bani Adam*). Thus the "ways" are many, and differ all the more among themselves the closer they are to their starting-point on the circumference; but their end is one, as there is only one center and one truth. Strictly speaking, the initial differences are effaced along with "individuality" itself (*al-innīya*, from *ana*, "I"); in other words, when the higher states of the being have been attained, and when the attributes (*sifāt*) of the creature (*'abd*, "slave")—which are really limitations—disappear (*al-fanā'*, "extinction"), leaving only those of Allah (*al-baqā'*, "permanence"), the being becoming identified with the latter [Divine attributes] in his "personality" or "essence" (*adh-dhāt*).

Esoterism, considered thus as comprising both *ṭarīqah* and *ḥaqīqah*, namely means and end, is designated in Arabic by the general term *taṣawwuf*, which can only be translated precisely as "initiation"—a point to which we will return later. Although *taṣawwuf* can be applied to any esoteric and initiatic doctrine, regardless of the traditional form to which it belongs, Westerners have coined the [derivative] term "Sufism" to designate Islamic esoterism; but, apart from being completely conventional, this term has the unfortunate disadvantage of inevitably suggesting by its "ism" suffix, the idea of a doctrine proper to a particular school, whereas this is not the case in reality, the only schools in question being the *ṭuruq*, which basically represent different methods, without there being any possibility of a fundamental difference of doctrine, for "the doctrine of Unity is unique" (*at-tawḥīdu wāḥid*). As for the derivation of the terms *taṣawwuf* and "Sufism", they obviously come from the word *ṣūfī*, and here it must first be said that no one can ever call himself a *ṣūfī*, except from pure ignorance, for he proves thereby that he is not truly so, this quality necessarily being a secret (*sirr*) between the true *ṣūfī* and Allah; one can only call oneself a *mutaṣawwuf*, a term applied to anyone who has entered upon the initiatic "way", whatever the "degree" he may have reached; but the *ṣūfī*, in the true sense of the term, is only the one who has reached the supreme degree.

Some have sought to assign the most diverse origins to the Arabic word *ṣūfī*; but this question is undoubtedly unsolvable from our present position, and we freely admit that the word has too many proposed etymologies, of equal plausibility, for only one to be true; in reality, we must rather see herein a purely symbolic name, a sort of "cipher", which, as such, requires no linguistic derivation strictly speaking; and this is not unique, for one can find comparable cases in other traditions. As for the so-called etymologies, these are basically only phonetic resemblances, which, moreover, according to the laws of a certain symbolism, effectively correspond to relationships between various ideas which have come to be grouped more or less as accessories around the word in question. But given the character of the Arabic language (a character which it shares with Hebrew), the primary and fundamental meaning of a word is to be found in the numerical values of the letters; and in fact, what is particularly remarkable is that the sum of the numerical values of the letters which form the word *ṣūfī* has the same number as *al-Hikmatu'l-ilahiya*, "Divine Wisdom". The true *ṣūfī* is therefore the one who possesses this Wisdom, or, in other words, he is *al-'ārif bi 'Llāh*, that is to say "he who knows through God", for God cannot be known except by Himself; and this is the supreme or "total" degree of knowledge or *haqīqah*.[1]

From the preceding, we can draw several important consequences, the foremost being that "Sufism" is not something that was "added" to Islamic doctrine as an afterthought and from outside, but, on the contrary, is an essential part of it, since without it, Islamic doctrine would be manifestly incomplete, and, what is more, incomplete "from above", that is to say in regard to its very principle. The completely gratuitous supposition of a foreign origin—Greek, Persian, or Indian—is in any case formally contradicted by the fact that the means of expression of Islamic esoterism are intimately linked with the very constitution of the Arabic language; and if there are incontestable similarities with doctrines of the same order existing elsewhere, these can be explained quite naturally and without recourse to hypothetical "borrowings", for, truth being one, all traditional doctrines

---

[1] In a work on *taṣawwuf*, written in Arabic, but from a very modern perspective, a Syrian writer so ill acquainted with us as to mistake us for an "orientalist", has taken it into his head to address a rather singular reproach to us: having somehow read *al-Sūfiah* in place of *Ṣūfī* (in a special issue of *Cahiers du Sud* in 1935 on "Islam and the West"), he imagined that my calculation was inexact; wishing then to make the calculation himself according to his own lights, he managed, by way of several errors in the numeric value of the letters, to arrive (this time as equivalent to *al-Sūfī*, which is still wrong) at *al-hakīm al-ilahī*, without, moreover, perceiving that, one *ya* being equal to two *ha*'s, these words form exactly the same total as *al-hakmah al-ilahiya*! We know well enough that academic teaching of the present day is ignorant of the *abjad* [the alphabet], and is only familiar with the simple grammatical order of the letters; but just the same, when someone undertakes to treat these questions, such ignorance passes beyond the acceptable limits. Be that as it may, *al-hakīm al-ilahī* and *al-hakmah al-ilahiya* have basically the same meaning; but the first of these two expressions has a somewhat unusual character, while the second, as we have indicated, is, on the contrary, completely traditional.

are necessarily identical in their essence, whatever the diversity of the forms in which they are clothed. As regards this question of origins, it is of little importance whether the word *ṣūfī* and its derivatives (*taṣawwuf, mutaṣawwuf*) have existed in the language from the beginning or have appeared at some later juncture, this being a great subject for discussion among historians; the thing may well have existed before the word, or under another name, or even without it having been found necessary to give it one. In any case—and this ought to settle the matter for anyone not regarding things merely from the outside—tradition expressly indicates that esoterism, as well as exoterism, proceeds directly from the very teaching of the Prophet, and, in fact, every authentic and regular *ṭarīqah* possesses a *silsilah* or "chain" of initiatic transmission that ultimately goes back to him through a varying number of intermediaries. Even if, subsequently, some *ṭuruq* really did "borrow", or, better said, "adapt", certain details of their particular methods, this has a very secondary importance, and in no way affects what is essential; and here again similarities may equally well be explained by the possession of the same knowledge, especially as regards the "science of rhythm" in its various branches. The truth is that "Sufism" is as Arab as the Koran itself, in which it has its direct principles; but in order to find them there, the Koran must be understood and interpreted according to the *ḥaqāʾiq* (plural of *ḥaqīqah*) which constitute its deepest meaning, and not simply by the linguistic, logical, and theological procedures of the *ʿulamā aẓ-ẓāhir* (literally the "doctors of the outward") or doctors of the *shariʿah*, whose competence extends only to the exoteric realm. It is a question here of two clearly different domains, and this is why there can never be any contradiction or any real conflict between them; it is moreover obvious that one cannot in any way oppose exoterism and esoterism, since on the contrary the second finds its foundation and point of departure in the first, and since they are really no more than the two aspects or the two faces of one and the same doctrine. . . .

In its essence, initiatic doctrine is purely metaphysical in the true and original meaning of this term; but in Islam, as in other traditional forms, it also includes a complex ensemble of "traditional sciences" by way of more or less direct applications to various contingent realms. These sciences are as if suspended from the metaphysical principles on which they depend and from which they derive, and draw from this attachment (and from the "transpositions" which it permits) all their real value; they are thereby an integral part of the doctrine itself, although to a secondary and subordinate degree, and not more or less artificial and superfluous accretions. There seems to be something here that is particularly difficult for Westerners to understand, doubtless because their own environment offers no point of comparison in this regard; nevertheless there were analogous Western sciences in antiquity and the Middle Ages, but these are entirely forgotten by modern men, who ignore the true nature of things and often are not even aware of their existence. . . . Such is the science of numbers and of letters, of which we gave an example in the interpretation of the term *ṣūfī*, and which, in a comparable form, can be found only in the Hebrew *Kabbalah*, by virtue of the close affinity of the languages which are the vehicles of expression for these two traditions, languages of which only this science can give the most profound understanding. Such are also the various "cosmological" sciences which are included in part in what is called "Hermeticism"; and in this connection we must note that alchemy is taken in a "material" sense only by the ignorant, for whom symbolism is a dead letter, those very people whom the true alchemists of the Middle Ages stigmatized as "puffers" and "charcoal burners", and who were the true precursors of modern chemistry, however unflattering such an origin may be for the latter. Likewise astrology, another cosmological science, is in reality something entirely other than the "divining art" or the "science of conjecture" which alone is what modern people see in it. Above all it has to do with the knowledge of "cyclical laws" which play an important role in all traditional doctrines. Moreover, there is a certain correspondence between all these sciences which, since they proceed from essentially the same principles, may be regarded as various representations of one and the same thing from a certain point of view. Thus, astrology, alchemy, and even the science of letters do nothing but translate the same truths into the languages proper to different orders of reality, united among themselves by the law of universal analogy, the foundation of every symbolic correspondence; and, by virtue of this same analogy, these sciences, by an appropriate transposition, find their application in the realm of the "microcosm" as well as in that of the "macrocosm", for the initiatic process reproduces in all its phases the cosmological process itself. To have a full awareness of all these correlations, it is necessary to have reached a very high degree in the initiatic hierarchy, a degree which is called that of "red sulfur" (*al-Kebrīt al-ahmar*); and whoever possesses this degree may, by means of the science known as *sīmiyā* (a word that must not be confused with *kīmiyā*), and by operating certain mutations on letters and numbers, act on the beings and things that correspond to these in the cosmic order. *Jafr*, which according to tradition owes its origin to Seyidna 'Alī himself, is an application of these same sciences to the prevision of future events; and this application, in which the cyclical laws to which we alluded just now naturally intervene, exhibits all the rigor of an exact and mathematical science for those who can understand and interpret it (for it possesses a kind of "cryptography", which in fact is no more astonishing than algebraic notation). One could mention many other "traditional sciences", some of which might seem even stranger to those who are not used to such things; but we must content ourselves with this, and restrict ourselves to generalities, in keeping with the scope of this exposition.

Finally, we must add one last observation of capital importance for understanding the true character of initiatic doctrine: this doctrine has nothing to do with "erudition" and could never be learned by the reading of books in the manner of ordinary or "profane" knowledge. The writings of the greatest masters themselves can only serve as "supports" for meditation; one does not become a *mutaṣawwuf* simply by having read them, and in any case they remain mostly incomprehensible to those who are not "qualified". Indeed, it is necessary above all to possess certain innate dispositions or aptitudes which no amount of effort can replace; then, it is necessary to have an attachment to a regular *silsilah*, for the transmission of the "spiritual influence" that is obtained by this attachment is, as we have already said, the essential condition, failing which there is no initiation, even of the most elementary degree. This transmission, which is acquired once and for all, must be the point of departure of a purely inward work for which all the outward means are no more than aids and supports, albeit necessary, given that one must take the nature of the human being such as it actually is into account; and it is by this inward work alone that a being, if capable of it, will ascend from degree to degree, to the summit of the initiatic hierarchy, to the "Supreme Identity", the absolutely permanent and unconditioned state beyond the limitations of all contingent and transitory existence, which is the state of the true *ṣūfī*.

30

Taoism and Confucianism

For the most part, ancient peoples bothered little about establishing a strict chronology for their history; some even used only symbolic numbers, at least for the most remote epochs, and we would be seriously mistaken in taking these as dates in the ordinary and literal sense of that word. In this respect, however, the Chinese constitute a remarkable exception and are perhaps the only people to have taken constant care, from the very origin of their tradition, to date their annals by means of precise astronomical observations, including the description of the state of the heavens at the moment when the events recorded took place. Thus we can be more definite regarding China and its ancient history than in many other cases, and know that the tradition we may properly call Chinese originated around 3,700 years before the Christian era. By a rather curious coincidence, this same epoch is also the beginning of the Hebrew era, although for this latter it would be difficult to say what event really marks its starting-point.

However remote such an origin may appear when one compares it with that of the Greco-Roman civilization and with the dates of so-called "classical" antiquity, it is in fact still fairly recent. What was the state of the yellow race, which at that time probably inhabited certain regions of central Asia, before 3,700 BC? In the absence of sufficiently explicit data it is impossible to say with any precision; it seems that for an indeterminate length of time this race went through a period of obscurity, and was roused from this slumber at a moment also marked by changes important for other sectors of humanity. It is then possible—and indeed is the only thing that can be affirmed outright—that what appears as a beginning may in reality have been the awakening of a much earlier tradition, which, moreover, had to be put in another form at that time to adapt to new conditions. However that may be, the history of China, or of what is so named today, only begins with Fu-Hsi, who is regarded as its first emperor; and it must immediately be added that the name of Fu-Hsi, to which is linked the whole body of sciences that make up the very essence of the Chinese tradition, in reality seems to designate a whole period lasting for several centuries.

To fix the principles of the tradition, Fu-Hsi made use of linear symbols that were both simple and at the same time as synthetic as possible, that is, the continuous line and the broken line, respectively signs of *yang* and *yin*, that is, of the two principles, active and passive, which, proceeding from a sort of polarization of the supreme metaphysical Unity, give birth to the whole of universal manifestation. From the combinations of these two signs in all their possible arrangements, are formed the eight *kua* or "trigrams", which have always remained the fundamental symbols of the Far-Eastern tradition. It is said that "before tracing the trigrams, Fu-Hsi looked at the Heaven, then lowered his eyes to the Earth, observed its details, considered the characteristics of the human body and of all external things".[1] This text is especially interesting in that it contains the formal expression of the "Great Triad": Heaven and Earth, or the two complementary principles from which all beings spring, and man, who, by his nature partaking of both, is the middle term of the triad, the mediator between Heaven and Earth.[2] Here we should specify that we refer to "true man", that is, he who having reached the full development of his higher faculties "can assist Heaven and Earth in the maintenance and transformation of beings, and by that very fact constitute a third power along with Heaven and Earth".[3] It is also said that Fu-Hsi saw a dragon emerge from the river, uniting in itself the powers of Heaven and Earth, and bearing the trigrams inscribed on its back, which is another way of expressing the same thing symbolically.

Thus the whole tradition was first contained essentially and as if in germ in the trigrams, symbols marvelously adapted to serving as support for an indefinitude of possibilities; it only remained to draw from them all the necessary developments, whether in the domain of pure metaphysical knowledge itself, or in its diverse applications to the cosmic and human orders. To this end Fu-Hsi wrote three books, of which only the last, the *I Ching*, or "Book of Changes", has survived. The text of this book is so synthetic that it can be understood in many senses, nonetheless perfectly concordant among themselves,

---

[1] *The Book of the Rites of the Kingdom of Chou.*

[2] See *The Great Triad*, especially chap. 3. ED

[3] *Ch'ung Yung*, chap. 22.

according to whether one keeps strictly to the principles themselves or applies them to this or that determinate order. Thus, besides the metaphysical sense, there are a multitude of contingent applications of unequal importance which constitute as many traditional sciences. In this way it can be applied to logic, mathematics, astronomy, physiology, social organization, and so on; and there is even a divinatory application, which, however, is considered the most inferior of all, and the practice of which is left to wandering minstrels. Besides, it is characteristic of all traditional doctrines that from the outset they contain within themselves the possibilities of all conceivable developments, including those of an indefinite variety of sciences of which the modern West has not the slightest idea, and of all the adaptations that might be required by later circumstances. There is thus no cause to be astonished that the teachings contained in the *I Ching*, which Fu-Hsi himself claimed to have drawn from a past very ancient and difficult to date, should in turn have become the common basis of the two doctrines in which the Chinese tradition has been maintained to the present, and which, by reason of the completely different domains to which they relate, seem at first sight to have no point of contact, namely Taoism and Confucianism.

What were the circumstances that after roughly three thousand years rendered a re-adaptation of the traditional doctrine necessary, that is to say, a change not in the foundation, which in itself always remained strictly the same, but as it were in the forms into which this doctrine was incorporated? This is another point that it would doubtless be difficult to elucidate fully, for in China and elsewhere such things scarcely leave a trace in recorded history, where exterior effects are much more apparent than the profound causes. What seems certain in any case is that the doctrine such as it had been formulated in the time of Fu-Hsi had generally ceased to be understood in its most essential aspects; and doubtless, too, the applications which had been drawn from it in the past, especially concerning social matters, no longer corresponded to the racial conditions of existence, which must have been changed perceptibly in the interval.

It was then the sixth century before the Christian era, and it is notable that this century saw considerable change among almost all peoples, so that it would seem that what happened in China at that time should be attributed to a cause, perhaps difficult to define, that affected the whole of terrestrial humanity. What is remarkable is that in a general way the sixth century can be considered as the beginning of the properly "historical" period. When one goes farther back, it is impossible to establish even an approximate chronology, except in a few exceptional cases, as, for example, precisely that of China. On the other hand, beginning with this epoch, dates of events are everywhere known with a fair degree of accuracy, which is assuredly a fact deserving our attention. Moreover, the changes that took place at the time present different characteristics according to the country. India, for instance, saw the birth of Buddhism, that is, a revolt against the traditional spirit going as far as the negation of all authority, even to veritable anarchy in the intellectual and social orders;[4] in China, on the contrary, the two new doctrinal forms, which were given the names Taoism and Confucianism, were constituted simultaneously and strictly within the line of tradition.

The founders of these two doctrines, Lao Tzu and Kung Tzu (whom Westerners call Confucius) were thus in fact contemporaries, and history tells us that one day they met:

> "Hast thou discovered Tao?" asked Lao Tzu. "I have sought it twenty-seven years", replied Kung Tzu, "and I have not yet found it." Whereupon Lao Tzu gave his visitor these few precepts. "The sage loves obscurity; he does not throw himself at every comer; he studies times and circumstances. If the moment is propitious, he speaks; otherwise, he keeps silent. Whoever possesses a treasure does not display it before the whole world; in the same way, one who is truly a sage does not unveil his wisdom to the whole world. That is all I have to say to you; make what profit you can out of it!"

---

[4] Guénon later revised his views on Buddhism, largely through the influence of A. K. Coomaraswamy and Marco Pallis. In his last revision of *The Crisis of the Modern World* (chap. 1, n. 4), in which the identical statement regarding Buddhism is found, Guénon added the following note: "The question of Buddhism is by no means so simple as this brief account of it might suggest; and it is interesting to note that if, as far as their own tradition is concerned, the Hindus have always condemned the Buddhists, this is not the case with the Buddha himself, for whom many of them have a great reverence, some going so far as to see in him the ninth *Avatāra*. As for Buddhism such as it is known today, one should be careful, in dealing with it, to distinguish between its *Mahāyāna* and its *Hīnayāna* forms, that is, between the 'Greater' and the 'Lesser' Vehicles; in general one may say that Buddhism outside India differs markedly from the original Indian form, which began to lose ground rapidly after the death of Ashoka and eventually disappeared." ED

On returning from this interview Kung Tzu said, "I have seen Lao Tzu; he is like the dragon. As for the dragon, I know not how it can be borne by winds and clouds and raise itself to Heaven."

This anecdote, reported by the historian Ssu-Ma-Chi'en, perfectly delineates the respective positions of the two doctrines, or rather of the two branches of the doctrine, into which the Far-Eastern tradition would henceforth be divided: the one essentially consisting of pure metaphysics, to which are joined all the traditional sciences of which the scope is strictly speaking speculative, or rather "cognitive"; the other, confined to the practical domain and keeping exclusively to the field of social applications. Kung Tzu himself admitted that he was not at all "born to Knowledge", that is, that he had not attained to knowledge *par excellence*, which is that of the metaphysical and supra-rational order; he was acquainted with traditional symbols, but he had not penetrated their deepest meaning. That is why his work was necessarily to be limited to one particular and contingent domain, which alone was within his competence; but at least he was careful not to deny what lay beyond his understanding. His later disciples did not always imitate him in this, and at times some of then exhibited a narrow exclusivism—a defect widespread among "specialists" of all kinds—and this brought forth various ripostes of scathing irony on the part of the great Taoist commentators of the fourth century such as Lieh Tzu, and more especially Chuang Tzu. However, it must not be inferred from such disputes that Taoism and Confucianism are rival schools, for this they never were and never could be, since each has its proper and clearly distinct domain. Their co-existence is thus perfectly normal and regular, and in some respects their distinction corresponds fairly exactly to what in other civilizations is that between the spiritual authority and the temporal power.

We have already said, moreover, that the two doctrines share a common root, namely the earlier tradition. Neither Kung Tzu nor Lao Tzu ever intended to expound conceptions of their own, which, as such, would have lacked all authority and any real influence. "I am a man who has loved the ancients and who has bent all his efforts toward acquiring their sciences", said Kung Tzu;[5] and this attitude,

[5] *Liun-Yu*, chap. 7.

which is the very opposite of the individualism of modern Westerners with their pretensions to "originality" at any cost, is the only one compatible with the establishment of a traditional civilization. The word "re-adaptation" which we have used before is therefore the one that indeed fits here; and the social institutions that resulted from it were endowed with a remarkable stability, for they lasted twenty-five centuries and survived all the periods of disorder that China underwent until recently. We have no wish to dwell further on these institutions, which moreover are fairly well-known in broad outline; but it is worth recalling that their essential characteristic is to take the family as foundation and from there to extend itself to the race, which is the totality of families belonging to one and the same original stock. One of the special characteristics of the Chinese civilization is in fact that it is founded on the idea of race and the solidarity that unites its members among themselves, whereas other civilizations, which generally include men belonging to diverse or poorly-defined races, rest on completely different principles of unity.

Usually when one speaks in the West of China and its doctrines, it is almost exclusively Confucianism that comes to mind. This is not to say that it is always interpreted correctly, for some make of it a kind of Eastern "positivism", whereas in reality it is something totally different, first by reason of its traditional character, and then also because, as we have said, it is an application of superior principles, whereas "positivism", on the contrary, implies a negation of such principles. As for Taoism, it is generally passed over in silence, and many seem to be ignorant of its very existence, or at any rate to believe that it disappeared long ago and today presents only an historical or archaeological interest. In what follows, we shall see the reasons for this mistake.

Lao Tzu wrote only one treatise, which, moreover, was extremely concise, called the *Tao Te Ching* or "Book of the Way and of Rectitude"; all other Taoist texts are either commentaries on this fundamental book or later versions of various complementary teachings that originally had been purely oral. The *Tao*, which is translated literally as "Way", and which gave its name to the doctrine itself, is the supreme Principle envisaged from a strictly metaphysical standpoint; it is both the origin and the end of all beings, as is very clearly indicated by the ideographic character that represents it. The *Te*—which we prefer to render as "Rectitude" rather than "Virtue", as is sometimes done, so as not to seem to give it a "moral" meaning that is not at all in keeping with the outlook of Taoism—is what could be called a "specification" of the *Tao* with respect to a determinate being, such as the human being for instance; it is the direction which that being must follow in order that its existence in its present state shall be according to the Way, or, in other words, in conformity with the Principle. Thus, at the outset Lao Tzu takes his stand in the universal order and then descends to an application; but although this application is specifically made to the case of man, it is in no way done from a social or moral point of view; what is always and exclusively envisaged is the connection with the Supreme Principle, so that in reality we never leave the metaphysical domain.

Consequently Taoism does not attribute importance to outward action, which it ultimately holds as unimportant, and it expressly teaches the doctrine of "non-action". In general, Westerners have some difficulty grasping this doctrine in its true significance, but they could be helped by recalling the Aristotelian theory of the "unmoved mover" which has essentially the same meaning, but from which they never seem to have drawn all the consequences. "Non-action" is not inertia, but on the contrary implies the fullness of activity, but an activity that is transcendent and altogether interior, non-manifested, in union with the Principle, and thus beyond all the distinctions and appearances that most people mistakenly take for reality itself, whereas they are only more or less distant reflections of it. Moreover, we should also note that Confucianism itself, though its point of view is that of action, nonetheless speaks of the "invariable middle", that is, of the state of perfect equilibrium shielded from the incessant vicissitudes of the outer world. Now in the case of Confucianism this can only be the expression of a purely theoretical ideal, and in its contingent realm it can at most grasp a mere image of true "non-action", whereas for Taoism it is a question of something altogether different, namely, a fully effective realization of this transcendent state. Placed at the center of the cosmic wheel, the perfect sage moves it invisibly by his presence alone, without participating in its movement and untroubled by the need to exercise any action whatsoever; his absolute detachment makes him master of all things because he can no longer be affected by anything.

He has attained such perfect impassibility, for him life and death are alike indifferent, and the collapse of the world would move him not at all. By penetration he has reached the Immutable Truth, the Knowledge of the One Universal Principle. He lets all the beings roll on according to their destinies, while himself he keeps to the Immobile Center of all destinies. . . . The outward sign of this inner state is imperturbability, not that of the warrior who for love of glory swoops down upon an army ranged in battle, but that of the spirit, superior to Heaven, to Earth, and to all beings, who dwells in a body for which he cares not, taking no account of the images perceived by his senses and knowing all, in his immobile unity, by a knowledge all-embracing. This absolutely independent spirit is the master of men; if it pleased him to summon them all together, all would run to his bidding on the day appointed; but he does not care to be served.[6]

If a true sage, much in spite of himself, had to take charge of an empire, keeping himself to non-action, he would make use of the leisure of his non-intervention by giving free rein to his natural propensities. The empire would prosper for having been put in the hands of this man. Without bringing his faculties into play, without using his bodily senses, seated motionless, he would behold all with his transcendent eye; absorbed in contemplation, he would shake all like thunder; the sky would conform obediently to the motions of his spirit; all beings would follow the impulse of his non-intervention, as dust follows the wind. Why should this man seek to guide the empire, when letting it go on is enough?[7]

We have insisted particularly on this doctrine of "non-action", for besides the fact that it is one of the most important and most characteristic aspects of Taoism, there are other more particular reasons for doing so that will be better understood from what follows. But one question that arises is this: how can one attain the state described as that of the perfect sage? Here, as in all analogous doctrines found in other civilizations, the answer is very clear. One attains it exclusively through knowledge, but this knowledge, which Kung Tzu admitted to never having obtained, is of an order altogether different from

[6] Ibid., chap. 5.

[7] Ibid., chap. 11.

ordinary or "profane" knowledge, and has no connection whatsoever with the exterior learning of the "scholars", and even less so with science as understood by modern Westerners. This is not a case of incompatibility, although, by reason of the barriers which it sets and of the mental habits it imposes, ordinary science may often be an obstacle to the acquisition of true knowledge; but whoever possesses the latter is bound to hold as negligible the relative and contingent speculations with which most men rest content, the detailed analyses and researches in which they lose themselves, and the many divergent opinions that inevitably result.

> Philosophers lose themselves in their speculations, sophists in their distinctions, investigators in their researches. All these men are caught within the limits of space and blinded by particular beings.[8]

The sage, on the contrary, has passed beyond all the distinctions inherent in external points of view; at the central point where he abides, all opposition has disappeared, having been resolved into a perfect equilibrium.

> In the primordial state, these oppositions did not exist. They all derived from the diversity of beings and from their contacts caused by the universal gyration. They would cease, if difference and motion were to cease. They cease at once to affect the being that has reduced his distinct individuality and his particular motion to almost nothing. This being no longer enters into conflict with any other being, for he is established in the infinite, effaced in the indefinite. He has reached the point from which start all transformations, wherein are no conflicts, and there he abides. By concentrating his nature, by nourishing his vital spirit, by bringing together all his powers, he is united to the principle of all births. Inasmuch as his nature is whole, and his vital spirit intact, no being can harm him.[9]

It is for this reason and not from any kind of skepticism, which is obviously excluded by the degree of knowledge he has attained, that

---

[8] Ibid., chap. 24.

[9] Ibid., chap. 19.

the sage keeps himself entirely outside of all discussions that agitate the generality of men; for him, in fact, all contrary opinions are equally valueless, because, by very reason of their opposition, they are all equally relative.

> His own viewpoint is one where this and that, yes and no, seem still to be undistinguished. This point is the hinge of the norm; it is the immobile center of a circumference on whose contours all contingencies, distinctions, and individualities roll; hence one sees only one infinity, which is neither this nor that, neither yes nor no. To see everything in as yet undifferentiated primordial unity, or from such a distance that all dissolves into one, is true intelligence. Let us not busy ourselves with distinguishing, but let us see everything in the unity of the norm. Let us not debate in order to get the better, but let us use, toward others, the method of the monkey-trainer. This man said to the monkeys he was training: "I will give you three taros in the morning and four in the evening." But not one of the monkeys was satisfied. "So be it", said he, "I will give you four in the morning and three in the evening." All the monkeys were satisfied. Thus not only did he satisfy them, but also he gave them only the seven taros a day which he had intended for them in the first place. Thus does the sage; he says yes and no, for the sake of peace, and remains calm at the center of the Universal Wheel, indifferent as to the direction of its turning.[10]

We need hardly say that the state of the perfect sage with all that this implies (which we cannot discuss at length here), cannot be attained at one stroke, and that even the degrees inferior to this state, which are as it were so many preliminary stages, are only accessible at the price of efforts of which very few men are capable. The methods employed to this end by Taoism are, moreover, particularly difficult to follow, and the help they furnish is much more restricted than that found in the traditional teaching of other civilizations such as India, for example; they are in any case almost impracticable for men belonging to races other than that for which they are particularly adapted. Moreover, even in China, Taoism has never been very widespread, nor has it ever sought to be, having always abstained from propagandizing

---

[10] Ibid., chap. 2.

since its very nature imposes this reserve on it; it is a very closed and essentially "initiatic" doctrine, which as such is destined for an elite only, and could not be propounded to everyone without distinction, for not all are suited to understand it, and still fewer to "realize" it. It is said that Lao Tzu entrusted his teaching to two disciples only, who themselves instructed ten others; after writing the *Tao Te Ching*, he disappeared toward the West, doubtless taking refuge in some almost inaccessible retreat in Tibet or the Himalayas, and, says the historian Ssu-Ma-Chi'en, "no one knows how or where he ended his days".

The doctrine common to all, and which everyone must study and put into practice according to his capacity, is Confucianism, which, embracing everything to do with social relations, is fully sufficient for the needs of ordinary life. However, since Taoism represents principial knowledge from which all the rest derives, in a way Confucianism is really only an application thereof to a contingent order and is by right subordinate by its very nature; but this is something that need not concern the masses and that they may not even suspect since only the practical application falls within their intellectual horizon; and the masses we speak of certainly include the great majority of Confucian "scholars" themselves. All questions of form aside, this *de facto* separation between Taoism and Confucianism, between the inner and the outer doctrine, constitute one of the most notable differences between the civilizations of China and India; the latter has only one body of unified doctrine, namely Brāhmanism, which includes both the principle and all its applications, so that there is no break in continuity from the lowest to the highest degrees. To a great extent this difference reflects the mental conditions of the two peoples; however, it is very probable that the continuity that has been maintained in India, and no doubt in India alone, also formerly existed in China, from the epoch of Fu-Hsi up to that of Lao Tzu and Kung Tzu.

It is now clear why Taoism is so little known to Westerners; outwardly it is unlike Confucianism, which has visible effects on all circumstances of social life; rather it is the exclusive attribute of an elite perhaps fewer in number today than ever before, which in no way seeks to communicate to outsiders the doctrine of which it is the guardian; finally, its very point of view, its mode of expression, and its methods of teaching are as foreign as possible to the spirit of the modern West. Some people, while aware of the existence of Taoism and admitting that it is still living, nevertheless imagine that its influence on the whole of Chinese civilization is practically negligible, if not altogether null, because of its closed character; this again is a grave error, and it now remains for us to explain the true situation as far as possible.

Referring back to the texts quoted above concerning "non-action", it will be readily understood, at least in principle if not in the modalities of its application, that the role of Taoism must be one of invisible direction, dominating events rather than taking part in them directly, and all the more efficacious for not being clearly evident in exterior movements. As stated above, Taoism fulfills the function of the "unmoved mover"; it does not seek to interfere in action, and is even entirely uninterested in it insofar as it sees in action a mere momentary and transitory modification, an infinitesimal element of the "current of forms", a point on the circumference of the "cosmic wheel". Taoism, on the other hand, is like the pivot around which the wheel turns, or the norm by which its motion is regulated, precisely because it does not participate in that movement, and this is so even without express intervention on its part. Everything that is carried along in the revolutions of the wheel changes and passes; only that remains which, being united with the Principle, abides invariably at the center, immovable as the Principle itself; and the center, which nothing can affect in its undifferentiated unity, is the starting-point of the indefinite multitude of modifications that constitute universal manifestation.

Since the perfect sage is the only being actually to have reached the center, we should immediately add that what we have just said regarding his state and function applies in all strictness only to the supreme degree of the Taoist hierarchy; the other degrees are like intermediaries between the center and the outer world, and, just as the spokes of a wheel start from the hub and join it to the circumference, so these degrees assure the uninterrupted transmission of influence emanating from the invariable point where "non-acting action" resides. The word "influence", and not "action", is the most suitable here, although one might also speak of an "action of presence"; and even the lower degrees, though very far from the fullness of "non-action", nevertheless still partake of it in a certain way. Besides, the means by which this influence is communicated necessarily escape those who only see the outside of things; they would be as unintelligible to the Western mind, and for the same reasons, as are the methods by which accession is gained to the various degrees of the hierarchy. It would thus be perfectly useless to dwell upon what are called "temples without doors" and "colleges without teachers", or upon the constitution of organizations that have none of the character-istics of a "society" in the European sense of the word, and that have no definite outward form, and sometimes not even a name, which nevertheless forge the most effective and the most indissoluble link that can exist between their members—all this would mean nothing to the Western imagination, since it is familiar with nothing that could furnish any valid term of comparison.

At the most exterior level, organizations no doubt exist that seem more comprehensible since they are engaged in the domain of action, although they may still be as secret as all the Western associations which, with more or less justification, claim to possess such a char-acter. These organizations generally have only a temporary existence; formed for a specific purpose, they disappear without a trace as soon as their mission has been accomplished; in fact they are only emana-tions of other, more profound and permanent organizations from which they receive their real direction, even when their apparent leaders are entirely outside the Taoist hierarchy. Some of these leaders who played a considerable role in the distant past, have left in the popular mind memories that are expressed in legendary form; thus we have heard it said that in the past the masters of a particular secret organization would take a handful of pins and throw them on the ground, and that from them would spring so many armed soldiers. This is precisely the story of Cadmus sowing the teeth of the dragon; and these legends conceal beneath their ingenuous appearance a very real symbolic value which only the common man makes the mistake of taking literally.

It can often happen that the associations in question, or at least those that are most outward, stand in opposition to or even in con-flict with one another. As a result superficial observers will not fail to object to what we have just said, and to conclude that unity of direc-tion cannot exist in such conditions. These people will have forgotten only one thing, which is that the direction in question is "beyond" the opposition they point to, and not in the domain in which this oppo-sition occurs and where alone it is valid. If we had to reply to such objections, we would limit ourselves to recalling the Taoist teaching of the equivalence of the "yes" and the "no" in the primordial indistinction, and, as for putting this teaching into practice, we would simply refer them to the fable of the monkey-trainer.

We think we have said enough to make it understood that the real influence of Taoism can be extremely important, while yet remaining invisible and hidden; it is not only in China that things of this sort exist, but there they seem to be in more constant use than anywhere else. It will also be understood that those who have some knowledge of the part played by this traditional organization must be wary of appearances and very reserved in assessing events such as those presently taking place in the Far East, which too often one judges by comparison with events in the West, thus placing them in a completely false light. Chinese civilization has weathered many other crises in the past, and it has always found its equilibrium again in the end; in fact, there is nothing to indicate that the present crisis is more serious than preceding ones, and even if it were, this would still be no reason for supposing that it must necessarily penetrate to that which is deepest and most essential in the tradition of the race, and which moreover a very small number of men would suffice to preserve intact in periods of trouble, for things of this order do not depend on the brute force of the multitude. Confucianism, which represents only the exterior aspect of the tradition, might even disappear should social conditions happen to change to the point of requiring the establishment of an entirely new form; but Taoism is beyond such contingencies. Let us not forget that the sage, according to the Taoist teachings we have cited, "remains at rest at the center of the cosmic wheel", whatever may be the circumstances, and that "even the collapse of the universe would not cause him any emotion".

31

Rite and Symbol

... Rites and symbols, both of which are essential elements of every initiation, and, more generally are associated with everything traditional, are in fact closely linked by their very nature. All the constituent elements of a rite necessarily have a symbolic sense, whereas, inversely, a symbol produces—and this indeed is its essential purpose—in one who meditates upon it with the requisite aptitudes and disposition, effects rigorously comparable to those of rites properly speaking, with the reservation of course that when this meditation is undertaken there be, as a preliminary condition, that regular initiatic transmission failing which the rites would be in any case nothing more than a vain counterfeit, as with their pseudo-initiatic parodies. We must also add that the origin of authentic rites and symbols (anything less does not deserve the name, since it amounts in the end to entirely profane and fraudulent imitations) is likewise "non-human". Thus the impossibility of assigning to them any definite author or maker is not due to a lack of information, as profane historians suppose (that is, if for want of a better solution they have not been driven to look on them as the product of a sort of "collective consciousness", which, even if it existed, would in any case be quite incapable of producing things of a transcendent order, such as these), but is a necessary consequence of that very origin, something that can only be contested by those who completely misunderstand the true nature of tradition and of all its integral parts, as is evidently the case with rites and symbols.

If the fundamental identity of rites and symbols is more closely examined, it will first be noted that a symbol, understood as a "graphic" figuration, as it is most commonly, is only as it were the fixation of a ritual gesture.[1] In fact it often happens that for a symbol to be regular, its actual tracing must be accomplished under conditions that confer upon it all the characteristics of a true rite. A very clear

---

[1] These considerations relate directly to what we have called the "theory of gestures", to which we have alluded on several occasions but have not had occasion to explain until now.

example of this in a lower domain, that of magic (which is nonetheless a traditional science), is provided by the preparation of talismanic figures; and in the order that more immediately concerns us the tracing of *yantra*s in the Hindu tradition provides a no less striking example.[2]

But this is not all, for the above-mentioned concept of the symbol is really much too narrow: there are not only figurative or visual symbols but also auditory symbols, two fundamental categories that in the Hindu doctrine are called the *yantra* and the *mantra*.[3] Their respective predominance characterizes the two categories of rites that originally related to the traditions of sedentary peoples in the case of visual symbols and to those of nomadic peoples in the cause of auditory ones; it should of course be understood that no absolute separation can be made between the two (for which reason we speak only of predominance), for every combination is possible as a result of the multiple adaptations that have arisen with the passage of time and produced the various traditional forms we know today. These considerations clearly show the bond that exists in general between rites and symbols, but we may add that in the case of *mantra*s this bond is more immediately apparent, for once it has been traced out, the visual symbol remains or may remain in a permanent state (which is why we have spoken of a fixed gesture), while the auditory symbol, on the contrary, is manifested only in the actual performance of the rite. This difference is attenuated, however, when a correspondence is established between visual and auditory symbols, as in writing, which represents a true fixation of sound (not of sound as such, of course, but of a permanent possibility of reproducing it); and it need hardly be recalled in this connection that all writing, at least in its origin, is essentially symbolic figuration. The same is true of speech itself, in which the symbolic character is no less inherent by its very nature, for it is quite clear that every word is nothing more than a symbol of the

---

[2] This can be likened to the *tracing board* of the Lodge in early Masonry (and also, perhaps by corruption, to the *trestle-board*), which in effect constituted a true *yantra*. The rites concerned with the construction of monuments intended for traditional uses might also be cited as an example here, for monuments of this sort necessarily have a symbolic character.

[3] See *Reign of Quantity*, chap. 21.

idea it is intended to express. Thus all language, whether spoken or written, is truly a body of symbols, and it is precisely for this reason that language, despite all the "naturalistic" theories contrived in modern times to explain it, cannot be a more or less artificial human creation nor a simple product of man's individual faculties.[4]

Among visual symbols themselves there is an example very similar to that of auditory symbols. These are symbols that are not permanently traced but only employed as signs in initiatic rites (notably the "signs of recognition" . . .)[5] and even in religious ones (the "sign of the cross" is a typical example known to all),[6] where the symbols are truly one with the ritual gesture itself.[7] It would in any case be altogether futile to make of these signs yet a third category of symbols distinct from those of which we have already spoken; certain psychologists would probably consider them to be such, and call them "active" symbols, or some such thing, but they are obviously made to be visually perceptible and thus belong to the category of visual symbols; among these, by reason of their "instantaneity", if one may put it so, are those that are most similar to the complementary category of auditory symbols. In any case, a "graphic" symbol, we repeat, is itself the fixation of a gesture or a movement (that is, the actual movement, or the totality of more or less complex movements, required to trace it, which in their specialized jargon psychologists would no

---

[4] It goes without saying that the distinction between "sacred languages" and "profane languages" arises only secondarily; for languages as well as for the sciences and the arts, the profane character is only the result of a degeneration that arose earlier and more readily in the case of languages on account of their more current and more general use.

[5] "Words" that serve a similar purpose, passwords for example, naturally fall into the category of auditory symbols.

[6] This sign was, moreover, a veritable "sign of recognition" for the early Christians.

[7] A sort of intermediate case is that of the symbolical figures traced at the beginning of a rite or preparatory to it and effaced immediately after its accomplishment; this is true with many *yantras*, and was formerly so with the *tracing board* of the Lodge in Masonry. This practice does not represent a mere precaution against profane curiosity, which as an explanation is far too "simple" and superficial, for it should be regarded above all as a consequence of the intimate bond uniting symbols and rites, which implies that the former have no reason for visual existence apart from the latter.

doubt call an "action gestalt"),[8] and with auditory symbols one can also say the movement of the vocal organs required to produce them, whether it be a matter of uttering ordinary words or musical sounds, is as much a gesture as all the other kinds of bodily movements, from which in fact it can never be entirely isolated.[9] Thus the notion of the gesture, in its widest meaning (which indeed accords better with the real meaning of the word than the more restricted meanings currently allowed), brings all these different cases back to unity, so that we can discern in them their common principle; and this fact has a profound significance in the metaphysical order which we cannot enlarge upon without straying far from the subject of our present study.

It will now be easy to understand that every rite is literally made up of a group of symbols which include not only the objects used or the figures represented, as we might be tempted to think if we stopped at the most superficial meaning, but also the gestures effected and the words pronounced (the latter, as we have said, really consti-tuting moreover only a particular case of the former); in a word, all the elements of the rite without exception; and these elements then have a symbolic value by their very nature and not by virtue of any superadded meaning that might attach to them from outward circum-stances without really being inherent to them. Again, it might be said that rites are symbols "put into action", or that every ritual gesture is a symbol "enacted",[10] but this is only another way of saying the same thing. Highlighting more particularly the rite's characteristic that,

---

[8] This is especially evident in a case such as that of the "sign of recognition" among the Pythagoreans, where the pentagram was traced out at one stroke.

[9] On the subject of the correspondences between language and gesture (the latter taken in its ordinary and restricted sense) it should be remarked that the works of Marcel Jousse, though their point of departure is quite different from ours, are none-theless in our opinion worthy of interest insofar as they touch on the question of cer-tain traditional modes of expression related, in a general way, to the constitution and usage of the sacred languages, but are almost lost or entirely forgotten in the vernacular languages, which have in fact been diminished to the most narrowly restricted of all forms of language.

[10] Note especially in this connection the role played in rites by gestures called *mudrās* in the Hindu tradition, which constitute a veritable language of movements and atti-tudes; the "handclasps" used as "means of recognition" in initiatic organizations in the West as well as in the East are really only a particular case of *mudrās*.

like every action, it is something necessarily accomplished in time,[11] whereas the symbol as such can be envisioned from a timeless point of view. In this sense one could speak of a certain pre-eminence of symbols over rites; but rites and symbols are fundamentally only two aspects of a single reality, which is, after all, none other than the "correspondence" that binds together all the degrees of universal Existence in such a way that by means of it our human state can enter into communication with the higher states of being.

---

[11] In Sanskrit the word *karma*, of which the primary meaning is "action" in general, is also used in a "technical" sense to mean "ritual action" in particular; what it then expresses directly is this same characteristic of the rite we are here indicating.

32

The Symbolism of Weaving

. . . In Eastern doctrines, traditional books are frequently referred to by terms which in their literal sense are connected with weaving. Thus, in Sanskrit, *sūtra* properly means "thread":[1] a book may be formed by a connection of *sūtra*s, as a fabric is formed by a tissue of threads; *tantra* also has the meaning of "thread" and that of "fabric", and denotes more particularly the "warp" of a fabric.[2] Similarly in Chinese *king* is the "warp" of a material, and *wei* is its "weft"; the first of these two words denotes at the same time a fundamental book, and the second denotes the commentaries on it.[3] This distinction between the "warp" and the "weft", in the corpus of traditional scriptures, corresponds to the distinction drawn in Hindu terminology between *Shruti*, which is the fruit of direct inspiration, and *Smriti*, which is the product of reflection upon the contents of *Shruti*.[4]

If the meaning of this symbolism is to be clearly grasped, it should first be observed that the warp, formed as it is by threads stretched upon the loom, represents the immutable, principial ele-

[1] This word is identical with the Latin *sutura*, the same root, with the meaning of "to sew", being found in both languages. It is at least curious to note that the Arabic word *sūrat*, which denotes chapters of the Koran, is composed of exactly the same elements as the Sanskrit *sūtra*; this word has in addition the kindred sense of "row" or "line", and its derivation is unknown.

[2] The root *tan* of this word expresses in the first place the idea of extension.

[3] The use of knotted cords, which took the place of writing in China at a very distant period, is also attached to the weaving symbolism; these cords were of the same kind as those used by the ancient Peruvians and called by them *quipos*. Though it has sometimes been maintained that these were merely for counting, it seems clear that they also expressed far more complex ideas, especially since we are told that they formed the "annals of the empire", and since the Peruvians never had any other mode of writing, whereas they possessed a highly perfected and refined language. This kind of ideography was made possible by multiple combinations in which the use of threads of different colors played an important part.

[4] See *Man and His Becoming*, chap. 1 and also *Spiritual Authority and Temporal Power*, chap. 8.

ments, whereas the threads of the weft, which pass between those of the warp by the to-and-fro movement of the shuttle, represent the variable and contingent elements, in other words the applications of the principle to this or that set of particular conditions. Again, if one thread of the warp and one of the weft are considered, it will at once be seen that their meeting forms the cross, of which they are respectively the vertical line and the horizontal; and every stitch in the fabric, being thus the meeting-point of two mutually perpendicular threads, is thereby the center of such a cross. Now, following . . . the general symbolism of the cross, the vertical line represents that which joins together all the degrees of Existence by connecting their corresponding points to one another, whereas the horizontal line represents the development of one of these states or degrees. Thus the horizontal direction may be taken as depicting, for example, the human state, and the vertical direction that which is transcendent in relation to that state. This transcendence clearly belongs to *Shruti*, which is essentially "non-human", where *Smriti* involves applications to the human order and is produced by the exercise of the specifically human faculties.

At this point another observation may be made which will bring out still more clearly the concordance of different symbolisms which are more closely connected than might be supposed; this concerns the aspect of the cross in which it symbolizes the union of complements. In this aspect, as we have seen, the vertical line represents the active or masculine principle (*Purusha*), and the horizontal one the passive or feminine principle (*Prakriti*), all manifestation being produced by the "actionless" influence of the first upon the second. Now, in another context, *Shruti* is likened to direct light, depicted by the sun, and *Smriti* to reflected[5] light, depicted by the moon; but, at the same time, the sun and moon, in nearly all traditions, also respectively symbolize the masculine and feminine principles in universal manifestation.

The weaving symbolism is not applied merely to traditional scriptures; it is also used to represent the world, or more precisely the aggregate of all the worlds, that is, the indefinite multitude of the states or degrees that constitute universal Existence. Thus, in the *Upanishads*, the supreme *Brahma* is called "That upon which the

---

[5] The double meaning of the word "reflection" is worthy of note.

worlds are woven, as warp and weft", or by other similar formulas;[6] here again, warp and weft naturally have the respective meanings just defined. Again, according to the Taoist doctrine, all beings are subject to the continual alternation of the two states of life and death (condensation and dissipation, vicissitudes of *yang* and *yin*);[7] and the commentators call this alternation "the to-and-fro motion of the shuttle upon the cosmic loom".[8] Actually, these two applications of one and the same symbolism are even more closely akin, since in certain traditions the Universe itself is sometimes symbolized by a book; in this connection, one need only recall the *Liber Mundi* of the Brotherhood of the Rose-Cross, and also the well-known Apocalyptic symbol of the *Liber Vitae*.[9] From this standpoint again, the threads of the warp, by which the corresponding points in all states are connected, form the sacred book which is the prototype (or rather, archetype) of all traditional scriptures, and of which these scriptures are merely expressions in human language.[10] The threads of the weft, each of which is

---

[6] *Muṇḍaka Upanishad* II.2.5; *Brihad-Āranyaka Upanishad* III.8.7-8. The Buddhist monk Kumarajīva translated into Chinese a Sanskrit work entitled *The Net of Brahma* (*Fan-wang-king*), according to which the worlds are arranged like the meshes of a net.

[7] *Tao Te Ching*, chap. 16.

[8] Chang-Hung Yang also compares this alternation to breathing, the active inspiration corresponding to life and the passive expiration to death, the end of the one being moreover the beginning of the other. The same commentator also makes use of the lunar rotation as a term of comparison, the full moon signifying life and the new moon death, with two intermediate periods of waxing and waning. As regards breathing, what is said here refers to the two phrases of existence of a being as if he himself were the breather; in the universal order, on the other hand, out-breathing corresponds to the development of manifestation, and in-breathing to the return to the non-manifested. . . ; according as things are considered in respect of manifestation or in respect of the Principle, one must not forget to apply the "inverse sense" in analogy.

[9] . . . In certain representations the book sealed with seven seals, with the lamb lying upon it, is placed, like the "Tree of Life", at the common source of the four rivers of Paradise. We also remarked upon the relationship between the symbolism of the tree and that of the book: the leaves of the tree and the characters in the book alike represent all the beings in the Universe (the "ten thousand beings" of the Far-Eastern tradition).

[10] This is expressly affirmed of the *Veda* and the Koran; the idea of the "Eternal Gospel" also shows that this same conception is not wholly foreign to Christianity.

the development of events in a certain state, form the commentary, in the sense that they give the applications relating to the different states; all events, envisaged in the simultaneity of the "timeless", are thus inscribed in the Book, of which each represents as it were one character, being also identified with one stitch in the fabric. On this symbolism of the book, the following passage from Muḥyi 'd-Dīn ibn al-'Arabī may also be quoted: "The Universe is a vast book; the characters of this book are all written, in principle, with the same ink and transcribed on to the eternal Tablet by the Divine Pen; all are transcribed simultaneously and inseparably; for that reason the essential phenomena hidden in the 'secret of secrets' were given the name of 'transcendent letters'. And these same transcendent letters, that is to say all creatures, after having been virtually condensed in the divine Omniscience, were carried down on the divine Breath to the lower lines, and composed and formed the manifested Universe."[11]

Another form of the symbolism of weaving, also found in the Hindu tradition, is the image of the spider weaving its web; this image is even more exact, since the spider spins the thread out of its own substance.[12] By reason of the web's circular shape, which may be considered as the plane section of the cosmogonic spheroid, that is, of the non-closed sphere. . . , the warp is here represented by the threads radiating from the center, and the weft by the threads arranged in concentric circles.[13] To return from this to the ordinary representation of weaving, it is only necessary to consider the center as being indefinitely remote, so that the radii become parallel in the vertical direction, while the concentric circles become straight lines perpendicular to these radii, that is, horizontal lines.

To sum up, the warp may be said to represent the principles that bind together all the worlds or all the states, each of its threads forming the connection between corresponding points in these different states, whereas the weft represents the chains of events that are produced in

[11] *Al-Futūhāt al-Makkiyah.* One might compare the part likewise played by letters in the cosmogonic doctrine of the *Sepher Yetsirah.*

[12] Commentary of Shankarāchārya on the *Brahma-Sūtras* II.1.25.

[13] The spider, at the center of its web, corresponds to the sun surrounded by its rays; it can thus be taken as a figure of the "Heart of the World".

each of the worlds, each thread being thus the development of events in a given world. From another point of view it may be said that the manifestation of a being in a certain state of existence, like any other event, is determined by the meeting of a thread of the warp with a thread of the weft. Each thread of the warp is then a being envisaged in its essential nature, which insofar as it is a direct projection of the principial "Self" provides the connecting link between all its states, and maintains its unity through their indefinite multiplicity. In this case, the thread of the weft which this thread of the warp meets at a given point corresponds to a definite state of existence, and the intersection of the two threads determines the relation of the being, as regards its manifestation in that state, with the cosmic environment in which it is thus situated. The individual nature of a human being, for instance, is the resultant of the meeting of these two threads; in other words, it will always be necessary to distinguish in him two kinds of elements which will have to be referred to the vertical and the horizontal directions respectively: the first are the elements that properly belong to the being in question, whereas the second proceed from the environmental conditions.

By a different but equivalent symbolism, the threads of which the "world fabric" is formed are also termed the "hair of Shiva"; they might be metaphorically described as the "lines of force" of the manifested Universe, and the directions of space represent them in the corporeal order. It will readily be seen in how many different ways all these considerations are capable of being applied; but the sole purpose of this chapter was to indicate the essential meaning of the symbolism of weaving, which apparently is very little known in the West.[14]

---

[14] Nevertheless, traces of a symbolism of the same kind are to be found in Greco-Roman antiquity, notably in the myth of the Fates; but this really seems to relate rather to the threads of the weft alone, and its "fateful" character may in fact be explained by the absence of the notion of the warp, that is, by the fact that the being is envisaged solely in its individual state, without any conscious intervention (for that being) of its transcendent personal principle. This interpretation is further justified by the way in which Plato regards the vertical axis in the myth of Er the Armenian (*Republic*, Book X): according to him, in fact, the luminous axis of the world is the "spindle of Necessity"; it is an axis of diamond, surrounded by a number of concentric sheaths, of different dimensions and colors, which correspond to the different planetary spheres; the Fate Clotho makes it turn with her right hand, hence from right to left, which is also the most usual and normal direction of rotation of the *swastika*. Apropos of this

"diamond axis", the Tibetan symbol of the *vajra*, a name which means both "thunder-bolt" and "diamond", is also related to the "World Axis".

33

The Sword of Islam (*Sayf al-Islām*)

In the Western world it is customary to consider Islam as essentially a warrior tradition and, consequently, when the saber or the sword (*as-sayf*) is involved, this word is taken only in its most literal sense, with no thought as to whether it is in reality a question of something else. Moreover, although it is incontestable that there is in Islam a certain warlike aspect, this same aspect, far from constituting a characteristic peculiar to Islam, is also to be found in most other traditions, Christianity included. Even without recalling that Christ himself said "I came not to bring peace, but a sword",[1] which, on the whole, can be understood figuratively, the history of Christianity in the Middle Ages, that is, at the time when it was effectively realized in social institutions, furnishes ample proofs of this. Moreover, the Hindu tradition itself, which certainly cannot be considered particularly warlike, since one tends rather to reproach it for allotting but little place to action, nevertheless also contains this aspect, as becomes evident in reading the *Bhagavad-Gītā*. Short of being blinded by certain prejudices, it is easy to understand that this must be so, for in the social domain, war, as long as it is directed against those who create disorder and aims at bringing them back to order, constitutes a legitimate function, which is fundamentally but one aspect of the function of "justice" understood in its fullest meaning. However, this is only the most outward aspect of things, and thus the least essential. From the traditional point of view, what gives all its validity to warfare thus understood, is that it symbolizes the struggle man must carry on against the enemies he bears within himself, that is, against all those elements within him that are contrary to order and to unity. In both cases, moreover, whether it is a question of the outward social order or the inward spiritual order, warfare must always tend equally to the establishment of equilibrium and harmony (which explains why it is related properly to "justice"),

---

[1] Matt. 10:34.

and thereby to unifying in a certain measure the multiplicity of elements that are in opposition among themselves. This amounts to saying that its normal outcome, and in the final analysis its only *raison d'être*, is peace (*as-salām*), which can only truly be obtained by submission (*al-islām*) to the divine will, each element being put in its place in order to make them all work toward the conscious realization of one and the same plan; and there is hardly need to point out how closely these two terms *al-islām* and *as-salām* are related to one another in the Arabic language.[2]

In Islamic tradition, these two meanings of warfare, as well as the real relationship between them, are expressed as clearly as possible by a *ḥadīth* of the Prophet uttered on the return from an expedition against outward enemies: "We have returned from the lesser holy war to the greater holy war" (*Raja'nā min al-jihādi l-aṣghar ila l-jihādi l-akbar*). If outer warfare is thus only the "lesser holy war",[3] whereas the inner war is the "greater holy war", it is because the first has only a secondary importance in relation to the second, of which it is merely a perceptible image. It goes without saying that in these conditions, whatever serves for outer warfare may be taken as symbol of what concerns inner war,[4] and this is particularly so in the case of the sword.

Those who disregard this meaning, even if they are ignorant of the *ḥadīth* we have just cited, could at least note in this regard that during the sermon, the *khaṭīb* [preacher], whose function obviously has nothing warlike about it in the ordinary sense of the word, holds in his hand a sword, which in such cases can only be a symbol—quite apart from the fact that this sword is usually of wood, which obviously renders it useless for outer combat, and thereby emphasizes even further its symbolic character.

---

[2] We have treated these questions more fully in *The Symbolism of the Cross*, chap. 8.

[3] It must be understood, of course, that this is so only when it is dictated by motives of a traditional order; all other warfare is *ḥarb* and not *jihād*.

[4] Naturally, this is no longer true for the weaponry of modern wars, if only because of its "mechanical" character, which is incompatible with any true symbolism; it is for a similar reason that the exercise of mechanical trades cannot serve as basis for a development of the spiritual order.

The wooden sword, moreover, dates back to a very remote past in traditional symbolism, for in India it is one of the objects that figured in the Vedic sacrifice;[5] this sword (*sphya*), the sacrificial post, the chariot (or more precisely, the axle, its essential element), and the arrow, are said to be born of the *vajra* or thunderbolt of Indra:

> When Indra hurled the thunderbolt at Vritra, it became, at his hurling of it, fourfold. . . . The Brahmins use two of these four forms during the sacrifice, while the Kshatriyas use the other two in battle. . . .[6] When the sacrificer brandishes the wooden sword, it is the thunderbolt that he hurls at the enemy. . . .[7]

The relationship of this sword with the *vajra* is especially to be noted in view of what follows. In this connection we should add that the sword is generally compared to lightning or regarded as deriving from this latter;[8] the well-known "flaming sword" represents it in a perceptible manner, independently of other meanings that the sword may have at the same time, for it must be clearly understood that true symbols always contain a plurality of meanings, which, far from being mutually exclusive or contradictory, harmonize on the contrary and complete one another.

To return to the sword of the *khatīb*, we can say that it symbolizes above all the power of the word, as should be obvious enough, all the more so in that this is a meaning quite commonly attributed to the sword, and one not foreign to the Christian tradition either, as these texts from Revelation clearly show: "In his right hand he held seven stars, from his mouth issued a sharp two-edged sword, and his

---

[5] See A. K. Coomaraswamy, "Le Symbolisme de l'épée", in *Études Traditionnelles*, January 1938; the citation which follows is taken from that article.

[6] Here the function of the Brahmins and of the Kshatriyas may be said to correspond respectively to inner and outer warfare, or, according to Islamic terminology, to the "greater holy war" and to the "lesser holy war".

[7] *Satapatha Brāhmana* I.2.4.

[8] In Japan, notably, according to the Shinto tradition, "the sword is derived from a lightning-flash archetype, of which it is the descendant or hypostasis" (A. K. Coomaraswamy, ibid.).

face was like the sun shining in full strength."[9] "From his mouth[10] issues a sharp sword with which to smite the nations. . . ."[11] The sword issuing from the mouth obviously can have no other meaning than this, all the more so when the being described in these two passages is none other than the Word himself, or one of his manifestations; as for the sword's double edge, it represents a twofold power of the Word, creative and destructive, which takes us back precisely to the *vajra*. Indeed, the latter also symbolizes a force that, although one in its essence, is manifested under two aspects that are contrary in appearance, although complementary in reality. These two aspects, just as they are represented by the two edges of the sword or other similar weapons,[12] are here represented by the two opposite points of the *vajra*; this symbolism is moreover valid for the totality of cosmic forces, so that its application to speech is only one particular case, but one which, by reason of the traditional conception of the Word and of all that it implies, may itself be taken to symbolize in their totality all the other possible applications.[13]

Not only is the sword compared symbolically to lightning, but also, like the arrow, to the solar ray; this is what is clearly referred to in the first of the two apocalyptic passages just cited: the one from whose mouth a sword issues has a face "shining like the sun". In this relationship, moreover, it is easy to establish a comparison between Apollo killing the serpent Python with his arrows and Indra killing the dragon Vritra with the *vajra*; and this parallel should leave no doubt about the equivalence between these two aspects of weapon

[9] Rev. 1:16. We see here the union of polar symbolism (the seven stars of the Great Bear, or the *sapta-riksha* of Hindu tradition) and solar symbolism, as we are going to find in the traditional meaning of the sword itself.

[10] The one in question is "he who was mounted on the white horse", the *Kalki-avatāra* of the Hindu tradition.

[11] Ibid., 19:15.

[12] Mention must be made here of the Aegean and Cretan symbol of the double axe; we have already explained that the axe is especially a symbol of lightning and therefore a strict equivalent of the *vajra*.

[13] On the double power of the *vajra* and other equivalent symbols (in particular the "power of the keys") see our treatment in *The Great Triad*, chap. 6.

symbolism, which are finally only two different modes of expression for one and the same thing. On the other hand, it is important to note that most symbolic weapons, and more particularly the sword and lance, are also frequently symbols of the "World Axis"; it is then a question of a "polar"—and no longer a "solar"—symbolism, but, although these two points of view should never be confused, there are however certain relationships between them allowing for what might be called "transfers" from one to the other, the axis itself being sometimes identical to a "solar ray".[14] With this axial meaning, the two opposing points of the *vajra* are related to the duality of the poles, considered to be the two extremities of the axis, whereas in the case of two-edged weapons, the duality, marked off in the same direction of the axis, refers more expressly to the two inverse currents of the cosmic force, also represented by symbols such as the two serpents of the caduceus. Since the two currents are themselves represented respectively in relation to the two poles and the two hemispheres,[15] it can thereby be seen that, despite their apparent differences, the two representations actually agree as to their essential meaning.[16]

Axial symbolism brings us back to the idea of harmonization conceived as the goal of "holy war", both in its outer and inner acceptations, for the axis is the place where all oppositions are reconciled and vanish, or in other words the place of perfect equilibrium, which Far-Eastern tradition designates as the "Invariable Middle".[17] Thus, in this respect—which in reality corresponds to the most profound point of view—the sword represents not only the means, as its most immediately apparent meaning might lead us to believe, but also the very end to be attained, being in a sense a synthesis of both as to its total meaning. In any event, we have done no more here than to gather a few remarks on this subject, which could give rise to many other lines

---

[14] Without being able to dwell upon this question here, we ought to at least recall by way of example the relationship of the two points of view in the Greek symbolism of Hyperborean Apollo.

[15] On this point too, see our treatment in *The Great Triad*, chap. 5.

[16] See *Symbols of Sacred Science*, chap. 26.

[17] This is also represented by the sword positioned vertically along the axis of a balance, the ensemble constituting the symbolic attributes of justice.

of thought; but we think that, such as they are, they show sufficiently how far it is from the truth to attribute to the sword no more than a "material" significance, whether it be in the context of Islam or of any other traditional form.

34

The Heart and the Cave

We have already alluded to the close relationship that exists between the symbolisms of the cave and of the heart, which explains the role played by the cave as a representation of a spiritual center from the initiatic point of view. Indeed, the heart is essentially a symbol of the center, whether it be the center of a being or, analogically, that of a world—that is to say whether the standpoint taken be microcosmic or macrocosmic. It is therefore natural, by virtue of this relationship, that the same meaning be attached to the cave, but the symbolic connection itself now calls for a fuller explanation.

The "cave of the heart" is a well-known traditional expression: the Sanskrit word *guha* generally designates a cave, but is applied also to the inner cavity of the heart, and consequently to the heart itself. This "cave of the heart" is the vital center in which reside not only the *jīvātmā* but also the unconditioned *Ātmā*, which is in reality identical with *Brahma* itself, as we have explained elsewhere.[1] This word *guha* derives from the root *guh*, meaning "to cover" or "to hide", which is also the sense of another similar root, *gup*, whence *gupta*, applied to everything of a secret character, everything not outwardly manifested; it is the equivalent of the Greek *kruptos*, which gives the word "crypt", synonymous with cave. These ideas refer to the center considered as the innermost and consequently most hidden point; at the same time, they refer also to the initiatic secret, whether in itself or insofar as it is symbolized by the arrangement of the place where the initiation is accomplished, a place that is hidden or "covered",[2] that is, inaccessible to the profane, whether access be barred by a "labyrinthine" structure or in any other way (as for example, the "temples without doors" of Far-Eastern initiations), and always looked upon as an image of the center.

---

[1] *Man and His Becoming according to the Vedānta*, chap. 3 (see *Chāndogya Upanishad*, III.14.3 and VIII.1.1).

[2] Cf. the Masonic expression, "to be under cover".

On the other hand, it is important to note that this hidden or secret character of spiritual centers or of their figurative representation implies that the traditional truth itself in its totality is no longer accessible to all men equally, which indicates that the period concerned is one of "obscuration", at least in a relative sense. This allows us to "situate" such a symbolism in the course of the cyclic process; but this is a point we shall have to consider more fully when we turn to the relationships between the mountain and the cave, insofar as both are taken as symbols of the center. For the moment we will just point out in this connection that the schema of the heart is a downward-pointing triangle (the "triangle of the heart" is yet another traditional expression). This same schema is applied also to the cave, whereas that of the mountain, or of the pyramid which is its equivalent, is on the contrary an upward-pointing triangle, which shows that here we have a relationship that is both inverse and in a certain sense complementary. Concerning this representation of the heart and the cave as an inverted triangle, we should add that this is a case where clearly there is no suggestion of "black magic", contrary to the claims of those whose acquaintance with symbolism is altogether insufficient.

That said, let us now return to what, according to Hindu tradition, is hidden in the "cave of the heart", that is, the very principle of the being which, in this state of "envelopment" and with regard to manifestation, is compared to what is smallest (the word *dahara*, designating the cavity wherein it resides, also refers to this same idea of smallness). In reality, however, it is what is greatest, just as the point is spatially infinitesimal and even non-existent, even though it is the principle by which all space is produced; or again, just as the number one appears as the smallest of numbers, although it contains all principially, and produces from itself the entire, indefinite series. So here too we find the expression of an inverse relationship in that the principle is envisaged from two different points of view; of these, the point of view of extreme smallness relates to its hidden and so to speak "invisible" state, which, for the being in question, is as yet only a "virtuality", but from which the spiritual development of this being will begin. Thus it is here that we find, properly speaking, the "beginning" (*initium*) of this development, that relates directly to initiation in the etymological sense of this word; and it is precisely from this point of view that the cave can be regarded as the place of the "second birth". In this respect we find texts such as the following: "Know that this *Agni*, who is the foundation of the eternal [principial] world, and through whom that world can be attained, is hidden in the cave [of the heart]",[3] which, in the microcosmic order, refers to the "second birth", and, by transposition to the macrocosmic order, to its analogue, which is the birth of the *Avatāra*.

We have said that what resides in the heart is at one and the same time *jīvātmā* from the point of view of individual manifestation, and unconditioned *Ātmā* or *Paramātmā* from the principial point of view. These two are only distinguishable in an illusory mode, that is to say relative to manifestation itself, while being but one in absolute reality. They are the "two who have entered into the cave" and who at the same time are also said to "dwell on the highest summit", so that the two symbolisms of cave and mountain are here united.[4] The text adds that "those who know *Brahma* call them shadow and light", which refers particularly to the symbolism of *Nara-nārāyana*, which we have discussed in connection with the *Ātmā-Gītā*,[5] citing this very same text. *Nara*, the human or the mortal, who is *jīvātmā*, is identified with Arjuna; and *Nārāyana*, the divine or immortal, which is *Paramātmā*, is identified with Krishna; now, according to their proper meanings, *Krishna* denotes darkness of hue and *Arjuna* lightness, or night and day, respectively, when they are considered as the non-manifested and the manifested.[6] An exactly similar symbolism found elsewhere is that of the Dioscuri [Castor and Pollux] with respect to the two hemispheres, one dark, the other light, as we have indicated in connection with the meaning of the "double spiral".[7] From another angle, these "two", that is, *jīvātmā* and *Paramātmā*, are also the "two birds" mentioned in other texts as "abiding on the same tree" (just as Arjuna and Krishna are mounted in the same chariot), and said to be "inseparably

---

[3] *Katha Upanishad* I.14.

[4] *Katha Upanishad* III.1; cf. *Brahma-Sūtra*s 1.2.11-12

[5] See *Studies in Hinduism*, chap. 1. ED

[6] Cf. A. K. Coomaraswamy, "The Darker Side of Dawn" [*Smithsonian Miscellaneous Collections* (1935), 94:1] and "Angel and Titan, an Essay in Vedic Ontology", *Journal of the American Oriental Society* (1935), 55, pp. 373-419.

[7] *The Great Triad*, chap. 5.

united" because, as we said above, they are really one, the distinction between them being no more than illusory.[8] We should point out here that the symbolism of the tree, like that of the mountain, is essentially "axial"; and the cave, inasmuch as it is considered to be located under the mountain or within it, is also on the axis, for in every case, and from whatever point of view it is envisaged, it is there that the center, which is the place of the union of the individual and the Universal, must always and necessarily be located.

Before leaving this subject, we will draw attention to a linguistic point to which we should perhaps not attach too much importance, although it is curious just the same. The Egyptian word *hor*, which is the very name *Horus*, properly seems to mean "heart"; *Horus* would thus be the "Heart of the World", according to a designation found in most traditions, which is in perfect keeping with its symbolism as a whole, insofar as that can be determined. At first sight one might be tempted to connect this word *hor* with the Latin *cor*, which has the same meaning, the more so in that in different languages similar roots denoting the heart are equally found with either the aspirate or the guttural as initial letter. Thus, on the one hand, *hrid* or *hridaya* in Sanskrit, *heart* in English, *herz* in German, and on the other, *kēr* or *kardion* in Greek, and *cor* itself (genitive *cordis*) in Latin; but the common root of all these words, including the last mentioned, is in reality HRD or KRD, and it does not appear that this can be the case with the word *hor*, so that here we are dealing, not with the same root, but only of a sort of phonetic convergence, although one rather striking nonetheless. But what is perhaps more remarkable, and in any case is directly related to our subject, is that in Hebrew the word *hor* or *hūr*, written with the letter *heth*, signifies cave; we do not say that there is an etymological link between these Hebrew and Egyptian words, although they may have a common origin in the more or less distant past; but this is basically of little importance, for when one realizes that there can be no such thing as pure chance, the resemblance will seem most interesting. Nor is this all: again in Hebrew, *hor* or *har*, written this time with the letter *hē*, means "mountain". Now since among aspirates *heth* is a stronger or reinforced *hē*, a sort of "compression", and moreover since *heth* expresses in itself, ideographically, a notion of

---

[8] *Muṇḍaka Upanishad* III.1.1; *Shvetāsvatara Upanishad* IV.6.

limit or enclosure, we see that the very relationship between the two words points to the cave as the enclosed place within the mountain, which is quite exact, literally as well as symbolically; and we are thus brought back once again to the relationships between the mountain and the cave. . . .

35

Initiatic Affiliation

Most of our contemporaries, at least in the West, find certain matters so hard to understand that we are obliged to return to them repeatedly; and quite often these matters, which are at the root of all that is related to the traditional point of view in general or more especially to the esoteric and initiatic point of view in particular, are also of an order that ought normally to be regarded as rather elementary. Such for example is the question of the role and inherent efficacy of rites; and perhaps it is at least in part because of its rather close involvement with rites that the question of the need for initiatic affiliation seems to be in the same situation. Indeed, when one understands that initiation consists essentially in the transmission of a certain spiritual influence, and that this transmission can only be operated by means of a rite, which is precisely what effectuates the affiliation one has to an organization that as its chief function conserves and communicates this influence, it does seem that there should no longer be any difficulty in this respect, for transmission and affiliation are fundamentally only the two inverse aspects of one and the same thing, according to whether it is envisaged as descending or ascending the initiatic "chain". Recently, however, we have had occasion to ascertain that this difficulty exists even for some who in fact have such an affiliation; this may seem rather astonishing, but we doubtless see here one result of the "speculative" diminishment that the organization to which they belong has undergone, for it is obvious that for anyone who confines himself to this single "speculative" point of view, questions of this order, as well as all those that might properly be called "technical", will only appear in a very indirect and distant perspective, and it is also clear that by this very fact their fundamental importance risks being more or less completely misunderstood. We might even say that such an example enables us to measure the distance separating "virtual" from "effective" initiation; not of course that the former can be regarded as negligible, for quite the contrary, it is this that constitutes initiation properly speaking, the indispensable "beginning" (*initium*) that carries with it the possibility of all later developments. But we have to recognize that especially under present conditions, it is very far indeed from this virtual initiation to the slightest hint of realization. However this may be, we think we have already sufficiently explained the need for initiatic affiliation,[1] but in the face of certain questions still being asked on this topic it will be useful to add a few points of detail to complement what we have already said.

We must first of all set aside the objection that some might be tempted to draw from the fact that the neophyte in no way experiences the spiritual influence at the actual moment of its reception; to tell the truth, this case is quite comparable to that of certain rites of an exoteric order, such, for example, as the religious rites of ordination, where a spiritual influence is also transmitted, and, at least in a general way, is no longer experienced either—which does not prevent it from being truly present and conferring upon those who receive it certain aptitudes that they would not have possessed without it. But in the initiatic order, we must go further; in a way it would be contradictory for the neophyte to be aware of the transmitted influence, since with respect to this influence as well as by definition he is still in a purely potential and "non-developed" state, whereas the capacity to experience it would on the contrary necessarily imply a certain degree of development or actualization; and this is why we have just said that one must begin with a *virtual* initiation. But in the exoteric domain there is in fact no disadvantage in not having any conscious awareness of the influence received, even indirectly and in its effects, since in this domain it is not a matter of obtaining an effective spiritual development as a result of the effected transmission; on the other hand, it is an altogether different matter when it is a question of initiation, and hence the interior work of the initiate, for ultimately the effects of this work should be felt, and this is precisely what constitutes the passage to effective initiation, at whatever degree it may be envisaged. This is at least what ought to take place normally if the initiation is to yield the results rightly expected from it. It is true that in most cases initiation remains forever virtual, which amounts to saying that the above-mentioned effects remain in a latent state indefinitely; but if this is the

---

[1] See *Perspectives on Initiation*, especially chaps. 5 and 8.

case, it is nonetheless an anomaly from a strictly initiatic point of view, and due only to certain contingent circumstances,[2] as, for instance, an initiate's insufficient qualifications (that is, the limitation of those possibilities which he bears within himself, and for which nothing external can make up), or again the state of imperfection or degeneration to which certain initiatic organizations are reduced at the present time, and which prevents them from furnishing sufficient support for the attainment of effective initiation, so that even the existence of such an initiation is unsuspected by those who might otherwise be qualified for it, although these organizations do remain capable of conferring a virtual initiation, that is, of assuring the initial transmission of a spiritual influence to those who possess the minimum of the indispensable qualifications.

Incidentally, . . . this transmission does not and cannot have anything "magical" about it for the very reason that it is essentially a matter of a spiritual influence, whereas everything of a magical order is concerned exclusively with the manipulation of psychic influences. Even if it happens that the spiritual influence is accompanied secondarily by certain psychic influences, this changes nothing, for it amounts to no more than a purely accidental result, due only to the correspondence that always necessarily obtains between different orders of reality; in all cases, initiatic rites do not act on or by means of these psychic influences, but stem solely from spiritual influences, and precisely insofar as they are initiatic, could not have any *raison d'être* outside of the latter. The same is also true moreover in the exoteric domain concerning religious rites;[3] and regarding these as well as initiatic rites, whatever differences there may be between spiritual influences, either in themselves or with respect to the various ends to which they are directed, it is still properly a matter of spiritual influences. This suffices to show that they have nothing in common with magic, which

---

[2] One could say in a general way moreover that in the conditions of an age like ours it is almost always the truly normal case that from the traditional point of view appears as the exception.

[3] It goes without saying that the same holds true for exoteric rites in traditions other than those clothed in a religious form; if we speak more particularly of religious rites here, it is because, in this domain, they represent the most generally known case in the West.

is only a secondary traditional science of an altogether contingent and even of a very inferior order, and which is, we repeat, entirely foreign to everything that has to do with the spiritual domain.

We now come to what seems the most important point, one that touches most closely on the very root of the question, which, seen from this angle, might be formulated thus: nothing can be separated from the Principle, for if it were it would truly be without existence or reality, even in the smallest degree; how then can one speak of an affiliation, whatever may be the intermediaries by which it is effected, for ultimately this could only be conceived of as a link to the Principle itself, which, to take the word in its literal meaning, seems to imply the re-establishment of a link that had been broken? A question of this type is quite similar to another that has also been asked: Why do we need to make an effort to attain Deliverance, since the "Self" (*Ātmā*) is immutable and remains always the same, and could not in any way be modified or affected by anything whatsoever? Those who raise such questions show that they have stopped at a much too exclusively theoretical and thereby one-sided view of things, or else that they have confused two points of view which, however, are clearly distinct, although complementary to each other in a certain sense—the principial point of view and that of manifested beings. Assuredly, from the metaphysical point of view one could if need be confine oneself to the principial aspect only and as it were neglect all the rest; but the properly initiatic point of view, on the contrary, must start from conditions that are those of manifested beings here and now, and more precisely, of human individuals as such, the very conditions, that is, from which it would have them liberate themselves; thus it must necessarily take into consideration—and this is what distinguishes this point of view from that of pure metaphysics—what might be called a "state of fact", and in some way link it to the principial order. To avoid any ambiguity on this point we should say this: it is evident that in the Principle nothing could ever be subject to change, and so it is not the "Self" that must be liberated, since it is never "conditioned" or subject to any limitation, but rather the "ego", and it can only be liberated by dissipating the illusion that makes it seem separate from the "Self". Similarly, it is not really the link with the Principle that must be re-established, since it always exists and cannot cease to exist,[4] but for the manifested being, it is the effective consciousness of this link that has to be realized; and, in view of the present condition of humanity, there are no other possible means for this than those provided by initiation.

Hence one can understand that the necessity for an initiatic affiliation is not one of principle but only of fact, though one that is nonetheless rigorously indispensable in our present state and which we are consequently obliged to take as a starting-point. Besides, for the men of primordial times initiation would have been useless and even inconceivable, since spiritual development in all its degrees was accomplished among them in an altogether natural and spontaneous way by reason of their proximity to the Principle; but as a result of the "descent" that has occurred since then, in conformity with the inevitable process of all cosmic manifestation, the conditions of the cyclic period in which we find ourselves at present are altogether different, and this is why the restoration of the possibilities of the primordial state is the first of the goals that initiation sets for itself.[5] It is therefore in taking account of these conditions such as they are in fact that we must affirm the necessity of an initiatic affiliation, and not in a general way and without further qualification as to the conditions of the age or, even more, of the world concerned. In this connection we would call attention more especially to what we have said elsewhere about the possibility that living beings might be born of themselves, without parents;[6] this "spontaneous generation" is indeed a possibility in principle, and we can very well conceive a world where it would actually be so; but this is not an actual possibility in our world, at least, to be more precise, in its present state. It is the same for the attainment of

---

[4] This link is basically none other than the *Sūtrātmā* of the Hindu tradition, which we have mentioned in other studies.

[5] On initiation considered in connection with the "lesser mysteries" as enabling the accomplishment of a "re-ascent" of the cycle by successive stages back to the primordial state, cf. *Perspectives on Initiation*, chap. 40.

[6] *Perspectives on Initiation*, chap. 4.

certain spiritual states, which moreover is also a kind of "birth",[7] and this comparison seems both the most exact and the best suited to help us understand what is involved. In the same order of ideas, we will also say this: in the present state of our world, the earth is unable to produce a plant of itself and spontaneously, except from a seed deriving necessarily from a pre-existing plant;[8] nevertheless the former case must have obtained at one time, for otherwise there could have been no beginning, although at present this possibility is no longer among those susceptible of manifestation. In the conditions in which we now in fact exist, no one can reap without first having sown, and this is just as true spiritually as it is materially; now, the seed that must be planted in our being in order to make possible our subsequent spiritual development is precisely the influence which, in a state of virtuality and "envelopment" exactly comparable to that of a plant seed,[9] is communicated to us by initiation.[10]

At this point it will be profitable to point out an error of which several examples have turned up recently: some people believe that affiliation with an initiatic organization is in some way merely a first step "toward initiation". This would only be true on condition that we clearly specify that this is the case with effective initiation; but the people in question do not make any distinction between virtual

---

[7] In this regard there is hardly need to recall everything we have said elsewhere on initiation considered as a "second birth"; moreover, this manner of envisaging things is common to all traditional forms without exception.

[8] Let us point out, without being able to stress the point just now, that this is not unrelated to the grains of wheat of Eleusis, or, in Masonry, to the password of the grade of Companion; the initiatic application is moreover obviously closely related to the idea of "spiritual posterity". In this respect it is perhaps not without interest to note also that the word "neophyte" means literally "new plant".

[9] It is not that the spiritual influence in itself can ever be in a state of potentiality, but that the neophyte receives it in a manner somehow proportioned to his own state.

[10] We could even add that, by reason of the correspondence that obtains between the cosmic order and the human order, there can be between the two terms of comparison that we have just indicated not just a similarity, but a much closer and more direct relationship, of such a nature as to justify it even more completely; and from this we can begin to see that the biblical text in which fallen man is represented as condemned to being no longer able to harvest anything from the soil without hard labor (Gen. 3:17-19) may well correspond to a truth, even in its most literal sense.

initiation and effective initiation, and perhaps do not even have the faintest notion of such a distinction, which, however, is of the greatest importance and even, one might say, altogether essential; besides, it is quite possible that they have been more or less influenced by certain conceptions of occultist or Theosophist provenance concerning the "great initiates" and other things of this kind, which are assuredly apt to cause or maintain many confusions. In any case, such people obviously forget that initiation is derived from *initium*, a word that properly means "entrance" and "beginning": it is the entrance into a way that will be traversed thereafter, or again the beginning of a new existence in the course of which possibilities of another order will be developed, possibilities beyond the narrow confines of the ordinary life. Understood in its strictest and most precise sense, initiation is in reality nothing other than the initial transmission of a spiritual influence in its seed state, or in other words, initiatic affiliation itself.

Recently, another question concerning initiatic affiliation has been raised, but to correctly assess its scope we should first of all say that it particularly concerns cases where initiation is obtained outside the ordinary and normal channels, and it must be clearly understood above all that such cases are never anything but exceptional, and that they occur when certain circumstances render normal transmission impossible, since their *raison d'être* is precisely to substitute in some measure for that transmission. We say "in some measure" because such a thing can only happen with individuals possessing qualifications far beyond the ordinary and aspirations strong enough to in a way attract to themselves the spiritual influence that they would not find if left to their own devices, and also because for such individuals it is even rarer still—for lack of the assistance provided by constant contact with a traditional organization—that the results obtained through such an initiation are anything but fragmentary and incomplete. This cannot be insisted on too much, and yet to speak of such a possibility is nevertheless perhaps still not entirely without danger, if only because too many people have a tendency to entertain illusions in this regard; let an event occur in their lives that is a little extraordinary—or so it seems to them—but that is really rather commonplace, and they interpret it as a sign that they have received this exceptional initiation; and present-day Westerners in particular are all too easily tempted to seize upon the flimsiest pretext of this kind in order to dispense with a regular affiliation, which is why we are quite justified in insisting that as long as this latter is not in fact impossible to obtain one should not expect to receive any other kind of initiation apart from it.

Another very important point is this: even in such a case, affiliation with an initiatic "chain" and the transmission of a spiritual influence is always involved, whatever may otherwise be the means and modalities, which no doubt can differ greatly from what they are in normal cases, and may for example imply an activity outside of the ordinary conditions of time and place; but at any rate there is necessarily a real contact, which assuredly has nothing in common with "visions" or reveries that arise only from the imagination.[11] In certain well-known cases, such as that of Jacob Boehme, to which we have alluded elsewhere,[12] this contact was established by an encounter with a mysterious personage who did not reappear thereafter; whoever this personage may have been,[13] what we have here is a perfectly "positive" fact, and not simply a more or less vague and ambiguous "sign" to be interpreted as one likes. But it must be understood that an individual initiated by such means may not have any clear awareness of the true nature of what he has received or to what he has thus been affiliated. What is more, lacking "instructions" that could enable him to gain some idea, however imprecise, on all of this, he himself may be quite incapable of explaining the matter; he may not even have heard of initiation, the word and the thing itself being totally unknown in his milieu, but this is basically of small concern and obviously does not in any way affect the reality of that initiation itself, provided we understand that this kind of initiation presents certain inevitable disadvantages with respect to normal initiation.[14]

---

[11] It should be kept in mind further that when questions of an initiatic order are involved one cannot be too distrustful of the imagination; whatever has to do only with "psychological" or "subjective" illusions is completely worthless in this respect, and should not be allowed to intervene in any way or to any degree.

[12] *Perspectives on Initiation*, chap. 10.

[13] It may have been an instance, though certainly not necessarily so, of the appearance assumed by an "adept" acting, as we were just saying, outside of the ordinary conditions of time and place. To better understand possibilities of this order, cf. *Perspectives on Initiation*, chap. 42.

[14] Among other consequences, these disadvantages often give the initiate, especially as regards his manner of expression, a certain exterior resemblance to the mystics, which

Having said this, we now come to the question alluded to previously, for these few remarks enable us to answer it more easily: is it not possible that certain books, of which the contents are of an initiatic order, can, for particularly qualified individuals who study them with the requisite frame of mind, serve by themselves as vehicles for the transmission of a spiritual influence, so that in such an instance their reading would suffice, without there being any need for direct contact with a traditional "chain", to confer on them an initiation of the type mentioned above? The impossibility of an initiation through books is yet again a point we thought we had sufficiently explained elsewhere, and we must admit that we had not anticipated that the reading of any books whatsoever could be envisaged as constituting one of those exceptional ways that sometimes replace the ordinary means of initiation. Besides, even outside of those particular and special cases where it is properly a matter of the transmission of an initiatic influence, there is here something clearly opposed to the fact that an oral transmission is always and everywhere considered a necessary condition of true traditional teaching, so much so that putting this teaching in writing can never dispense with it;[15] and this because, to be really valid, its transmission implies the communicating of a "vital" element as it were, for which books could not serve as a vehicle.[16] But what is perhaps most astonishing is that this question was raised in connection with a passage about "bookish" studies (a passage in which we thought that matters were explained with sufficient clarity

---

may even cause him to be taken as such by those who do not go to the heart of things, as was precisely the case with Jacob Boehme.

[15] In a book the content itself, as a body of words and sentences expressing certain ideas, is therefore not the only thing that really matters from the traditional point of view.

[16] It might be objected that according to some accounts referring especially to the Rosicrucian tradition, certain books were charged with influences by the authors themselves, which is indeed possible for a book as well as for any other object; but even admitting the reality of this fact, it could in any case only be a question of specific copies especially prepared to that end; moreover, each of these copies would have been destined exclusively for a given disciple, to whom it was directly entrusted, not to take the place of an initiation, which that disciple would have already received, but solely to furnish him with more effective help when, in the course of his personal work, he would use the contents of the book as a support for meditation.

to preclude any misunderstanding), where we indicated that precisely those books having an initiatic content were apt to give rise to such misunderstandings;[17] and so it would not seem useless to return to this topic and to explain more completely what we had wanted to say.

It is obvious that there are many different ways of reading one and the same book, and that the results will vary accordingly; in the case of a tradition's sacred scriptures, for example, a person who is profane in the most complete sense of the word, such as the modern "critic", will view it only as "literature", from which he will only be able to derive that kind of exclusively verbal knowledge which constitutes pure and simple erudition, without the addition of any real comprehension of even the most exterior kind, since he does not know and does not even ask whether what he is reading is the expression of a truth; and this is the kind of knowledge that can be qualified as "bookish" in the strictest sense of the term. Anyone affiliated to the tradition in question, even if he knows only its exoteric side, will already see something altogether different in its scriptures, although his comprehension may still be limited to the literal sense alone; but what he finds there will be incomparably more valuable for him than any erudition, and this remains equally true for those at the lowest level, who, through an incapacity to understand doctrinal truths, regard them simply as rules of conduct which at least enable them to participate in the tradition to the extent of their possibilities. And yet someone like the theologian who aims at assimilating the exoterism of the doctrine as completely as possible and is thus situated at a very much higher level, is still only concerned with the literal sense, and may not even suspect the existence of other more profound meanings—in short, those of esoterism—whereas on the contrary someone having no more than a theoretical grasp of esoterism will, with the help of certain commentaries or otherwise, be able to begin to perceive the plurality of meanings contained in the sacred texts, and hence be in a position to discern the "spirit" hidden beneath the "letter"; his comprehension therefore will be of a much more profound and lofty order than that which is aspired to by the most learned and accomplished of the exoterists. The study of such texts can then form an important part of the doctrinal preparation that normally must precede all realization; but

---

[17] *Perspectives on Initiation*, chap. 34.

if the one devoting himself to this does not also receive an initiation, he will always be left with an exclusively theoretical knowledge, no matter what predisposition he brings to it, which no amount of study will of itself enable him to surpass.

If instead of the sacred scriptures we consider certain writings of a properly initiatic character, as for example those of Shankarāchārya or Muḥyi 'd-Dīn ibn al-ʿArabī, we could, except on one point, say almost exactly the same thing, and so, to take one instance, the only gain that an orientalist could derive from reading them would be to know that such an author (indeed, they are for him "authors" and nothing more) has said such or such a thing; furthermore if he wishes to express this material in his own words rather than resting content to repeat it verbatim by a simple act of memory, there is the greatest risk that he will deform it, since he has not assimilated its real meaning to any degree. This only differs from what we mentioned earlier in that there is no longer any reason to consider the case of the exoterist since these writings relate to the esoteric domain alone and as such are entirely beyond his competence; were he truly able to understand them, he would by that very fact already have crossed the boundary separating exoterism from esoterism, and then we would in fact be in the presence of a "theoretical" esoterist, of whom we could only repeat unaltered what we have already said on this subject.

Nothing remains now but to focus on one last difference, which however is not the least important from our present point of view: this is the difference between the reading of one and the same book by both the "theoretical" esoterist just mentioned (who, we will suppose, has not yet received any initiation) and by someone who already possesses an initiatic affiliation. The latter will naturally see in it things of the same order as the former, though perhaps more completely, and above all they will appear to him in a different light as it were; moreover, it goes without saying that as long as his is only a virtual initiation, he can do no more than simply pursue, to a more profound degree, a doctrinal preparation that had remained incomplete until then; but it is altogether different once he enters into the way of realization. For him the content of the book is then properly no more than a support for meditation, in the sense one might call "ritual", and in exactly the same way as the various kinds of symbols he uses to assist and sustain his inner work; surely it would be inconceivable for traditional writings, which by their very nature are necessarily symbolic in the strictest sense of this term, not to play such a role as well. Beyond the "letter", which has now as it were disappeared for him, he will truly see nothing but the "spirit", and thus possibilities altogether different from those inherent in a simple theoretical understanding will be as open to him as when he meditates by concentrating on a *mantra* or a ritual *yantra*. But if this is so, it is only, we repeat, by virtue of the initiation received, which constitutes the necessary condition without which, whatever qualifications an individual might otherwise possess, there cannot be the slightest beginning of realization—which in short amounts simply to saying that every effective initiation necessarily presupposes a virtual initiation. And we can add further that if it happens that someone meditating on an initiatic piece of writing really enters into contact by its means with an influence emanating from the author thereof (which is in fact possible if the writing originates in a traditional form, and especially from the particular "chain" to which he himself is attached), this too, far from taking the place of an initiatic affiliation, can on the contrary never be anything but a consequence of a prior affiliation. However we look at it then, there can be absolutely no initiation through books, but only, under certain circumstances, an initiatic use of books, which is obviously something altogether different. We hope that this time we have sufficiently stressed this point so that not even the slightest ambiguity remains, and that no one will continue to think that there might be something here which lends itself, even if only under exceptional circumstances, to dispensing with the need for an initiative affiliation.

36

True and False Spiritual Teachers

We have often emphasized the distinction that should be made between initiation properly speaking, which is the pure and simple affiliation with an initiatic organization, implying essentially the transmission of a spiritual influence, and the means that can thereafter be used to make effective what at first was only virtual, means the efficacy of which is naturally subordinate in all cases to the indispensable condition of a prior affiliation. Insofar as they constitute an aid brought from without to the interior work from which the spiritual development of the being should result (and of course they can never take the place of this work itself), these means can in their totality be designated by the term initiatic teaching, taking this latter in its widest sense and not limiting it to the communication of certain ideas of doctrinal order, but including in it everything that in one way or another is of a nature to guide the initiate in the work he is accomplishing to achieve spiritual realization of whatever degree.

What is most difficult, especially in our time, is certainly not obtaining an initiatic affiliation—which may sometimes be only too easy[1]—but finding an instructor who is truly qualified, that is, as we have just said, one really capable of discharging the function of a spiritual guide by applying all the suitable means to the disciple's particular possibilities, apart from which it is clearly impossible, even for the most perfect master, to obtain any effective result. Without such an instructor, . . . the initiation remains merely virtual save for rare exceptions, although it is certainly valid in itself from the time that the spiritual influence has really been transmitted by means of the appropriate rite.[2] What further aggravates the difficulty is that those who claim

---

[1] By this we wish to allude to the fact that certain initiatic organizations have become much too "open", which is moreover always a cause of degeneration for them.

[2] We must recall here that the initiator who acts as a "transmitter" of the influence attached to the rite is not necessarily fit to play the role of teacher; if the two functions are normally combined where traditional institutions have suffered no diminution, they are in fact far from always being so in present-day conditions.

to be spiritual guides without being at all qualified for this role, have probably never been as numerous as they are today, and the resulting danger is all the greater because in fact these people generally have very powerful and more or less abnormal psychic powers, which obviously prove nothing from the point of view of spiritual development and in this respect are ordinarily even rather an unfavorable indication, but which are nonetheless capable of creating an illusion and imposing it on all who are insufficiently informed and consequently cannot make the essential distinctions. Therefore, one cannot be too much on guard against such false teachers, who can only lead astray those who let themselves be seduced by them, and who ought to consider themselves fortunate if they suffer nothing more than a waste of their time. Moreover, whether they be mere charlatans, of which there are only too many at present, or whether they delude themselves before deluding others, it goes without saying that this changes nothing as to the results, and in a certain way those who are more or less sincere (for there can be many degrees here) are perhaps even more dangerous for their very unconsciousness. We hardly need add that the confusion of the psychic with the spiritual, unfortunately so widespread among our contemporaries, and which we have often denounced, greatly contributes to render possible the worst misunderstandings in this regard; and when one adds to this the attraction of alleged "powers" and a taste for extraordinary "phenomena", which moreover almost inevitably go together, one has a fairly complete explanation for the success of certain false teachers.

There is nonetheless a characteristic by which many if not all such false teachers can be easily recognized, and although this is only a direct and necessary consequence of what we have persistently said on the subject of initiation, we believe that, given questions that have been posed to us recently concerning various more or less suspect personages, it will not be useless to state it again more explicitly. Whoever presents himself as a spiritual teacher, without attaching himself to a definite traditional form, or without conforming to the rules established by the latter, cannot truly possess the qualifications he attributes to himself; according to the case, he may either be a common imposter or a "deluded" person ignorant of the real conditions of initiation, and in this latter case even more than in the former it is greatly to be feared that he is only too often nothing more than an instrument in the service of something that he himself may not suspect. We can say as much of anyone who claims to dispense indiscriminately an initiatic teaching to all, even to the merely profane, and who proceeds according to methods that do not conform to those of any traditionally recognized initiation (moreover, these cases are identical to the first up to a point). If one knows how to apply these few indications and always hold strictly to them, the promoters of "pseudo-initiations", of whatever cast, would find themselves almost immediately unmasked;[3] only the danger that can come from deviant, though real, initiations that have departed from the line of traditional orthodoxy, would still remain; but such cases are certainly much less prevalent, at least in the Western world, so that it is clearly much less urgent to worry about them in the present circumstances. Furthermore, we can at the very least say that the "teachers" affiliated with such initiations, in common with the others we have mentioned, generally share the habit of showing off their psychic "powers" at every opportunity and without any valid reason (for we cannot consider valid the desire to attract disciples or to retain them by such means, which is the end they usually have in mind), and attribute the preponderance of such displays to an excessive and more or less disordered development of possibilities of that order, something that is always detrimental to any true spiritual development.

As for true spiritual teachers on the other hand, the contrast they strike with false teachers in the different respects we have just noted, can make them, if not recognizable with complete certainty (in the sense that these conditions, although necessary, can nonetheless be insufficient), at least help greatly to that end. But here it is appropriate to make another remark in order to dispel other false ideas. Contrary to what many people seem to imagine, it is not always necessary that, in order to be able to fulfill this role within certain limits, someone must himself have arrived at a complete spiritual realization; indeed, it should be quite evident that much less than this is required to be capable of guiding a disciple validly through the first stages of his

---

[3] As we have explained on other occasions, one must naturally not forget to count among the "pseudo-initiations" all that claim to base themselves on traditional forms that no longer have any effective existence; the former at least are clearly recognizable at first sight, and without there being any need to examine things more closely, whereas this may not always be the case for the latter.

initiatic journey. Of course, once the disciple has reached the point beyond which the former cannot guide him, the teacher worthy of the name will never hesitate to let him know that henceforth he can do no more for him and in order that he may continue his work in the most favorable conditions, direct him either to his own master, if this is possible, or to another teacher whom he recognizes as more completely qualified than himself; and when this is the case, there is really nothing astonishing or even abnormal in that disciple's finally surpassing the spiritual level of this first teacher, who, if he is truly what he ought to be, will be satisfied to have contributed his part, however modest it may be, in leading his former disciple to this result. Indeed, individual jealousies and rivalries can find no place in the true initiatic domain, whereas, on the contrary, they almost always play a very great part in the actions of false teachers; and it is solely these latter who should be fought and denounced whenever circumstances require, not only by authentic spiritual masters, but also by all who are to any degree conscious of what initiation really is.

Conclusion to
Introduction to the Study of the Hindu Doctrines

If a few people in the West, through reading the preceding pages, could become conscious of all that is lacking to them intellectually, if they could, we do not say understand, but only just catch a glimpse and a suspicion of it, then this work would not have been written in vain. We do not mean to refer only to the priceless personal gain that would accrue to those who were thus led to study the Eastern doctrines, wherein, if they were endowed with the smallest aptitude of the necessary kind, they would discover knowledge the like of which exists nowhere in the West, and compared to which philosophies that there are looked upon as the sublime creations of genius are but as child's play: there is no common measure between truth comprehended in its fullness, by means of a conception opening out upon limitless possibilities and accompanied by a correspondingly effective realization, and any hypothesis whatsoever that has been propounded by the essentially limited imagination of an individual. Other results can also follow, more general in scope, and related to the former as its more or less distant consequences; here we are alluding to the doubtless long drawn out but nonetheless effective preparation for an intellectual understanding between East and West.

When speaking of the divergence of the West in relation to the East, which has become increasingly marked in modern times, we said that we did not think this divergence could go on developing indefinitely, in spite of all appearances. In other words, it seems difficult to believe that the West, both in respect of its mentality and all its characteristic tendencies, can continue to draw further and further away from the East, as it is now doing, without sooner or later calling forth a reaction which might, under certain circumstances, have the happiest results; indeed, such an uninterrupted divergence seems to us all the more unlikely since the realm within which modern Western civilization is developing is, by its very nature, the most restricted of any. Furthermore, the changeful and unstable character peculiar to the West permits us to entertain the hope that a considerable and even a radical change of direction may occur one day, in which case the remedy would emerge from that very thing which seems to us the chief sign of inferiority. But we must repeat that such a change would only provide a remedy under certain circumstances, in default of which the condition of the world could not fail to become still worse than it is at present. This may appear a somewhat vague statement, and we fully recognize that it is not easy to make it as explicit as one might wish, even by adopting the standpoint of the West and trying to speak to it in its own language; nevertheless it is worth attempting, but with the warning that the explanations we are about to offer do not cover the whole of our thoughts on the subject.

First of all, what we know of the mental characteristics of certain Westerners compels us to say plainly that we have no intention of uttering a single word that could possibly be described as a "prophecy"; it would perhaps not be difficult to create such an impression by publishing the results of a process of deduction couched in suitable terms, but this proceeding would savor of charlatanism, unless one happened to have a predisposition toward a kind of auto-suggestion: of these two choices, the first inspires disgust while the second condition is fortunately not our own. We shall therefore under all circumstances avoid statements that cannot be substantiated, and that are as dangerous as they are useless; we are not one of those who believe that a detailed knowledge of the future would be advantageous to mankind, and in our opinion the discredit attaching in the East to the practice of the arts of divination is fully justified. This, in itself, is a sufficient reason for condemning occultism and other similar speculations that attach importance to this kind of thing, quite apart from additional and far more serious and decisive reasons of a doctrinal nature, which impose a downright rejection of conceptions that are both chimerical and dangerous.

We admit that it is not at present possible to foresee the circumstances that could determine a change of direction in the development of the West; but the possibility of such a change can only be denied by those who believe that development on the present lines constitutes "progress" in an absolute sense. This notion of progress in the absolute is really meaningless, and we have already pointed out the mutual incompatibility of certain lines of development, resulting, on the one hand, in relative progress in a given field and inevitably, on the other hand, in a corresponding retrogression in other fields; we said "corresponding", not equivalent, since one cannot use the latter term when referring to things that are neither similar in nature nor of the same order. This is what has occurred in Western civilization: researches carried out solely with a view to practical applications and material advancement have necessarily been accompanied by retrogression in the purely speculative and intellectual order; and since there is no common measure between these two realms, the loss on the one side has been incomparably greater than any supposed gain on the other; a man must be suffering from all the mental distortion that afflicts the vast majority of modern Westerners to be able to regard things in any other light. But however that may be, if one only considers the fact that a one-track development is necessarily subject to certain limiting conditions, which are all the narrower when that development takes place in the material sphere, it will be realized that a change of direction such as we have been discussing is almost sure to take place sometime or other.

As for the nature of the events that will lead up to this reorientation, it is possible that people will one day begin to notice that things which now appear all-important are unable to yield the results expected of them; but this in itself would presuppose a certain change in the general mental trend, even though the disillusion were chiefly sentimental in character, arising for instance from having come to realize the non-existence of a "moral progress" running parallel with the progress called scientific. Indeed, if they are not to be supplied from an outside source, the means of change will necessarily be as mediocre in quality as the mentality they are called upon to influence; but this mediocrity would not augur very well for the results to follow. It is also possible to suppose that mechanical inventions, developed ever further and further, may reach a point where they will seem so dangerous that men will feel impelled to renounce them, either from the terror gradually aroused by some of their consequences, or else following on a cataclysm which everyone is at liberty to picture as he pleases. Even in the latter case, the motive force of the change would be of a sentimental nature, but derived from that side of feeling which relates most closely to the physiological order; and it might be added, but without over-stressing the point, that symptoms connected with both the above-mentioned possibilities have already appeared, though on a very small scale, as a result of the recent events that have shaken Europe [World War I]; however, these events have not yet assumed sufficiently large proportions, whatever people may think, to bring about deep and lasting effects in the direction we are discussing. Furthermore, changes such as we have in mind could either come about slowly and gradually, requiring several centuries in which to mature, or on the other hand they might occur rapidly after sudden and unforeseen upheavals; however, even in the first case, it is probable that a moment will come when a more or less violent rupture will take place, amounting to a real severing of continuity with the pre-existing state. In any case, we fully admit that it is impossible to calculate the date of such a change beforehand, even approximately; however, truth compels us to add that those who possess some knowledge of the cyclic laws and their application to historical epochs might allow themselves at least a few forecasts in order to determine periods comprised within certain limits; but here we shall abstain entirely from entering into questions of this kind, the more so since a knowledge of the laws we have just alluded to has sometimes been falsely claimed by persons who found it all the easier to speak of such things the less they understood them: this last observation must not be taken for a paradox, for it expresses something that is literally a fact.

The next question to be asked is this: supposing certain events bring about a reaction in the West at some date as yet unspecified, causing those things to be given up that form the substance of present-day European civilization—what results must then be expected to follow? Several eventualities are possible, and it is well worth pausing to consider the various hypotheses corresponding to them: the most unfavorable result would occur if nothing were introduced to take the place of the civilization in question, so that, as it disappeared, the West, abandoned to its own fate, would sink into the lowest forms of barbarism. To understand this possibility, it is enough to call to mind several examples of civilizations that have been entirely obliterated, even without having to go back beyond what are called historical times. Some of these civilizations belonged to peoples who disappeared along with them, but this fate could hardly apply except to fairly localized cultures; in the case of civilizations enjoying a widespread extension it is more likely that the survivors would find themselves reduced to a degenerate state more or less comparable with that which . . . is represented by certain of the present-day savages; it is hardly necessary to spend a long time pointing out the disquieting nature of the picture called up by this first hypothesis.

The second eventuality is the one in which representatives of other civilizations, namely Eastern peoples, in rescuing the Western world from this incurable decay, would assimilate it by consent or by force, either as a whole or in respect of some of its component parts—that is assuming that the thing were possible and that the East were willing to do this. It is to be hoped that no one is so blinded by Western prejudice as not to recognize how much this hypothesis is to be preferred to the first one: under such circumstances there would doubtless be a transitional period of extremely painful ethnic revolutions, which are difficult to picture but which in their final result would be of a nature to compensate for the damage certain to be sustained during a catastrophe of this kind; but in that case the West would have had to forego its own character and would find itself absorbed purely and simply.

For these reasons a third possibility may be regarded as being far more favorable from the Western point of view, though merely equivalent, truth to tell, from the general point of view of humanity, since, were it to be fulfilled, its effect would be to have brought about the disappearance of the Western anomaly, not by suppression as in the first case, but, as in the second, by a return to true and normal intellectuality; but this return, instead of being imposed under duress, or at most accepted and experienced through external influence, would in this case be effected voluntarily and as it were spontaneously. It is easy to see what this last possibility implies, if it is to be realizable: it would mean that the West, at the very moment when its development in the present direction was nearing its end, had succeeded in discovering within itself the principles of a development in a different direction, which it would thenceforth carry out in quite a natural manner; and this fresh development, by turning its civilization into something comparable with those of the East, would allow of its occupying in the world, not a position of preponderance to which it is not entitled and which it owes at present only to its employment of brute force, but at least the position that it would lawfully occupy as one civilization among others, a civilization moreover which, under these conditions, would cease to be an element of maladjustment and of oppression for the rest of mankind.

It must not indeed be supposed that the Western domination can be otherwise looked upon by the peoples of different civilizations at present subject to it; we are not referring, of course, to certain degenerate tribes, though even in the latter case Western influence is probably more harmful than useful, since they tend to copy only the worst traits of their conquerors. As for the Easterners, we have already explained on several occasions how justifiable their contempt for the West appears in our eyes, all the more justifiable the oftener the European race insists on repeating its odious and absurd claims to a quite non-existent mental superiority, and the greater its efforts to force all men into an assimilation which its own unstable and ill-defined characteristics fortunately prevent it from consummating. Only a delusion and a blindness begotten of the most ridiculous prejudice could allow a man to believe that the Western mentality can win over the East, or that men who acknowledge no real superiority save that of the intellect will allow themselves to be seduced by mechanical inventions, which inspire them with a strong disgust and with not the slightest admiration. It may well happen that the Easterners will accept or rather submit to certain unavoidable effects of the present age, but they will look on them as purely temporary, and much more inconvenient than advantageous, and at heart they will only be waiting for an opportunity to get rid of all this material "progress", which can never be of any real interest to them. There are, it is true, many individual exceptions to be found among those who have undergone an entirely Western education; otherwise, generally speaking, defections in this sense remain far more superficial than outside observers, judging only by appearances, might be led to believe, and this is true despite the most ardent and untimely efforts expended by Western proselytism. Intellectually, it is in every way in the interest of the Easterners not to change today any more than they have changed in the course of preceding centuries; all we have said here goes to prove it, and this is one of the reasons why a real and deep understanding can only arise, as is logical and normal, out of a change taking place on the Western side.

We must now return once more to the three hypotheses we have outlined, in order to lay down more explicitly the conditions that would determine the realization of any one of them; everything clearly depends on the mental state of the Western world at the moment when it reaches the furthest term of its present civilization. If that mental state were then the same as it is now, the first hypothesis must perforce be realized, since nothing would be found to replace those things that were about to be given up, and because, on the other hand, no assimilation by other civilizations would be possible, the differences of mentality amounting to direct opposition. The assimilation which corresponds to our second hypothesis would require, as a minimum condition, the existence in the West of an intellectual kernel, even if it were only constituted by a numerically small elite, but one strong enough to provide the indispensable intermediaries for guiding back the mentality of the people toward the sources of true intellectuality, by imparting to it a direction which would however in no wise need to be consciously felt by the masses. From the moment that it is admitted that a term to the present Western civilization is a possibility, the preliminary establishment of this elite necessarily appears as alone capable of saving the West from chaos and dissolution at the appointed moment; and besides, in order to enlist the interest of the accredited representatives of the Eastern traditions in the fate of the West, it would be essential to prove to them that although their severest strictures on Western intellectuality as a whole were not unde-served, yet there might be at least a few honorable exceptions to be found, as evidence that the degradation of that intellectuality was not entirely beyond remedy.

We have said that the realization of the second hypothesis would not be free from certain unpleasant features, at any rate temporarily, and in this case the function of the elite would be confined to sup-plying the pivot of an action in which the West would not take the initiative; but that function would be quite a different story if events allowed the elite time to exercise such an activity directly and on its own responsibility, an eventuality that would then correspond to the realization of the third hypothesis. One can in fact imagine how the intellectual elite, once constituted, might act rather after the fashion of a "leaven" in the Western world, with the purpose of preparing the way for a transformation which, once effected, would allow the West to treat with the authorized representatives of the Eastern civiliza-tions if not as one equal with another, then at least as an autonomous power. In that case the transformation would have an appearance of spontaneity, all the more so since it could then operate without shock, provided the elite had really gained sufficient influence to be in a position to direct the general outlook; besides, the support of the Easterners would not be denied it in this task, for they will always be favorable, as is only natural, to an understanding brought about on such a basis, all the more so since they too would have an interest in it which, though quite of another order from that animating the Westerners, would be by no means negligible; but it would perhaps be rather difficult, and moreover useless, to try to define the nature of this interest here. Howbeit, the point we wish to stress is that in order to prepare the way for the changes in question it is in no wise necessary for the mass of Westerners, or for the generality of so-called intellectuals even, to take part in the work at the outset; even were this not quite impossible, it would in certain respects do more harm than good; it is enough, therefore, as a start, for a few individuals to understand the need for such a change, but of course on condition that they understand it truly and thoroughly.

We have shown the essentially traditional character of all the Eastern civilizations; the absence of an effective attachment to a tradition is the fundamental cause of the Western deviation. A return to a traditional civilization, both in principle and in respect of the whole body of institutions, is obviously the basic condition for the transformation we have been speaking about, or rather it is identical with that transformation itself, which will have been achieved from the moment that this return to tradition is fully effective. Under such conditions it would be possible to preserve whatever really valuable elements the present Western civilization may contain under any heading, always provided that before that time things had not reached a pass where there was no other alternative left but a complete renunciation. This return to tradition appears then as the most essential of the objects to which the intellectual elite ought to devote its activities; the difficulty would be to give effect to all that this implies in the various orders of activity, and also to determine the precise means which would have to be employed to that end. We can only say that the Middle Ages afford us an example of a traditional development that was truly Western; ultimately it would be a case not purely and simply of copying or reconstructing what existed then, but of drawing inspiration from it in order to bring about an adaptation to suit the actual circumstances. If there exists a "Western tradition", that is where it must be looked for, and not in the fantasies of occultists and pseudo-esoterists; this tradition was formerly conceived after the religious mode, and we do not see that the West is suited to conceive it otherwise, now less so than ever; it would be enough if a few minds became conscious of the essential unity of principle of all the traditional doctrines, as must formerly have been the case, judging by many suggestive signs and notwithstanding the absence of tangible or written proofs; the absence of such documents is quite natural under the circumstances and objections based on the "historical method" are quite irrelevant. . . .

Many things are still lacking from this concluding chapter before it can be considered complete, and these are the things that concern the deepest, and therefore the most truly essential characteristics of the Eastern doctrines and of the results that may be obtained from their study by those who are capable of carrying it far enough. The nature of these results can be sensed, in some measure, from the few words we have said on the subject of metaphysical realization; we have explained our reasons for not dwelling on things of this nature at greater length, especially in an introductory treatise like the present one; perhaps we shall come back to this question on another occasion, but it is above all in a case like this that one must bear in mind the Far-Eastern saying that "he who knows ten should only teach nine." However that may be, such things as can be expounded without reservation, that is to say whatever ideas can be expressed on the purely theoretical side of metaphysics, are more than enough to enable those who can understand them, even if they go no further, to see through the analytical and fragmentary speculations of the West; these will then appear to them in their true colors, namely as a vain and illusory research without principle and without ultimate goal, a pursuit yielding mediocre results that are worth neither the time nor the effort of any man whose intellectual horizon is wide enough to preserve him from such a cramping of his activities.

René Guénon (1886-1951)

APPENDIX 1: BIOGRAPHY OF RENÉ GUÉNON[1]

René Guénon was born in Blois, France, in 1886. He grew up in a strict Catholic environment and was schooled by Jesuits. As a young man he moved to Paris to take up studies in mathematics at the College Rollin. However, his energies were soon diverted from academic studies and in 1905 he abandoned his formal higher education studies. Guénon submerged himself in certain currents of French occultism and became a leading member in several secret organizations such as theosophical, spiritualistic, masonic, and "gnostic" societies. In June, 1909 Guénon founded the occultist journal *La Gnose*. It lasted a little over two years and carried most of Guénon's writings from this period.

Although Guénon was later to disown the philosophical and historical assumptions on which such occultist movements were built, and to contrast their "counterfeit spirituality" with what he came to see as genuine expressions of traditional esoterism, he always steadfastly opposed contemporary European civilization. There have been suggestions that during this period Guénon received either a Taoist or an Islamic initiation—or both. Whitall Perry has suggested that the "catalyzing element" was Guénon's contact with representatives of the *Advaita* school of Vedanta.[2] It was during this period that he embarked on a serious study of the doctrines of Taoism, Hinduism, and perhaps Islam.

Guénon emerged now from the rather secretive and obscure world of the occultists and moved freely in an intensely Catholic milieu, leading a busy social and intellectual life. He was influenced by several prominent Catholic intellectuals of the day, among them Jacques Maritain, Fathers Peillaube and Sertillanges, and one M. Milhaud, who conducted classes at the Sorbonne on the philosophy of science. The years 1912 to 1930 are the most public of Guénon's life. He attended lectures at the Sorbonne, wrote and published widely, gave

---

[1] Adapted from Harry Oldmeadow, *Journeys East: 20th Century Western Encounters with Eastern Religious Traditions* (Bloomington, IN: World Wisdom, 2005), pp. 184-194. ED

[2] Whitall Perry, "The Revival of Interest in Tradition", in R. Fernando (ed.), *The Unanimous Tradition* (Colombo: Sri Lanka Institute of Traditional Studies, 1991), pp. 8-9.

at least one public lecture, and maintained many social and intellectual contacts. He published his first books in the 1920s and soon became well-known for his work on philosophical and metaphysical subjects.

Whatever Guénon's personal commitments may have been during this period, his thought had clearly undergone a major shift away from occultism and toward an interest in esoteric sapiential traditions within the framework of the great religions. One central point of interest for Guénon was the possibility of a Christian esoterism within the Catholic tradition. (He always remained somewhat uninformed on the esoteric dimensions within Eastern Orthodoxy). Guénon envisaged, in some of his work from this period, a regenerated Catholicism, enriched and invigorated by a recovery of its esoteric traditions, and "repaired" through a *prise de conscience*. He contributed regularly to the Catholic journal *Regnabit*, the Sacre-Coeur review founded and edited by P. Anizan. These articles reveal the re-orientation of Guénon's thinking in which "tradition" now becomes the controlling theme. Some of these periodical writings found their way into his later books.

The years 1927 to 1930 mark another transition in Guénon's life, culminating in his move to Cairo in 1930 and his open commitment to Islam. A conflict between Anizan (whom Guénon supported) and the Archbishop of Reims, and adverse Catholic criticism of his book *The King of the World* (1927), compounded a growing disillusionment with the Church and hardened Guénon's suspicion that it had surrendered to the "temporal and material". In January 1928 Guénon's wife died rather abruptly, and, following a series of fortuitous circumstances, Guénon left on a three-month visit to Cairo. He was to remain there until his death in 1951.

In Cairo Guénon was initiated into the Sufic order of Shadhilites and invested with the name Abdel Wahed Yahya. He married again and lived a modest and retiring existence. "Such was his anonymity that an admirer of his writings was dumbfounded to discover that the venerable next-door neighbor whom she had known for years as Sheikh Abdel Wahed Yahya was in reality René Guénon."[3]

---

[3] Whitall Perry, "Coomaraswamy: The Man, Myth, and History", in *Studies in Comparative Religion*, Vol. 11, No. 3, 1977, p. 160.

A good deal of Guénon's energy in the 1930s was directed to a massive correspondence that he carried on with his readers in Europe, people often in search of some kind of initiation, or simply pressing inquiries about subjects dealt with in his books and articles. Most of Guénon's published work after his move to Cairo appeared in *Études Traditionnelles* (until 1937 titled *Le Voile d'Isis*), a formerly theosophical journal that was transformed under Guénon's influence into the principal European forum for traditionalist thought. It was only the war that provided Guénon enough respite from his correspondence to devote himself to the writing of some of his major works including, *The Reign of Quantity* (1945).

In his later years Guénon was much more preoccupied with questions concerning initiation into authentic esoteric traditions. He published at least twenty-five articles in *Études Traditionnelles* dealing with this subject, from many points of view. Although he had found his own resting-place within the fold of Islam, Guénon remained interested in the possibility of genuine initiatic channels surviving within Christianity. He also never entirely relinquished his interest in Freemasonry, and returned to this subject in some of his last writings. Only shortly before his death did he conclude that there was no effective hope of an esoteric regeneration within either masonry or Catholicism.

Guénon was a prolific writer. He published seventeen books during his lifetime, and at least eight posthumous collections and compilations have since appeared. The *œuvre* exhibits certain recurrent motifs and preoccupations and is, in a sense, all of a piece. Guénon's understanding of tradition is the key to his work. As early as 1909 we find Guénon writing of "... the Primordial Tradition which, in reality, is the same everywhere, regardless of the different shapes it takes in order to be fit for every race and every historical period".[4] As Gai Eaton has observed, Guénon "believes that there exists a Universal Tradition, revealed to humanity at the beginning of the present cycle of time, but partially lost. . . . [His] primary concern is less with the detailed forms of Tradition and the history of its decline than with its

---

[4] René Guénon, "Le Démiurge", *La Gnose* 1909.

kernel, the pure and changeless knowledge which is still accessible to man through the channels provided by traditional doctrine."[5]

Guénon's work, from his earliest writings in 1909 onward, can be seen as an attempt to give a new expression and application to the timeless principles which inform all traditional doctrines. In his writings he ranges over a vast terrain—Vedanta, the Chinese tradition, Christianity, Sufism, folklore and mythology from all over the world, the secret traditions of gnosticism, alchemy, the Kabbalah, and so on, always intent on excavating their underlying principles and showing them to be formal manifestations of the one Primordial Tradition. Certain key themes run through all of his writings, and one meets again and again such notions as these: the concept of metaphysics as transcending all other doctrinal orders; the identification of metaphysics and the "formalization", so to speak, of gnosis (or *jñāna* if one prefers); the distinction between exoteric and esoteric domains; the hierarchic superiority and infallibility of intellective knowledge; the contrast of the modern Occident with the traditional Orient; the spiritual bankruptcy of modern European civilization; a cyclical view of time, based largely on the Hindu doctrine of cosmic cycles; and a contra-evolutionary view of history.

Guénon repeatedly turned to oriental teachings, believing that it was only in the East that various sapiential traditions remained more or less intact. It is important not to confuse this Eastward-looking stance with the kind of sentimental exotericism nowadays so much in vogue. As Coomaraswamy noted, "If Guénon wants the West to turn to Eastern metaphysics, it is not because they are Eastern but because this *is* metaphysics. If 'Eastern' metaphysics differed from a 'Western' metaphysics—one or the other would not be metaphysics."[6]

By way of expediency we may divide Guénon's writings into five categories, each corresponding roughly with a particular period in his life: pre-1912 articles in occultist periodicals; exposés of occultism, especially spiritualism and theosophy; expositions of Oriental metaphysics; treatments both of the European tradition and of initiation in

---

[5] Gai Eaton, *The Richest Vein* (Ghent, NY: Sophia Perennis et Universalis, 1995), pp. 188-189.

[6] A. K. Coomaraswamy, *The Bugbear of Literacy* (London: Perennial Books, 1979), pp. 72-73.

general; and lastly, critiques of modern civilization. This classification may be somewhat arbitrary, but it does help situate some of the focal points in Guénon's work.

Although his misgivings about many of the occultist groups were mounting during the 1909-1912 period, it was not until the publication of two of his earliest books that he launched a full-scale critique: *Theosophy: History of a Pseudo-Religion* (1921) and *The Spiritist Fallacy* (1923). As Mircea Eliade has noted: "The most erudite and devastating critique of all these so-called occult groups was presented not by a rationalist outside observer, but by an author from the inner circle, duly initiated into some of their secret orders and well acquainted with their occult doctrines; furthermore, that critique was directed, not from a skeptical or positivistic perspective, but from what he called 'traditional esoterism'. This learned and intransigent critic was René Guénon."[7]

Guénon's interest in Eastern metaphysical traditions had been awakened around 1909, and some of his early articles in La Gnose were devoted to Vedantic metaphysics. His first book, *Introduction to the Study of the Hindu Doctrines* (1921), marked Guénon as a commentator of rare authority. It also served notice of Guénon's formidable power as a critic of contemporary civilization. Of this book Seyyed Hossein Nasr has written, "It was like a sudden burst of lightning, an abrupt intrusion into the modern world of a body of knowledge and a perspective utterly alien to the prevalent climate and world view and completely opposed to all that characterizes the modern mentality."[8]

However, Guénon's axial work on Vedanta, *Man and His Becoming According to the Vedanta*, was published in 1925. Other significant works in the field of oriental traditions include *Oriental Metaphysics*, delivered as a lecture at the Sorbonne in 1925 but not published until 1939, *The Great Triad*, based on Taoist doctrine, and many articles on such subjects as Hindu mythology, Taoism and Confucianism, and doctrines concerning reincarnation. Interestingly, Guénon remained more or less incognizant of the Buddhist tradition

---

[7] Mircea Eliade, "The Occult and the Modern World", in *Occultism, Witchcraft and Cultural Fashions* (Chicago: University of Chicago, 1976), p. 51.

[8] S.H. Nasr, *Knowledge and the Sacred* (New York: Crossroad, 1981), p. 101.

for many years, regarding it as no more than a "heterodox development" within Hinduism, without integrity as a formal religious tradition. It was only through the influence of Marco Pallis, one of his translators, and Ananda Coomaraswamy, that Guénon decisively revised his attitude.

During the 1920s, when Guénon was moving in the coteries of French Catholicism, he turned his attention to some aspects of Europe's spiritual heritage. As well as numerous articles on such subjects as the Druids, the Grail, Christian symbolism, and folkloric motifs, Guénon produced several major works in this field, including *The Esoterism of Dante* (1925), *St. Bernard* (1929), and *The Symbolism of the Cross* (1931). Another work, *Spiritual Authority and Temporal Power* (1929), was occasioned by certain contemporary controversies.

The quintessential Guénon is to be found in two works that tied together some of his central themes: *The Crisis of the Modern World* (1927), and his masterpiece, *The Reign of Quantity and the Signs of the Times* (1945). The themes of these two books had been rehearsed in an earlier one, *East and West* (1924). The books mounted an increasingly elaborate and merciless attack on the foundations of the contemporary European world-view.

While Guénon's influence remains minimal in the Western academic community at large, he is the seminal influence in the development of traditionalism. Along with Coomaraswamy and Schuon, he forms what one commentator has called "the great triumvirate" of the traditionalist school. Like other traditionalists, Guénon did not perceive his work as an exercise in creativity or personal "originality", repeatedly emphasizing that in the metaphysical domain there is no room for "individualist considerations" of any kind. In a letter to a friend he wrote, "I have no other merit than to have expressed to the best of my ability some traditional ideas".[9] When reminded of the people who had been profoundly influenced by his writings, he calmly replied ". . . such disposition becomes a homage rendered to

---

[9] Whitall Perry, "The Man and His Witness", in S.D.R. Singam (ed.), *Ananda Coomaraswamy: Remembering and Remembering Again and Again* (Kuala Lumpur: privately published, 1974), p. 7.

the doctrine expressed by us in a way that is totally independent of any individualistic consideration".[10]

Most traditionalists regard Guénon as the "providential interpreter of this age".[11] It was his role to remind a forgetful world, "in a way that can be ignored but not refuted, of first principles, and to restore a lost sense of the Absolute".[12]

[10] Marco Bastriocchi, "The Last Pillars of Wisdom", in S.D.R. Singam (ed.), *Ananda Coomaraswamy*, p. 356.

[11] Frithjof Schuon, "René Guénon: Definitions", quoted by M. Bastriocchi, "The Last Pillars of Wisdom", p. 359.

[12] Whitall Perry, "Coomaraswamy: The Man, Myth, and History", p. 163.

APPENDIX 2: THE WORKS OF RENÉ GUÉNON

Books in French (Original Editions)

Introduction générale à l'Étude des doctrines hindoues. Paris: Éditions Trédaniel, 1921.

Le Théosophisme, histoire d'une pseudo-religion. Paris: Éditions Traditionnelles, 1921.

L'Erreur spirite. Paris: Éditions Traditionnelles, 1923.

Orient et Occident. Paris: Éditions Trédaniel, 1924.

L'Ésotérisme de Dante. Paris: Éditions Gallimard, 1925.

L'Homme et son devenir selon le Vedanta. Paris: Éditions Traditionnelles, 1925.

La crise du monde moderne. Paris: Éditions Gallimard, 1927.

Le Roi du Monde. Paris: Éditions Gallimard, 1927.

Autorité spirituelle et pouvoir temporel. Paris: Éditions Trédaniel, 1929.

Saint Bernard. Paris: Éditions Traditionnelles, 1929.

Le Symbolisme de la Croix. Paris: Éditions Trédaniel, 1931.

Les États multiples de l'Etre. Paris: Éditions Trédaniel, 1932.

La Métaphysique orientale. Paris: Éditions Traditionnelles, 1939.

Le Règne de la Quantité et les Signes des Temps. Paris: Éditions Gallimard, 1945.

La Grande Triade. Paris: Éditions Gallimard, 1946.

Les Principes du Calcul infinitésimal. Paris: Éditions Gallimard, 1946.

Aperçus sur l'Initiation. Paris: Éditions Traditionnelles, 1946.

Initiation et Réalisation spirituelle. Paris: Éditions Traditionnelles, 1952.

Aperçus sur l'ésotérisme chrétien. Paris: Éditions Traditionnelles, 1954.

Symboles de la Science sacrée. Paris: Éditions Gallimard, 1962.

Études sur la franc-maçonnerie et le compagnonnage, vol. 1. Paris: Éditions Traditionnelles, 1964.

Études sur la franc-maçonnerie et le compagnonnage, vol. 2. Paris: Éditions Traditionnelles, 1965.

Études sur l'Hindouisme. Paris: Éditions Traditionnelles, 1967.

Formes traditionnelles et cycles cosmiques. Paris: Éditions Gallimard, 1970.

Aperçus sur l'ésotérisme islamique et le taoïsme. Paris: Éditions Gallimard, 1973.

Mélanges. Paris: Éditions Gallimard, 1976.

Comptes rendus. Paris: Éditions Traditionnelles, 1986.

Articles et Comptes-Rendus. Paris: Éditions Traditionnelles, 2002.

Écrits pour Regnabit. Paris: Arché, 1999.

Psychologie: Notes de cours de philosophie (1917-1918) attribuées à René Guénon. Paris: Arché, 2001.

Books in English (Collected Works of René Guénon Series)
Introduction to the Study of the Hindu Doctrines. Hillsdale, NY: Sophia Perennis, 2002.
Theosophy, the History of a Pseudo-Religion. Hillsdale, NY: Sophia Perennis, 2003.
The Spiritist Fallacy. Hillsdale, NY: Sophia Perennis, 2003.
East and West. Hillsdale, NY: Sophia Perennis, 2001.
The Esoterism of Dante. Hillsdale, NY: Sophia Perennis, 2001.
Man and His Becoming According to the Vedanta. Hillsdale, NY: Sophia Perennis, 2001.
The Crisis of the Modern World. Hillsdale, NY: Sophia Perennis, 2001.
The King of the World. Hillsdale, NY: Sophia Perennis, 2001.
Spiritual Authority and Temporal Power. Hillsdale, NY: Sophia Perennis, 2001.
The Symbolism of the Cross. Hillsdale, NY: Sophia Perennis, 2002.
The Multiple States of the Being. Hillsdale, NY: Sophia Perennis, 2002.
The Reign of Quantity and the Signs of the Times. Hillsdale, NY: Sophia Perennis, 2002.
The Great Triad. Hillsdale, NY: Sophia Perennis, 2001.
Metaphysical Principles of the Infinitesimal Calculus. Hillsdale, NY: Sophia Perennis, 2001.
Perspectives on Initiation. Hillsdale, NY: Sophia Perennis, 2001.
Initiation and Spiritual Realization. Hillsdale, NY: Sophia Perennis, 2001.
Insights into Christian Esoterism [including *Saint Bernard*]. Hillsdale, NY: Sophia Perennis, 2001.
Symbols of Sacred Science. Hillsdale, NY: Sophia Perennis, 2004.
Studies in Freemasonry and the Compagnonnage. Hillsdale, NY: Sophia Perennis, 2004.
Studies in Hinduism [including *Oriental Metaphysics*]. Hillsdale, NY: Sophia Perennis, 2001.
Traditional Forms and Cosmic Cycles. Hillsdale, NY: Sophia Perennis, 2003.
Insights into Islamic Esoterism and Taoism. Hillsdale, NY: Sophia Perennis, 2003.
Miscellanea. Hillsdale, NY: Sophia Perennis, 2003.

LIST OF SOURCES

1. "The Dark Age": *The Crisis of the Modern World*. Hillsdale, NY: Sophia Perennis, 2001, pp. 7-20.
2. "Sacred and Profane Science": *The Crisis of the Modern World*. Hillsdale, NY: Sophia Perennis, 2001, pp. 42-54.
3. "A Material Civilization": *The Crisis of the Modern World*. Hillsdale, NY: Sophia Perennis, 2001, pp. 81-96.
4. "Introduction": *The Reign of Quantity and the Signs of the Times*. Hillsdale, NY: Sophia Perennis, 2002, pp. 1-10.
5. "Quality and Quantity": *The Reign of Quantity and the Signs of the Times*. Hillsdale, NY: Sophia Perennis, 2002, pp. 11-15.
6. "The Postulates of Rationalism": *The Reign of Quantity and the Signs of the Times*. Hillsdale, NY: Sophia Perennis, 2002, pp. 89-95.
7. "The End of a World": *The Reign of Quantity and the Signs of the Times*. Hillsdale, NY: Sophia Perennis, 2002, pp. 175-180.
8. "Civilization and Progress": *East and West*. Hillsdale, NY: Sophia Perennis, 2001, pp. 11-26.
9. "Eastern Metaphysics": *Studies in Hinduism*. Hillsdale, NY: Sophia Perennis, 2001, pp. 86-102.
10. "What is Meant by Tradition?": *Introduction to the Study of the Hindu Doctrines*. Hillsdale, NY: Sophia Perennis, 2002, pp. 54-57.
11. "Essential Characteristics of Metaphysics": *Introduction to the Study of the Hindu Doctrines*. Hillsdale, NY: Sophia Perennis, 2002, pp. 70-78.
12. "Metaphysical Realization": *Introduction to the Study of the Hindu Doctrines*. Hillsdale, NY: Sophia Perennis, 2002, pp. 114-118.
13. "*Sanātana Dharma*": *Studies in Hinduism*. Hillsdale, NY: Sophia Perennis, 2001, pp. 76-85.
14. "Some Remarks on the Doctrine of Cosmic Cycles": *Traditional Forms and Cosmic Cycles*. Hillsdale, NY: Sophia Perennis, 2003, pp. 1-11.
15. "Foundation of the Theory of the Multiple States": *The Multiple States of the Being*. Hillsdale, NY: Sophia Perennis, 2002, pp. 26-30.
16. "The Realization of the Being through Knowledge": *The Multiple States of the Being*. Hillsdale, NY: Sophia Perennis, 2002, pp. 77-80.
17. "On the Exact Meaning of the Word 'Hindu'": *Introduction to the Study of the Hindu Doctrines*. Hillsdale, NY: Sophia Perennis, 2002, pp. 121-126.
18. "Perpetuity of the *Veda*": *Introduction to the Study of the Hindu Doctrines*. Hillsdale, NY: Sophia Perennis, 2002, pp. 127-130.

19. "The Law of Manu": *Introduction to the Study of the Hindu Doctrines*. Hillsdale NY: Sophia Perennis, 2002, pp. 146-150.
20. "Principles Governing the Institution of Caste": *Introduction to the Study of the Hindu Doctrines*. Hillsdale, NY: Sophia Perennis, 2002, pp. 151-156.
21. "*Yoga*": *Introduction to the Study of the Hindu Doctrines*. Hillsdale, NY: Sophia Perennis, 2002, pp. 186-190.
22. "General Remarks on the *Vedānta*": *Man and His Becoming According to the Vedānta*. Hillsdale, NY: Sophia Perennis, 2001, pp. 7-20.
23. "The Vital Center of the Human Being: Seat of *Brahma*": *Man and His Becoming According to the Vedānta*. Hillsdale, NY: Sophia Perennis, 2001, pp. 31-38.
24. "The Degrees of Individual Manifestation": *Man and His Becoming According to the Vedānta*. Hillsdale, NY: Sophia Perennis, 2001, pp. 51-56.
25. "*Buddhi* or the Higher Intellect": *Man and His Becoming According to the Vedānta*. Hillsdale, NY: Sophia Perennis, 2001, pp. 57-60.
26. "Final Deliverance": *Man and His Becoming According to the Vedānta*. Hillsdale, NY: Sophia Perennis, 2001, pp. 153-159.
27. "*Kabbalah*": *Traditional Forms and Cosmic Cycles*. Hillsdale, NY: Sophia Perennis, 2003, pp. 33-37.
28. "The Symbolism of the Grail": *The King of the World*. Hillsdale, NY: Sophia Perennis, 2001, pp. 27-32.
29. "Islamic Esoterism": *Insights into Islamic Esoterism and Taoism*. Hillsdale, NY: Sophia Perennis, 2003, pp. 1-8.
30. "Taoism and Confucianism": *Insights into Islamic Esoterism and Taoism*. Hillsdale, NY: Sophia Perennis, 2003, pp. 52-66.
31. "Rite and Symbol": *Perspectives on Initiation*. Hillsdale, NY: Sophia Perennis, 2001, pp. 110-114.
32. "The Symbolism of Weaving": *The Symbolism of the Cross*. Hillsdale, NY: Sophia Perennis, 2002, pp. 75-80.
33. "The Sword of Islam": *Symbols of Sacred Science*. Hillsdale, NY: Sophia Perennis, 2004, pp. 179-184.
34. "The Heart and the Cave": *Symbols of Sacred Science*. Hillsdale, NY: Sophia Perennis, 2004, pp. 202-206.
35. "Initiatic Affiliation": *Initiation and Spiritual Realization*. Hillsdale, NY: Sophia Perennis, 2001, pp. 23-35.
36. "True and False Spiritual Teachers": *Initiation and Spiritual Realization*. Hillsdale, NY: Sophia Perennis, 2001, pp. 108-111.
    "Conclusion": *Introduction to the Study of the Hindu Doctrines*. Hillsdale, NY: Sophia Perennis, 2002, pp. 241-253.

BIOGRAPHICAL NOTES

JOHN HERLIHY works as a consultant at Khalifa University of Science, Technology, and Research in Abu Dhabi, United Arab Emirates. He was born into an Irish-American family in Boston, Massachusetts and completed studies at a Paulist seminary. He was educated at Boston University and Columbia University in New York City before converting to Islam in 1974. Twenty years after his conversion, he began to write about his experiences as a Muslim; his writings reflect upon the disparity between modernity and tradition and the pursuit of spirituality in today's anti-spiritual world. In addition to contributing to such traditional journals as *Sacred Web* and *Sophia*, he has written a number of books, including: *Borderlands of the Spirit: Reflections on a Sacred Science of Mind, Wisdom's Journey: Living the Spirit of Islam in the Modern World, Veils and Keys to Enlightenment*, and *Near and Distant Horizons*.

MARTIN LINGS (1909-2005) was a close friend and for many years the unofficial secretary of René Guénon. He was a leading member of the "Perennialist" or "Traditionalist" school and an acclaimed author, editor, translator, Arabist, and poet. In addition, he was an accomplished metaphysician and essayist who often turned to a number of the world's great spiritual traditions in his writings, though he is most likely best known for his work on Islam and its esoteric tradition, Sufism. Born in Lancashire, he took an English degree at Oxford and lectured on Shakespeare at the University of Cairo before becoming Keeper of Oriental Manuscripts at the British Library. The author of numerous books, including *What is Sufism?*, *A Sufi Saint of the Twentieth Century, Muhammad: His Life Based on the Earliest Sources*, and *Symbol & Archetype*, as well as the co-editor of *The Underlying Religion: An Introduction to the Perennial Philosophy*, he is considered an authority on tradition in general and on Sufism in particular.

INDEX

For a glossary of all key foreign words used in books published by World Wisdom, including metaphysical terms in English, consult: www.DictionaryofSpiritualTerms.org.
This on-line Dictionary of Spiritual Terms provides extensive definitions, examples, and related terms in other languages.

Titles in the Perennial Philosophy Series by World Wisdom

Titles in the
Collected Works of René Guénon Series
by Sophia Perennis